DIRECTORY

The Business Writing Process
general writing advice for planning, researching, organizing, drafting, and revising documents

Business Writing Forms and Elements
explanation of specific projects (with models) including proposals, various formal and informal reports, and their elements such as abstracts and executive summaries

Style and Clarity
advice on writing clear, concise, and jargon-free sentences appropriate for a business writing style

Correspondence and Job Application
explanation (with models) of various letters and memos, e-mail, résumés, and international correspondence

Grammar
explanations for writing grammatical sentences on topics such as subject-verb agreement, dangling modifiers, articles, and pronoun reference, plus a list of commonly misspelled words

Oral Communication
guidance on making effective oral presentations, conducting productive meetings, and building listening skills

Punctuation and Mechanics
explanations of all the punctuation marks plus rules on using abbreviations, contractions, and numbers

Format and Visual Aids
basics of document design with guidance on how to choose, plan, and create effective illustrations and graphics

Index
lists every entry and its location in the book

The
Business Writer's
Companion

The Business Writer's Companion

CHARLES T. BRUSAW
NCR Corporation (retired)

GERALD J. ALRED
University of Wisconsin–Milwaukee

WALTER E. OLIU
U.S. Nuclear Regulatory Commission

St. Martin's Press
New York

Editor: Nancy Lyman
Manager, publishing services: Emily Berleth
Senior editor, publishing services: Doug Bell
Project management: Omega Publishing Services, Inc.
Production supervisor: Scott Lavelle
Text design: Dorothy Bungert, EriBen Graphics
Cover design: Lucy Krikorian

Library of Congress Catalog Card Number: 95-72990

Manufactured in the United States of America.

09876
f e d c b

For information, write:
St. Martin's Press, Inc.
175 Fifth Avenue
New York, NY 10010

ISBN: 0-312-13316-2

Contents

Preface

The Business Writer's Companion combines the advantages of a rhetorically arranged handbook and an alphabetically arranged handbook. We believe this organization in a compact form makes the companion a flexible and handy supplement in the classroom or a quick reference on the job. First, the entries are divided into the following nine sections:

The Business Writing Process

Business Writing Forms and Elements

Correspondence and Job Application

Oral Communication

Format and Visual Aids

Usage

Style and Clarity

Grammar

Punctuation and Mechanics

These sections become nine individual, manageable handbooks for easy access to information. For example, "The Business Writing Process" groups together all the general information a writer needs about planning, organizing, drafting, and revising a document. Experienced writers, on the other hand, might only need models of specific letters, and they can find all the kinds of business letters in "Correspondence and Job Application."

Within these sections, the entries are organized alphabetically, so that readers can find immediately the topic at hand. The Business Writer's Companion provides two additional ways to find the information a user needs. Where appropriate within each entry, cross references guide the user to entries throughout the companion. Finally, the Index provides an exhaustive alphabetical list of the topics in all sections, indexed not only by the terms actually used in the entries but also by various other terms that readers might think of instead.

The Business Writer's Companion offers coverage far beyond the scope of conventional English handbooks. In addition to a thorough treatment of grammar, usage, style, format, and writing procedures (planning, research, outlining, methods of development, and so forth), it provides information on all types of business communication—reports of various kinds (including oral presentations), proposals, letters, and memorandums. It also covers the use of electronic mail, listening, page design, and graphics. It gives abundant examples, all drawn from business or industrial contexts, to provide the greatest possible relevance for professionally oriented readers.

The entries themselves are concise and focus on solutions to specific problems. Therefore, the general tone is prescriptive. For example, questions about the history of a term such as data and the controversy surrounding its use may be interesting, but they are secondary to the advice the user seeks. So, although debate over divided usage is acknowledged, a guideline is offered to get the writer on with the business of writing. The guidance offered in the entries will solve most of the problems users of this book will encounter. However, students should understand that some employers (much like instructors) have their own standards governing certain subjects dealt with in this book and their employees must conform to those standards.

The Business Writer's Companion shares not only its format but a majority of the topics with *The Concise Handbook for Technical Writing,* also published by St. Martin's Press. Within the alphabetical entries common to both books, however, the examples given, as well as portions of the text, are often different—illustrating the same principles but in language that reflects a business context in one and a technical context in the other. In a course combining both technical and business communication, either book might be used, the choice depending upon the emphasis the instructor thinks most appropriate.

We are deeply grateful to the many instructors, students, professional writers, and others who have helped us prepare *The Business Writer's Companion.* In particular, we appreciate the sound advice provided by Alma G. Bryant, University of South Florida; Chris Benson, Clemson University; Kenneth W. Davis, Indiana University–Purdue University, Indianapolis; and Philip Vassallo. We also express our appreciation to the following organizations for permission to use examples of their technical writing: Biospherics, Inc., *Chemical Engineering,* First Wisconsin National Bank, Harnischfeger Corporation, Johnson Service Company, NCR Corporation, and Professional Secretaries International. We are especially grateful to Doug Bell and Emily Berleth at St. Martin's Press and to Rich Wright at Omega Publishing Services for their energy, care, and professionalism in turning manuscript into bound books. Our greatest appreciation goes to Nancy Lyman who actually conceived this book and then worked closely with the authors to create it.

C.T.B.
G.J.A.
W.E.O.

The
Business Writer's
Companion

OVERVIEW

Many business people have difficulty writing because they do not know how to begin. They do not realize that skill in writing, like the business skills in which they are proficient, requires a disciplined and systematic approach. The best way to ensure that a writing task will be successful—whether it is a letter, a proposal, or a formal report—is to divide the writing process into the following five steps: preparation, research, organization, writing the draft, and revision.

Step 1. Preparation

Writing, like most business tasks, requires solid preparation. In fact, adequate preparation is as important as writing the draft. Preparation for writing consists of (1) establishing your purpose, (2) identifying your audience/reader, and (3) determining the appropriate scope of coverage. (See also the **preparation** entry in this tabbed section.)

Step 2. Research

The purpose of most business writing is to explain something—usually something that is complex. This kind of writing cannot be done by someone who does not understand the subject. The only way to be sure that you can deal adequately with a complex subject is to compile a complete set of notes during your research. For additional information see the **note taking** and **library research** entries on the BUSINESS WRITING FORMS AND ELEMENTS tab.

Step 3. Organization

Without organization, the material gathered during your research would be incomprehensible to your reader. Outlining makes large or complex subjects easier for you to organize by breaking them into manageable parts, and it ensures that your finished writing will move logically from idea to idea without omitting anything important. In addition, by forcing you to structure your thinking at an early stage, a good outline releases you to concentrate exclusively on writing when you begin the rough draft. (See also the **organization** entry in this tabbed section.)

Step 4. Writing the Draft

When you have established your purpose, your reader's needs, and your scope of coverage, and when you have completed your research and your outline, you will be prepared to write your first draft. To do so, simply expand the notes from your outline into paragraphs, without worrying about grammar, refinements of language, or such mechanical aspects of writing as spelling. Refinements will come with revision. The entry on **writing a draft** in this tabbed section describes tactics used by experienced writers to get started and keep moving. Discover which ones are the most helpful and appropriate for you.

Step 5. Revision

Revision, the obvious final step, requires a different frame of mind than writing the draft. Read and evaluate the draft from the reader's point of view. Be eager to find and correct faults, and be honest.

Don't try to do all your revising at once. Read your rough draft several times, each time looking for and correcting a different set of problems or errors. Check your draft for accuracy and completeness. Your draft should give readers exactly what they need, but it should not burden them with unnecessary information or sidetrack them into loosely related subjects. Check your draft for unity, transition, and the elements covered on the STYLE AND CLARITY tab such as coherence. Check your entire draft for appropriate word choice, referring as needed to the entries listed on the USAGE tab. Finally, check slowly and carefully for problems covered on the GRAMMAR and PUNCTUATION AND MECHANICS tabs. (See also the **revision** entry in this tabbed section.)

audience/readers

As a business writer, you must usually assume that your readers are less familiar with the subject than you are. You have to be careful, for example, when writing on a topic that is unique to your area of specialization for executives whose training is in other areas; such readers need definitions of specialized terms and explanations of principles that you, as a specialist, take for granted. Even if you write a journal article for others in your field, you must remember to explain new or special uses of standard terms and principles.

Always consider whether illustrations will help convey your message to your reader more effectively. If so, see the FORMAT AND VISUAL AIDS tab for help.

When you write for many readers with similar backgrounds, try to visualize a typical member of that group and write to that reader. You might also make a list of characteristics (experience, training, and work habits for example) of that reader to help you write at the appropriate level. This technique, used widely by professional writers, enables you to decide what should or should not be explained, according to the typical reader's needs.

When your reading audience includes people with widely varied backgrounds, however, consider aiming various sections of a document at different sets of readers. Recommendations, executive summaries, and abstracts can be aimed at executives who will be reading to understand the general implications of projects or technical systems. Appendixes containing tables, graphs, and raw technical data can be aimed at specialists who wish to examine or use such supporting data. The body of a report or proposal should be aimed at those readers with the most serious interest or who need to make decisions based on the details in the contents.

Routine memorandums and short reports that are written for one individual reader do not require such elaborate design. Simply remember that person's exact needs as you write.

collaborative writing

Collaborative writing occurs when two or more writers work together to produce a single document for which they share responsibility and decision-making authority. The collaborating writers make approximately equal contributions, and communication among them is among equals, never superior to subordinate.

Collaborative writing teams are formed when (1) the size of a project or the time constraints imposed on it requires collaboration, (2) the project needs multiple areas of expertise, or (3) the project requires the melding of divergent views to form a single perspective that is acceptable to the whole collaborating team or another group.

Although the collaborative writing team is composed of peers, its members recognize and take advantage of the expertise of each member. Team members must respect the professional capabilities of one another and be compatible enough to work together in harmony, although some conflict is a natural part of any group project.

The team must designate one person as its leader, although that person does not have decision-making authority (just the extra responsibility of coordinating the activities of the team members and organizing the project). Team leadership can be by mutual agreement of the team members, or it can be on a rotating basis if the team produces multiple documents.

TASKS OF THE COLLABORATIVE WRITING TEAM

The collaborative writing team normally has four tasks: planning the document, researching and writing the draft, reviewing the drafts of other team members, and revising the drafts on the basis of the reviewers' comments.

Planning. The team, collectively, should identify the audience, purpose, and scope of the project, as well as its goals and the most effective organization for the whole document. The team analyzes the overall project, conceptualizes the document to be produced, creates a broad outline of the document, divides the document into segments, and assigns different segments to individual team members (often on the basis of expertise).

In the planning stage, the team should produce a projected schedule and set any writing style standards that team members will be expected to meet. The agreed-on schedule should include the due dates for drafts, for reviews of the drafts by other team members, and for revisions. It is important that these deadlines be met, even if the drafts are not quite as polished as the individual author would like, because a missed deadline by one team member holds up the work of the entire team.

Research and Writing. Planning is followed by research and writing, a period of intense independent activity by the individual members of the team. Each member researches his or her assigned segment of the document, fleshes out the broad outline with greater detail, and produces a draft from the detailed outline. The writers revise their drafts until they are as good as the individual writers can make them. Then, by the deadline established for drafts, the individual writers submit copies of their drafts to all other members of the team for review.

Reviewing. During the review stage, team members assume the role of the reading audience and try to clear up in advance any problems that might arise for the reader. Each team member reviews the work of the other team members carefully and critically, but diplomatically. They evaluate the organization of each segment, as well as each sentence and paragraph. They offer any advice or help that will enable the individual writer to improve his or her segment of the document.

Revising. The individual writers evaluate the reviews of all other team members and accept or reject their suggestions. Writers must be careful not to let ego get in the way of good judgment. They must evaluate each suggestion objectively—on the basis of its merit—rather than emotionally. The ability to accept criticism and use it to produce a better product is one of the critical differences between an effective collaborator and an ineffective one.

Conflict. Members of a team never have exactly the same perspective on any subject, and differing perspectives can easily lead to conflict. A team that can tolerate some disharmony and yet work through conflicting opinions to reach consensus produces better results. Although mutual respect among team members is necessary, too much deference can inhibit challenges—and that actually reduces the team's creativity. Writers must be willing to challenge one another—tactfully and diplomatically.

It is important to the quality of the document being produced that all viewpoints be considered. Under such circumstances, conflicts will occur, ranging from relatively mild differences over minor points to major conflicts over the basic approach. Regardless of the severity of the conflict, it must be worked through to a conclusion or a compromise that all team members can accept, even though all might not entirely agree.

concluding

Concluding a document not only ties together all the main ideas, but can do so emphatically by making a final significant point. This final point may be to recommend a course of action, to make a prediction, to offer a judgment, to speculate on the implications of your ideas, or merely to summarize your main points.

The way you conclude depends on both the purpose of your writing and the needs of your reader. For example, a committee report about possible locations for a new manufacturing plant could end with a recommendation. A report on a company's annual sales figures might conclude with a judgment about why sales are up or down. A letter about consumer trends could end by speculating on the implications of these trends. A document that is particularly lengthy will often end with a summary of its main points. Study the following examples:

Recommendation   These results indicate that you need to alter your testing procedure to eliminate the impurities we found in specimens A through E.

Prediction   Although my original estimate on equipment ($20,000) has been exceeded by $2,300, my original labor estimate ($60,000) has been reduced by $3,500; therefore, I will easily stay within the limits of my original bid. In addition, I see no difficulty in having the arena finished for the December 23 Christmas program.

Judgment   Although our estimate calls for a substantially higher budget than in the three previous years, we believe that it is justified by our planned expansion.

Summary   As this letter has indicated, we would attract more recent graduates by (1) increasing our advertising in local student newspapers, (2) resuming our co-op program, (3) sending a representative to career day programs at local colleges, (4) inviting local college instructors to teach in-house courses here at the plant, and (5) encouraging our employees to attend evening classes at local colleges.

The concluding statement may merely present ideas for consideration, but also it may call for action or deliberately provoke thought.

Ideas for Consideration   The new prices become effective the first of the year. Price adjustments are routine for the company, but some of your customers will not consider them so. Please consider the needs of both your customers and the company as you implement these new prices.

Call for Action   Send us a check for $250 now if you wish to keep your account active. If you have not responded to our previous letters because of some special hardship, I will be glad to work out a solution with you personally.

*Thought-
Provoking
Statement*   Can we continue to accept the losses incurred by careless workmanship? Must we accept it as inevitable? Or should we consider steps to control it firmly now?

Be especially careful not to introduce a new topic when you conclude. A concluding thought should always relate to and reinforce the ideas presented in your writing.

conclusions

The conclusion section of a document pulls together the results or findings and interprets them in the light of the study's purpose and the methods by which it was conducted. The evidence for these findings makes up the discussions in the body of the document, and the conclusions must grow out of the information discussed there. Moreover, the conclusions must be consistent with what the introduction stated that the report would examine (its purpose) and how it would do so (its method). If the introduction stated that the report had as its objective to learn the economic costs of relocating a plant from one city to another, the conclusion should not discuss the social or aesthetic impacts the new plant could have on the new location.

The sample conclusion in Figure 1 comes from a report about how community growth and real estate values in four specific areas were affected by nearby nuclear power plants.

defining terms

Terms can be defined either formally or informally, depending on your purpose and on your readers.

A *formal definition* is a form of classification. A term is defined by placing it in a category and then identifying what features distinguish it from other members of the same category.

Term	Category	Distinguishing Features
A spoon is	an eating utensil	that consists of a small shallow bowl on the end of a handle.
An auction is	a public sale	in which property passes to the highest bidder through successively increased offers.
An annual is	a plant	that completes its life cycle, from seed to natural death, in one growing season.

CONCLUSIONS

Brief statement of purpose

This study was undertaken to test the hypotheses that nuclear power plants have an adverse effect on (1) community growth and (2) residential property values. Implicit in the second hypothesis is that prices paid for residential properties reflect perceptions of house and lot quality, community services and attributes, and environmental characteristics. If people in general perceive nuclear plants as a possible threat to health and safety, they will tend to avoid living close to them. Such actions should be reflected in the real estate market for residential properties, and everything else being equal, the closer to the plant, the lower the price for housing.

Findings based on methods specified in introduction

The following conclusions are apparent from an analysis of time series data on total assessed real property values from 1960 to 1976 and from a regression analysis of 540 single-family house sales in 1975, 1976, and 1977 in the vicinity of four nuclear power generating plants in the Northeast.

1. Assuming that the real (deflated) increase in total assessed property values is a good indicator of growth, the presence of the nuclear plants has had no adverse effects on the growth rates of communities in close proximity to such plants.
2. Because (a) growth rates were inversely related to distance from the plant and (b) annual growth rates for the years following plant construction were higher than for the years before plant construction, with the increase in the growth rate for the host communities being higher than the increase for the region as a whole, the presence of the nuclear plant may actually stimulate growth. The likely explanation for this is the lower tax rates in the host municipalities, which are made possible by the large tax assessments levied on the plants.
3. The presence of the nuclear power plants, at least in 1975, 1976, and 1977, exerted no influence on the price of single-family housing within 20 miles of these plants. Therefore, our hypothesis that residential property values are directly related to distance from the nuclear power plants must be rejected and the null hypothesis accepted.
4. For most people in these study areas, the proximity of a nuclear power plant does not appear as a factor in residential location choice. The fears for health and safety expressed by some individuals and groups in society are not reflected in the housing decisions of residents in communities near the nuclear plants studied.

Restatement of scope and its implications

These conclusions apply only to the four areas studied. Since the plants were preselected and do not represent a random sample of all nuclear plants, the findings cannot be used to predict influences on growth and property values at other plant sites. Moreover, society's perceptions and values change over time, and what may have been true in the mid-1970s may not hold true in the future.

Figure 1 *Sample Conclusion*

An *informal definition* explains a term by giving a familiar word or phrase as a synonym.

EXAMPLE An *invoice* is a *bill*.

Definitions should normally be stated positively; focus on what the term *is* rather than on what it is not. For example, "In a legal transaction, real property is not personal property" does not tell the reader exactly what real property is. The definition could just as easily be stated positively: "Real property is legal terminology for the right or interest a person has in land and the permanent structures on that land."

Avoid circular definitions, which merely restate the term to be defined and therefore fail to clarify it.

CIRCULAR   *Spontaneous combustion* is fire that begins spontaneously.

REVISED   *Spontaneous combustion* is the self-ignition of a flammable material through a chemical reaction.

Avoid "is when" and "is where" definitions. Such definitions fail to include the category and are too indirect.

"IS WHEN"   A *contract* is when two or more people agree to something

REVISED   A *contract* is a binding agreement between two or more people.

"IS WHERE"   A *day-care center* is where working parents can leave their preschool children during the day.

REVISED   A *day-care center* provides care during the work day for children of working mothers.

Even informal writing occasionally requires terms used in a special sense that your readers may not understand; such terms should always be defined.

EXAMPLE   In these specifications the term *safety can* refers to a five-gallon container having a spring-closing spout cover designed to relieve internal pressure.

description

Effective description uses words to transfer a mental image from the writer's mind to the reader's. The key to effective description is the accurate presentation of details.

Descriptions can be brief and simple, or they can be highly complex. Simple descriptions usually require only a simple listing of key features. A purchase order is a typical example of simple descriptive writing. Even an order for something as ordinary as trash compactor bags needed, in addition to the part number, five specific descriptive details.

PURCHASE ORDER		
Part No.	Description	Quantity
GL/020	Trash compactor bags, 31″ × 50″ tubular, non-transparent, 5-mil thickness, including 100 tie wraps per carton	5 cartons @ 100 per carton

Complex descriptions, of course, require even more details than do simple descriptions. The details you select should accurately and vividly convey what you are describing. If it is useful for your reader to visualize an object, for instance, include details—like color and shape—that appeal to the sense of sight. The following description of a corporate headquarters uses details, partly based on shapes, to convey an image to the reader. The writer assumes that the reader knows such terms as *colonial design* and *champaign elm*.

> Their corporate headquarters, which reminded me of a rural college campus, is located just north of the city in a 90-acre wooded area. It consists of five three-story buildings of colonial design. The buildings are spaced about 50 feet apart and are built in a U shape, with the main building at the bottom of the U. The driveway that runs in front of the buildings is lined with overarching champaign elms. Employee and visitor parking lots are nearly hidden behind each building.

For descriptions intended for readers unfamiliar with a topic, more details are needed. This type of description benefits from showing or demonstrating, as opposed to telling, primarily through the use of images and details. You can also use analogy to explain unfamiliar concepts in terms of familiar concepts. For example, the plastic device that holds the letters and symbols for some typewriters and word-processing printers is a wheel-shaped piece of plastic, with each letter and symbol positioned at the circumference of the wheel and attached to the hub at the center of the wheel by thin plastic strips. Using analogy, you can think of the strips as petals radiating from the center of a flower. Because the strips are uniform in length and width, similar to the petals of a daisy, the print elements are commonly referred to, in an extension of the flower analogy, as daisy wheel print elements.

emphasis

Emphasis is the principle by which ideas in writing are stressed according to their importance. The means of achieving emphasis are by:

- position within a sentence, paragraph, or document;
- the use of repetition;
- the selection of sentence type;
- variation in the length of sentences;
- the use of climactic order within a sentence;
- punctuation (use of the dash);
- the use of intensifiers;
- the use of mechanical devices, such as italics and capital letters; and
- direct statements (using such terms as *most important* and *foremost*).

Emphasis can be achieved by *position* because the first and last words of a sentence, paragraph, or document stand out in the reader's mind.

CHANGE   Because they reflect geological history, moon craters are important to understanding the earth's history.

TO   Moon craters are important to understanding the earth's history because they reflect geological history.

Notice that the revised version of the sentence emphasizes moon craters simply because the term is in the front part of the sentence and geological history because the term is at the end of the sentence. Similarly, the first and last sentences in a paragraph and the first and last paragraphs in a document tend to be the most emphatic to the reader.

Another way to achieve emphasis is to *vary sentence length,* following a very long sentence, or a series of long sentences, with a very short one (which will stand out in the reader's mind).

EXAMPLE   We have already reviewed the problem the bookkeeping department has experienced during the past year. We could continue to examine the causes of our problems and point an accusing finger at all the culprits beyond our control, but in the end it all leads to one simple conclusion. *We must cut costs.*

Emphasis can be achieved by the *repetition* of key words and phrases.

EXAMPLE   Similarly, atoms *come and go* in a molecule, but the molecule *remains;* molecules *come and go* in a cell, but the cell *remains;* cells *come and go* in a body, but the body *remains;* persons *come and go* in an organization, but the organization *remains.*

—Kenneth Boulding, *Beyond Economics* (Ann Arbor: U of Michigan P, 1968) 131.

Different emphasis can be achieved by the *selection of sentence type*—a compound sentence, complex sentence, or simple sentence.

EXAMPLES   The report turned in by the police detective was carefully illustrated, and it covered five pages of single-spaced copy. (This compound sentence carries no special emphasis because it contain two coordinate independent clauses.)

The police detective's report, which was carefully illustrated, covered five pages of single-spaced copy. (This complex sentence emphasizes the size of the report.)

The carefully illustrated report turned in by the police detective covered five pages of single-spaced copy. (This simple sentence emphasizes that the report was carefully illustrated.)

Emphasis can be achieved by a *climactic order* of ideas or facts within a sentence.

EXAMPLE   Over subsequent weeks the industrial relations department worked diligently, management showed tact and patience, and the employees finally accepted the new policy.

Emphasis can be achieved by setting an item apart with a *dash.*

EXAMPLE   Here is where all the trouble begins—in the American confidence that technology is ultimately the medicine for all ills.

Emphasis can be achieved by the *use of intensifiers (most, very, really)*, but this technique is so easily abused that it should be used only with caution.

EXAMPLE   The final proposal is *much* more persuasive than the first.

Although emphasis can be achieved by such *mechanical devices* as italics, underlining, and capital letters, this technique is also easily abused and should be used with caution.

garbled sentences

A garbled sentence is one that is so tangled with structural and grammatical problems that it cannot be repaired.

EXAMPLE   My job objectives are accomplished by my having a diversified background which enables me to operate effectively and efficiently, consisting of a degree in mechanical engineering, along with twelve years of experience, including three years in Staff Engineering-Packaging sets a foundation for a strong background in areas of analyzing problems and assessing economical and reasonable solutions.

A garbled sentence often results from an attempt to squeeze too many ideas into one sentence. Do not try to patch such a sentence; rather, analyze the ideas it contains, list them in a logical sequence, and then construct one or more entirely new sentence(s). An analysis of the previous example yields the following five ideas:

EXAMPLES   My job requires that I analyze problems and find economical and workable solutions to them.

My diversified background helps me accomplish my job.

I have a mechanical engineering degree.

I have twelve years of job experience.

Three of these years have been in Staff Engineering-Packaging.

Using these ideas, the writer might have described his job as follows:

EXAMPLE   My job requires that I analyze problems and find economical and workable solutions to them. Both my training and my experience help me achieve this goal. Specifically, I have a mechanical engineering degree and twelve years of job experience, three of which have been in the Staff Engineering-Packaging Department.

logic

In persuasive writing, logic (or correct reasoning) is essential to convincing your reader that your conclusion is valid. Errors in logic can quickly destroy your credibility with your reader. The following discussion points out some common errors in logic that you should watch for in your writing.

LACK OF REASON

When a statement violates the reader's common sense, that statement is not reasonable. If, for example, you stated "New York City is a small town," your reader might immediately question your logic. If, however, you stated "Although New York's population is over eight million, it is a city composed of small towns," your reader could probably accept the statement as reasonable.

SWEEPING GENERALIZATIONS

Sweeping generalizations are statements that are too large to be supportable; they generally enlarge an observation about a small group to a generalization about an entire population.

> **EXAMPLE** Management is never concerned about employees.

This statement ignores any possibility that some companies show great concern for employee welfare. Such generalizations are not true, and using them will weaken your credibility.

NON SEQUITUR

A statement that does not logically follow from a previous statement is called a *non sequitur.*

> **EXAMPLE** I arrived at work early today, so the weather is calm.

Common sense tells us that arriving early for work does not produce calm weather; thus, the second part of the sentence does not follow logically from the first. In your own writing, be careful that all points stand logically connected; non sequiturs cause difficulties for your reader.

POST HOC, ERGO PROPTER HOC

This term means literally "after this, therefore because of this," and it refers to the logical fallacy that because one event happened after another event, the first somehow caused the second.

> **EXAMPLE** I didn't bring my umbrella today. No wonder it is now raining.

In on-the-job writing, this error in reasoning usually results from a hasty conclusion that events are related, without the writer examining the logical connection between the two events.

BIASED OR SUPPRESSED EVIDENCE

A conclusion reached as a result of self-serving data, questionable sources, or purposely incomplete facts is illogical—and often dishonest. If you, in preparing a report on the acceptance of a new policy among employees, distributed questionnaires only to those who thought the policy effective, the resulting evidence would be biased. If you purposely ignored employees who did not believe the policy was effective, you would also be suppressing evidence.

FACT VERSUS OPINION

Distinguish between fact and opinion. Facts include verifiable data or statements, whereas opinions are personal conclusions that may or may not be based on facts. For example, it is a verifiable fact that distilled water boils at 100 degrees Centigrade; that it tastes better than tap water is an opinion. Distinguish your facts from your opinions in your writing so that your reader can clearly understand and judge your conclusions.

> EXAMPLES The new milling machines produce parts that are within 2 percent of specification. (This sentence is stated as a fact and can be verified by measurement.)
>
> The milling machine operators believe the new models are safer than the old ones. (The word *believe* identifies the statement as an opinion.)

LOADING

When you include an opinion in a statement and then reach conclusions that are based on that statement, you are loading the argument. Consider the following opening for a memorandum:

> EXAMPLE I have several suggestions to improve the poorly written policy manual. First, we should change . . .

By opening with the assumption that the manual is poorly written, the writer has loaded the statement to get readers to accept his arguments and conclusions. Be careful not to load arguments in your writing; conclusions reached with loaded statements are weak and ultimately unconvincing.

methods of development

After you have completed your research, but before beginning your outline, ask yourself how you can most effectively "unfold" your topic for your reader. An appropriate method of development will make it easy for your reader to see how your topic is organized and will move the topic smoothly from an introduction (or opening) to a conclusion. There are several common methods of development, each best suited to particular purposes.

If you are writing a set of instructions, you know that your readers need the instructions in the order that will enable them to perform some task. Therefore, you should use a *sequential* method of development. If you wished to emphasize the time element of a sequence, you would follow a *chronological* method of development.

If writing about a new topic that is in many ways similar to a familiar topic, you could develop the new topic by comparing it to the old one. By doing so, you are using a *comparison* method of development.

When describing a mechanical device, you may divide it into its component parts and explain each part's function and how all the parts work together. In this case, you are using a *division-and-classification* method of development. Or you may use a *spatial* method of development to describe the physical appearance of the device from top to bottom, from inside to outside, from front to back, and so on.

If you are writing a report for a government agency explaining an airplane crash, you might begin with the crash and trace backwards to its cause, or you could begin with the cause of the crash (for example, a structural defect) and show the sequence of events that led to the crash. Either way is the *cause-and-effect* method of development. You can also use this approach to develop a report dealing with the solution to a problem, beginning with the problem and moving on to the solution, or vice versa.

If you are writing about the software for a new computer system, you might begin with a general statement of the function of the software package, then explain the functions of the larger routines within the software package, and finally deal with the functions of the various subroutines within the larger routines. You would be using a *general-to-specific* method of development. (In another situation, you might use the *specific-to-general* method of development.)

To explain the functions of the departments in a company, you could present them in a sequence that reflects their importance within the company: the executive department first and the custodial department last, with all other departments arranged in the relative order of importance they are given in that company. You would be using the *decreasing-order-of-importance* method of development. (In another situation, you might use the *increasing-order-of-importance* method of development.)

Methods of development often overlap, of course. Rarely does a writer rely on only one method of development in a written work. The important thing is to select one primary method of development and base your outline on it. Then subordinate any other methods of development to it. For example, in describing the organization of a company, you could use elements from three methods of development: you could *divide* the larger topic (the company) into departments, present the departments *sequentially,* and arrange the departments by their *order of importance* within the company.

openings

If your reader is already familiar with your subject, or if what you are writing is short, you may not need to begin your writing project with a full introduction. You may simply want to focus the reader's attention with a brief opening. For many types of on-the-job writing, openings that simply get to the point are quite adequate, as shown in the following examples:

Correspondence

Mr. George T. Whittier
1720 Old Line Road
Thomasbury, WV 26401

Dear Mr. Whittier:

You will be happy to know that we have corrected the error in your bank balance. The new balance shows . . .

Progress Report Letter

William Chang, M.D.
Phelps Building
9003 Shaw Avenue
Parksville, MD 21221

Dear Dr. Chang:

To date, 18 of the 20 specimens you submitted for analysis have been examined. Our preliminary analysis indicates . . .

Longer Progress Report

PROGRESS REPORT ON REWIRING THE SPORTS ARENA

The rewiring program at the Sports Arena is continuing on schedule. Although the costs of certain equipment are higher than our original bid had indicated, we expect to complete the project without exceeding our budget, because the speed with which the project is being completed will save labor costs.

Work Completed

As of August 15, we have . . .

Memorandum

To: Jane T. Meyers, Chief Budget Manager
From: Charles Benson, Assistant to the Personnel Director
Date: June 12, 19--
Subject: Budget Estimates for Fiscal Year 19--

As you requested, I am submitting the personnel budget estimate for fiscal year 19--.

You may also use an intriguing or interesting opening to stimulate your reader's interest. Such openings have two purposes: to indicate the subject and to catch the interest of the reader.

STATEMENT OF THE PROBLEM

One way to give the reader the perspective of your report is to present a brief account of the problem that led to the study or project being reported.

> EXAMPLE   Several weeks ago a brewmaster noticed a discoloration in the grain supplied by Acme Farms, Inc. He immediately reported his discovery to his supervisor. After an intensive investigation, we found that Acme . . .

DEFINITION

Although a definition can be useful as an opening, do not define something with which the reader is familiar or provide a definition that is obviously a contrived opening (such as "Webster defines *business* as . . ."). A definition should be used as an opening only if it offers insight into what follows.

> EXAMPLE   *Risk* is a loosely defined term. It is used here in the sense of physical risk as a qualitative combination of the probability of an event and the severity of the consequences of that event.

INTERESTING DETAIL

Often an interesting detail of your subject can be used to gain the readers' attention and arouse their interest.

> EXAMPLE   From asbestos sheeting to zinc castings, from a chemical analysis of the water in Lake Maracaibo (to determine its suitability for use in steam injection units) to pistol blanks (for use in testing power charges), the purchasing department attends to the company's material needs. Approximately 15,000 requisitions, each containing from one to fourteen separate items, are processed each year by this department. Every item or service that is bought . . .

ANECDOTE

An anecdote can also be used to catch your reader's attention and interest.

> EXAMPLE   In his poem "The Calf Path," Sam Walter Foss tells of a wandering, wobbly calf trying to find its way home at night through the lonesome woods. It made a crooked path, which was taken up the next day by a lone dog that passed that way. Then "a bellwether sheep pursued the trail over vale and steep, drawing behind him the flock,

too, as all good bellwethers do." At last the path became a country road; then a lane that bent and turned and turned again. The lane became a village street, and at last the main street of a flourishing city. The poet ends by saying, "A hundred thousand men were led by a calf, three centuries dead."

Many companies today follow a "calf path" because they react to events rather than planning. . . .

BACKGROUND

The background or history of a subject may be interesting and put the subject in perspective for your reader. Consider the following example from a newsletter article describing the process of oil drilling:

EXAMPLE From the bamboo poles the Chinese used when the pyramids were young to today's giant rigs drilling in a hundred feet of water, there has been a lot of progress in the search for oil. But whether four thousand years ago or today, in ancient China or a modern city, in twenty fathoms of water or on top of a mountain, the object of drilling is and has always been the same—to manufacture a hole in the ground, inch by inch.

QUOTATION

Occasionally, you can use a quotation to stimulate interest in your subject. To be effective, however, the quotation must be pertinent—not some loosely related remark selected from a book of quotations.

EXAMPLE Richard Smith, president of P.R. Smith Corporation, recently said, "I believe that the Photon projector will revolutionize our industry." His statement represents a growing feeling among corporate . . .

OBJECTIVE

In reporting on a project or activity, you may wish to open with a statement of the project or activity's objective. Such an opening gives the reader a basis for judging the results.

EXAMPLE The primary objective of the project was to develop new techniques to measure heat transfer in a three-phase system. Our first step was to investigate . . .

SUMMARY

You can provide a summary opening by compressing the results, conclusions, or recommendations of your article or report. Do not start a summary, however, by writing "This report summarizes . . ."

CHANGE This report summarizes the advantages offered by the photon as a mean of examining the structural features of the atom. . . .

TO As a means of examining the structure of the atom, the photon offers several advantages. . . .

FORECAST

Sometimes you can use a forecast of a new development or trend to arouse the reader's interest.

EXAMPLE In the very near future, we may be able to call our local library and have a videotape of Hamlet replayed on our wall television. This project and others are now being developed at Acme industries. . . .

organization

Organization is achieved, first, by developing your topic in a way that will enable your reader to understand your message and then by outlining your material on the basis of that method of development.

A logical method of development satisfies the reader's need for a controlling shape and structure for your subject. For example, if you were writing a proposal to your manager, trying to get him or her to fund a project you wanted to undertake, you would probably use an order-of-importance method of developing the topic. You would start with the most important reason the project should be funded and end with the least important reason. On the other hand, if you were a Federal Aviation Administration agent reporting on an airplane crash, you would probably use a cause-and-effect method, starting with the cause of the crash and leading up to the crash (or starting with the crash and tracing back to the cause).

An appropriate method of development is the writer's tool for keeping things under control and the reader's means of following the writer's development of a theme. Many different methods of development are available to the writer. (See the **methods of development** entry in this tabbed section for different methods of development.) As the writer, you must choose the method of development that best suits your subject, your reader, and your purpose.

Outlining provides structure to your writing by ensuring that it has a beginning, a middle, and an end. It gives proportion to your writing by making sure that one step flows smoothly to the next without omitting anything important, and it enables you to emphasize your key points by placing them in the positions of greatest importance. Using an outline makes larger and more difficult subjects easier to handle by breaking them into manageable parts.

outlining

Outlining provides structure to your writing by ensuring that it has a beginning (introduction or opening), a middle (main body), and an end (conclusion or concluding section). An outline gives your writing proportion so that one part flows smoothly to the next without omitting anything important. Outlining also enables you to emphasize your key points by placing them in the positions of greatest importance.

Like a road map, an outline indicates a starting point and keeps you moving logically so that you don't get lost before arriving at your conclusion. Errors in logic are much easier to detect and correct in an outline than in a draft. Using an outline makes larger and more difficult subjects easier to handle by breaking them into manageable parts; therefore, the less certain you are about your writing ability or about your subject, the fuller your outline should be. The parts of an outline are easily moved about, so you can experiment to see what arrangement of your ideas is the most effective. Perhaps most important, creating a good outline frees you to concentrate on writing when you begin the rough draft.

Treat graphics as an integral part of your outline, noting approximately where each should appear throughout the outline. At each place, either make a rough pencil sketch of the visual or write "illustration of . . ." and enclose each suggestion in a box. Like other information in an outline, these boxes and sketches can be moved, amended, or deleted, as required. Planning your graphics requirements from the beginning stages of your outline ensures their harmonious integration throughout all versions of the draft to the finished document.

Two types of outlines are generally used: *topic outlines* and *sentence outlines*. The topic outline consists of short phrases that show the sequential order and relative importance of ideas; in this manner, a topic outline provides order and establishes the relationships of topics to one another. The topic outline alone is generally not sufficient for a large or complex writing job, but it may be used to structure the major and minor divisions of your topic in preparation for creating a sentence outline. (An outline for a small job is not as detailed as one for a larger job, but it is just as important; for example, a topic outline that lists your major and minor points can help greatly even in writing important letters.)

On a large writing project, it is wise to create a topic outline first and then use it as a basis for creating a sentence outline. In a sentence outline, the writer summarizes each idea in a single complete sentence that may become the topic sentence for a paragraph in the rough draft. The sentence outline begins with a main idea statement that establishes the subject and then follows with a complete sentence for each idea in the major and minor divisions. If most of your notes can be shaped into controlling topic sentences for paragraphs in your rough draft, you can be relatively sure before you begin its final composition that your paper will be well organized.

The following outlining technique is easy to master and well suited to unraveling the complexities of large and difficult subjects. The first step is to group naturally related items and write them down on note cards. Arrange them in the proper order, and label them with Roman numerals. For example, the major divisions for this discussion of outlining could be as follows:

> I. Advantages of outlining
> II. Types of outlining
> III. Effective outlining
> IV. Writing the draft from the outline

The second step is to establish your minor points by deciding on the minor divisions within each major head. Arrange them in the proper sequence under their major heads, and label them with capital letters. The major and minor heads for this discussion of outlining could be as follows:

> I. Advantages of outlining
> II. Types of outlining
>   A. The topic outline
>   B. The sentence outline
> III. Effective outlining
>   A. Establish major and minor heads
>   B. Sort note cards by major and minor head
>   C. Complete the sentence outline
> IV. Writing the draft from the outline

Of course, you will often need more than the two levels of heads illustrated here. If your subject is complicated, you may need four or five levels to keep all of your ideas straight and in proper relationship to one another. In that event, the following numbering scheme is recommended:

> I. First-level head
>   A. Second-level head
>   1. Third-level head
>   a. Fourth-level head
>   (1) Fifth-level head

The third step is to mark each of your note cards with the appropriate Roman numeral and capital letter. Sort the note cards by major and minor heads (Roman numerals and capital letters). Then arrange the cards within each minor head, and mark each with the appropriate sequential Arabic number. Transfer your notes to paper, converting them to complete sentences. You now have a complete rough sentence outline, and the most difficult part of the writing job is over.

The final step is to polish your rough outline. Check to ensure that the subordination of minor heads to major heads is logical. All major heads should be parallel with each other and all minor heads should be parallel.

CHANGE   A. Major and minor heads should be established. (passive voice)
        B. Note cards are sorted by major and minor heads. (passive voice)
        C. Complete the sentence outline. (active voice)

TO   A. Establish major and minor heads. (active voice)
    B. Sort note cards by major and minor heads. (active voice)
    C. Complete the sentence outline. (active voice)

Make certain that your outline follows your method of development. Check for unity. Does your outline stick to the subject, or does it stray into unrelated or only loosely related topics? Stay within your established scope of coverage. Resist the temptation to tell all you know unless it all is pertinent to your purpose. Check your outline for completeness; scan it to see whether you need more information in any of your divisions, and insert any information that is needed.

You now have a final, polished sentence outline. It isn't sacred, however; change it if you need to as you write the draft; the outline should be your point of departure and return. Return to it to find your place and your direction as you work.

paragraphs

A paragraph is a group of sentences that support and develop a single idea; it may be thought of as an essay in miniature, for its function is to expand the core idea stated in its topic sentence (which is italicized in the following example).

> *The cost of training new employees is high.* In addition to the cost of classroom facilities and instructors, an organization must pay employees a salary to sit in the classroom while they are learning. We have determined that for the company to break even on professional employees (such as engineers or systems analysts), they must stay in the job for which they have been trained for at least one year.

The paragraph performs three functions: (1) it develops the unit of thought stated in the topic sentence; (2) it provides a logical break in the material; and (3) it creates a physical break on the page, which provides visual assistance to the reader.

TOPIC SENTENCE

A topic sentence states the subject of a paragraph; the rest of the paragraph then supports and develops that statement with carefully related details. The topic sentence may appear anywhere in the paragraph—a fact that permits the writer to achieve emphasis and variety—and a topic sentence may be more than one sentence if necessary.

The topic sentence is most often the first sentence of the paragraph because it states the subject that the paragraph is to develop. The topic sentence is effective in this position because the reader knows immediately what the paragraph is about. In the following paragraph, the first sentence is the topic sentence:

> *One important objective of automation is the improvement of quality.* Cost alone is no longer the sole reason that U.S. industries are losing ground to international competition. Higher quality products from other countries are forcing U.S. firms to look for ways to improve the quality of their products. Computer-aided design and analysis systems permit better predictions of product performance. Inspection devices with computer-driven "eyes" can ensure that the product has been manufactured to specifications.

On rare occasions, the topic sentence logically falls in the middle of a paragraph.

> While the principles and techniques of system coordination can be taught in a one- to two-week training course, actual expertise cannot be developed until one has coordinated several systems. The reason for this is simple. *Coordination is at least 60% "art" and only 40% "science."* For any given system, there are many different and acceptable solutions, The business analyst performing coordination must have a depth of experience to select the optimum solution from the many choices.

Although the topic sentence is usually more effective early in the paragraph, when the reader's attention is greatest, a paragraph can lead up to the topic sentence, which is sometimes done to achieve emphasis.

> The way most office organizations work has usually developed over a number of years, through a process of continuing evolution. The employees need not understand how their organization works in order to do their part. Information-handling patterns are largely subconscious and change resistant, since they reflect how people in an organization think of themselves and their organization. Therefore, bringing in equipment and instructing employees in how to use it to do things differently from now on is likely not to work—at least not without careful preparation. *The barriers to the effective use of new information techniques, therefore, lie in the way that a company is organized and the ways people customarily work and think about themselves in the organization.*

Because multiple paragraphs are sometimes used to develop different aspects of an idea, not all paragraphs have topic sentences. In this situation, transition between paragraphs helps the reader know that the same idea is being developed through several paragraphs.

Topic sentence	*To conserve valuable memory space, a large portion of the software*
for all three	*for all three packages remains on disk; only the most frequently used*
paragraphs	*portion resides in internal memory all the time.* The disk-resident software is organized into small modules that are called into memory as needed to perform specific functions.

Transition   *The memory-resident portion of the operating system* maintains strict control of processing. It consists of routines, subroutines, lists, and tables that are used to perform common program functions, such as processing input/output operations, calling other software routines from disk as needed, and processing errors.

Transition   *The disk-resident portion of the operating system* contains routines that are used less frequently in system operation, such as the peripheral-related software routines that are useful for correcting errors encountered on the various units, and the log and display routines that record unusual operating conditions in the system log.

—*NCR Century Operating Systems Manual* (Dayton: NCR Corporation).

In this example, the reason for breaking the development of the idea expressed in the topic sentence into three paragraphs is to help the reader assimilate the fact that the main idea has two separate parts.

PARAGRAPH LENGTH

Paragraph length should aid the reader's understanding of ideas. A series of short, undeveloped paragraphs can indicate poor organization of material and sacrifice unity by breaking a single idea into several pieces. A series of long paragraphs, on the other hand, can fail to provide the reader with manageable subdivisions of thought. A paragraph should be just long enough to deal adequately with the subject of its topic sentence. A new paragraph should begin whenever the subject changes significantly. Occasionally, a one-sentence paragraph is acceptable if it is used as a transition between larger paragraphs or in letters and memorandums, in which one-sentence openings and closings are sometimes appropriate.

WRITING PARAGRAPHS

Careful paragraphing reflects the writer's accurate thinking and logical organization. Clear and orderly paragraphs help the reader follow the writer's thoughts more easily.

Outlining is the best guide to paragraphing. It is easy to group ideas into appropriate paragraphs when you follow a good working outline. Notice how the following outline plots the course of subsequent paragraphs:

Outline

I. Advantages of Chicago as location for new plant
   A. Transport facilities
      1. Rail
      2. Air
      3. Truck
      4. Sea (except in winter)

B. Labor supply
1. Engineering and scientific personnel
   a. Many similar companies in the area
   b. Several major universities
2. Technical and manufacturing personnel
   a. Existing programs in community colleges
   b. Possible special programs designed for us

Resulting Paragraphs

Probably the greatest advantage of Chicago as a location for our new plant is its excellent transport facilities. The city is served by three major railroads. Both domestic and international air cargo service is available at O'Hare International Airport; Midway Airport's convenient location adds flexibility for domestic air cargo service. Chicago is a major hub of the trucking industry, and most of the nation's large freight carriers have terminals there. Finally, except in the winter months when the Great Lakes are frozen, Chicago is a seaport, accessible through the St. Lawrence Seaway.

A second advantage of Chicago is that it offers an abundant labor force. An ample supply of engineering and scientific personnel is assured not only by the presence of many companies engaged in activities similar to ours but also by the presence of several major universities in the metropolitan area. Similarly, technicians and manufacturing personnel are in abundant supply. The colleges in the Chicago City College system, as well as half a dozen other two-year colleges in the outlying areas, produce graduates with associate degrees in a wide variety of technical specialties appropriate to our needs. Moreover, three of the outlying colleges have expressed an interest in establishing special courses attuned specifically to our requirements.

PARAGRAPH COHERENCE AND UNITY

A good paragraph has unity, coherence, and adequate development. Unity is singleness of purpose, based on a topic sentence that states the core idea of the paragraph. When every sentence in the paragraph contributes to developing the core idea, the paragraph has unity. Coherence is holding to one point of view, one attitude, one tense; it is the joining of sentences into a logical pattern. Coherence is advanced by the careful choice of transitional words so that ideas are tied together as they are developed.

Topic Sentence	*Any company which operates internationally today faces a host of difficulties.* Inflation is worldwide. Most countries are struggling
Transition	with other economic problems *as well. In addition,* there are many monetary uncertainties and growing economic nationalism directed
Transition	against multinational companies. *Yet* there is ample business available in most developed countries if you have the right products, services, and marketing organization. To maintain the growth we

Transition   have achieved overseas, we recently restructured our international operations into four major trading areas. *This* will improve the services and support which the corporation can provide to its subsid-

Transition   iaries around the world. *At the same time* it established firm management control, ensuring consistent policies around the world.

Transition   *So* you might say the problems of doing business abroad will be more difficult this year but we are better organized to meet those problems.

Simple enumeration (*first, second, then, next,* and so on) can also provide effective transition within paragraphs. Notice how the italicized words and phrases give coherence to the following paragraph:

> Most adjustable office chairs have nylon hub tubes that hold metal spindle rods. To ensure trouble-free operation, lubricate these spindle rods occasionally. *First,* loosen the set screw in the adjustable bell. *Then* lift the chair from the base so that the entire spindle rod is accessible. *Next,* apply the lubricant to the spindle rod and the nylon washer, using the lubrication sparingly to prevent dripping. *When you have finished,* replace the chair and tighten the set screw.

Sometimes a paragraph is used solely for transition, as in the following example:

> . . . that marred the progress of the company.
>
> *There were two other setbacks to the company's fortunes that year which contributed to its present shaky condition: the loss of many skilled workers through the early retirement program and the intensification of the devastating rate of inflation.*
>
> The early retirement program . . .

persuasion

Persuasion in writing attempts to convince the reader to adopt the writer's point of view. In persuasive writing, the way you present your ideas is as important as the ideas themselves. You must support your appeal with logic—a sound presentation of facts, statistics, and examples. You must also acknowledge any real or possible conflicting opinions, for only then can you demonstrate and argue for the merit of your point of view. Be careful not to wander from your main point—avoid ambiguity and never make trivial, irrelevant, or false claims.

The memorandum shown in Figure 1 was written to persuade a manager and others to accept a new computer system. Notice that the writer admits that the new printer may be noisier than the old one. In fact, by acknowledging negative details or opposing views, a writer gains credibility.

MEMORANDUM

Date: December 5, 19--
To: Harriet Sullivan, Office Manager
From: Christine Thomas, Administrative Assistant CT
Subject: Advantages of Expanding HVS Computing Facilities

Statement of position

Because our computing facilities currently operate at maximum capacity, we are turning away new customers in growing numbers and will soon have to deny our present customers computer time for emergencies or overload backups. But by purchasing a new VT-8000 minicomputer and expanding our staff, we could respond to new service requests, offer better service to valued customers, and attract new customers who would not have previously considered using our service.

Facts and statistics that support the writer's position

Last month we turned away 21 new service requests. At least six of them were equal to the largest accounts we currently serve. Furthermore, since our aging mainframe computer cannot handle the latest software available from VRX Systems, we can neither offer improved, faster services to our most profitable accounts (such as First International Savings and Loan) nor attract the new customers who are eager to take advantage of the most recent advances in computer technology.

The VT-8000 is a very fast, reasonably priced minicomputer with massive peripheral memory capacity in the form of removable disk packs. This machine would triple our current processing capacity and enable us to use the full range of the VRX software now available. The following details show how purchasing the VT-8000 System would triple our number of customers and pay for itself within two years:

Cost of New Equipment

VT-8000 minicomputer	$12,500
Two 3033 disks and disk drives	1,800
One VT80 computer terminal	980
New VRX software	1,050
Total cost of equipment	$16,330

Increases in Annual Operating Budget

Salaries: Computer Operator	$17,000
Data Entry Technician	$14,200
Total increase/annual operating budget	$31,200

Total Costs

First year	$47,530
Second year	$31,200
Two-year total cost	$78,730

Figure 1 *Persuasive Memo*

Increased Income Generated by Expansion

First-year estimate (45 new customers)	$28,100
Second-year estimate (50 new customers) plus the 45 of the first year	$59,322
Total increase	$87,422

Since the purchase of the VT-8000 system is a one-time investment, <u>a profit of over $8,500 will be generated by the end of the second year</u>. The estimates are based on the $578 average annual value of accounts over the past two years.

Other advantages of the VT-8000 minicomputer are as follows:

- It requires little maintenance and therefore has minimal downtime.
- It is easy to operate and thus requires less highly trained staff.
- It is extremely compact and will easily fit into space already available in our computer room.
- Additional peripheral equipment, such as disk drives and remote terminals, can be added at minimal cost if we decide to expand the facility again at a later date.

**Acknowledg-
ment of
disadvantage**

Because this system is reliable, easy to install, and easy to operate, we could have it running in three weeks with little disturbance of our normal office routine. More importantly, buying the VT-8000 will provide a cost-effective solution to the current problem of overburdened computing resources and will clear the way for meeting the demands of a growing base of customers. Because the VT-8000 printer is somewhat noisier than the VT-3400 printer, the computer room may have to be soundproofed.

On the basis of these details, I recommend that we expand HVS services by purchasing the VT-8000 system. An enclosed brochure describes the system in more detail. I will be happy to provide additional information about the system at your request.

mo
Enclosure

Figure 1 *Persuasive Memo (continued)*

point of view

Point of view indicates the writer's relation to the information presented, as reflected in the use of person. The writer usually expresses point of view in first-, second-, or third-person personal pronouns. The use of the first person indicates that the narrator is a participant or observer ("This happened to *me*," "*I* saw that"). The second and third person indicate that the narrator is writing about other people or something impersonal or is giving directions, instructions, or advice ("This happened to *her*, to *them*, to *it*"—third person; "Enter the data after pressing the ENTER key once"—second person).

Consider the following sentence, written from an impersonal point of view.

> **EXAMPLE** It is regrettable that your shipment of March 12 is not acceptable.

Now consider the same sentence written from the more personal, first-person point of view.

> **EXAMPLE** I regret that we cannot accept your shipment of March 12.

Although the meaning of both sentences is the same, the sentence with the personal point of view indicates that two people are involved in the communication. Years ago business people preferred the impersonal point of view because they thought it made writing sound more objective and professional. Unfortunately, the impersonal point of view often prevents clear and direct communication and can cause misunderstanding. Today, good business writers adopt a more personal point of view whenever it is appropriate.

Business writers should not avoid *I* by using *one* when they are really talking about themselves. They do not increase objectivity but merely make the statement impersonal.

> **CHANGE** *One* can only conclude that the absorption rate is too fast.
>
> **TO** *I* can only conclude that the absorption rate is too fast.

Writers should never use *the writer* to replace *I* in a mistaken attempt to sound formal or dignified.

> **CHANGE** *The writer* believes that this project will be completed by the end of June.
>
> **TO** *I* believe that this project will be completed by the end of June.

However, the personal point of view should not be used when an impersonal point of view would be more appropriate or more effective.

> **CHANGE** I am inclined to think that each manager should attend the final committee meeting to hear the committee's recommendations.
>
> **TO** Each manager should attend the final committee meeting to hear the committee's recommendations.

Whether the writer adopts a personal or an impersonal point of view should depend on the document's purpose and the reader. For example, in a business letter to an associate, you would most likely adopt a personal point of view. But in a report to a large group, you would probably choose to emphasize the subject by adopting an impersonal point of view. For the subject matter to receive more emphasis than either the writer or the reader, an impersonal point of view is needed.

EXAMPLE The evidence suggests that the absorption rate is too fast.

In a letter on company stationery, use of the pronoun *we* may be interpreted as reflecting company policy, whereas *I* clearly reflects personal opinion. Which pronoun to use should be decided according to whether the matter discussed in the letter is a corporate or an individual concern.

EXAMPLES *I* appreciate your suggestion regarding our need for more community activities.

We appreciate your suggestion regarding our need for more community activities.

preparation

The preparation stage of the writing process is analogous to focusing a camera before taking a picture. By determining who your reader is, what your purpose is, and what your scope of coverage should be, you are bringing your whole writing effort into focus before beginning to write the draft. As a result, your topic will be much more clearly focused for your reader.

PURPOSE

What exactly do you want your readers to know, believe, or be able to do when they have finished reading your document? When you can answer this question, you will have determined the purpose of your writing. A good test of whether you have formulated your purpose adequately is to state it in a single sentence. This statement may also function as the thesis statement in your outline. (For more details, see the **purpose/objective** entry in this tabbed section.)

READERS

Know who your readers are and learn certain key facts about them, such as their educational level, their knowledge of your subject, and their needs relative to your subject. Their level of knowledge, for example, should determine whether you need to cover the fundamentals of your subject and which terms you must define. (For more details, see the **audience/readers** entry in this tabbed section.)

SCOPE

If you know the purpose of your writing project and your readers' needs, you will know the type and amount of detail you must include in your writing to accomplish your purpose and meet your readers' needs. This is your required scope of coverage. (For more details, see the **scope** entry in this tabbed section.)

process explanation

Many kinds of business writing explain a process, an operation, or a procedure. An explanation involves putting in the appropriate order the steps that a specific mechanism or system uses to accomplish a certain result. The process itself might range from the legal steps necessary to form a corporation, to the steps necessary to develop a roll of film.

In your opening paragraph, you might sometimes want to tell your reader it is important to become familiar with the process you are explaining. Before you explain the steps necessary to form a corporation, for example, you could cite the tax savings that incorporation would permit. To provide your reader with a framework for the details that will follow, you might want to present a brief overview of the process. Finally, you might describe how the process works in relation to a larger whole.

Notice in Figure 1 how the method of obtaining a company tuition refund is described as a step-by-step process.

proofreading

To proofread effectively you must be critical and alert, and (like revising) proofreading requires that you look at your writing objectively. Remember, even if you have a spellchecker, it only identifies words that do not exist.

Following are useful tips for proofreading three types of material: short narratives (letters or memorandums), long narratives (manuals or reports of ten or more pages), and technical material and statistical tables. They are from "36 Aids to Successful Proofreading," by Ruth H. Turner.

SHORT NARRATIVES

Concentrate as you slowly read for errors. Speed reading does not help. To concentrate on typographical errors, read backwards (from right to left). Of course, this method will not reveal omissions or duplications, so you must read again for content.

Pay attention to dates; do not assume they are correct. Check the spelling of months and even the correctness of the year.

Do not overlook names, addresses, subject or reference lines, signature lines, or even the copies list.

MEMORANDUM

To: Walter Camburn
From: Leonard Fein *LF*
Date: March 25, 19--

Subject: Tuition Refund Procedure

**Why it is
important to
follow the
procedure**

As you requested in your memo of March 18, I checked with
Ron Manuszak, Tuition Refund Coordinator, about a tuition
refund for the two courses you plan to take this summer
at Parkland College. To obtain approval for the courses
and to receive the actual refund, you should follow the
procedure described below.

You must first gain the approval of your manager, Susan
Mueller, of the courses you wish to take. If she
approves, you must then meet with Mr. Manuszak in
Personnel Resources. He will notify you within one week
whether or not Personnel Resources has approved your
courses.

**Step-by-step
process**

If they approve, you should then complete Sections I and
II of the enclosed Form F-6970 and submit the form to
Personnel Resources. They will get Ms. Mueller's
signature, and Mr. Manuszak will then send you a memo
authorizing you to enroll in the courses.

Once the courses are over, you should send Mr. Manuszak a
copy of your grade report as evidence that you have
completed them successfully. Mr. Manuszak will then
complete Section III of Form F-6970 and send it on to you
with your tuition-refund check.

I know that Mr. Manuszak will be happy to answer any
specific questions you may have about certain courses.
His office is in the Blaylock West Building on River Road
and his phone number is extension 8709.

Good luck in your courses.

bb
Enclosure

Figure 1 *Explanation of a Process*

Examine the end and beginning of lines in the body of the letter or
memorandum to make sure that little words like *that* or *and* have not been
unnecessarily repeated.

LONG NARRATIVES

Proofread in steps. For example, check all the heads and titles first. Scan page numbers. Have you missed or duplicated any?

Read the body of the material against the original, sentence by sentence.

Make sure any references to other parts of the work are correct. For example, "See page 6 for a similar list"; possibly, through revision, the list moved to page 7.

Verify the title and page numbers of other reference materials, looking up each item if at all possible.

When proofreading from a draft that has handwritten inserts, make sure that none have been overlooked in the final draft.

TECHNICAL MATERIAL AND STATISTICAL TABLES

If the accuracy of your data is critical, use two people—one reading aloud, the other checking copy—to verify itemized data, codes, figures, and so on. Remember that spellcheckers are not 100 percent reliable. If the draft is typewritten, lay a ruler under each line. This technique will help you keep your place on both the original and the copy. It also helps when the inevitable interruptions occur.

When the columns of a table have been typed by tabulating across the page, proofread your copy down the columns, folding the original from top to bottom along the column and laying it next to the corresponding column of the copy.

Check for both vertical and horizontal alignment of table columns. Proofread across the page, folding the original beneath each line and laying it under the corresponding lines of typed entries so that you can easily read the original against your copy.

Count the number of entries in each table column, and compare the total with the number in your copy. If there is a difference, find the culprit.

PROOFREADING CHECKLIST

Check your final document for the following:

1. *Missing syllables.* Mentally repeat each syllable of long words with many vowels, such as *evaluation, responsibilities, continuously, individual.* It is easy to omit one.
2. *Double letters.* They are hard to remember, especially in words like *accommodation* and *occurrence.*
3. *Silent letters.* They are often forgotten, as in *rhythm, rendezvous, malign.*
4. *Punctuation.* Check all punctuation marks after completing all other proofreading. Be careful not to omit a closing parenthesis or quotation mark.
5. *Compound words.* Check the dictionary to determine whether to spell a compound word as two words, a hyphenated word, or one word.

If the dictionary does not list the word as hyphenated or separate words, write it as one word.

6. *Capital letters.* Be consistent and follow any established style for the type of document or subject matter. If an established style does not exist, adopt one of your own.

7. *Final advice*—proofread tomorrow what you worked on today.

purpose/objective

What do you want your readers to know, believe, or be able to do when they have read your finished writing project? When you have answered this question, you have determined the purpose or objective of your writing project. Too often, however, beginning writers state their purposes in broad terms that are of no practical value to them. Such a purpose as "to explain the Model 6000 Accounting System" is too general to be of any real help. But "to explain how to use a Model 6000 Accounting System" is a specific purpose that will help keep the writer on the right track.

The writer's purpose is rarely simply to "explain" something, although on occasion it may be. You must ask yourself, "*Why* do I need to explain it?" In answering this question, you may find, for example, that your purpose is also to persuade your reader to change his or her attitude toward the thing you are explaining.

A writer for a company magazine who has been assigned to write an article about cardiopulmonary resuscitation, in answer to the question *what*, could state the purpose as "to show the importance of CPR." In answer to the question *why*, the writer might state "so employees will sign up for evening CPR classes."

If you answer these two questions *exactly* and put your answers in writing as your stated purpose, not only will your job be made easier but also you will be considerably more confident of ultimately reaching your goal. As a test of whether you have adequately formulated your purpose, try to state it in a single sentence. If you find that you cannot, continue to formulate your purpose until you can state it in a single sentence.

Even a specific purpose is of no value, however, unless you keep it in mind as you work. Guard against losing sight of your purpose as you become involved with the other steps of the writing process.

revision

Allow a day or two, if possible, to go by without looking at the draft before beginning to revise it. Without a cooling period, you are too close to the draft to be objective in evaluating it.

Read and evaluate the draft with deliberation and objectivity, from the point of view of a reader. Be anxious to find and correct faults, and be honest. Do not try to do all your revision at once. Read through your rough draft several times, each time searching for and correcting a different set of problems.

REVISION CHECKLIST

Check your draft for the following:

1. *Completeness.* Your writing should give readers exactly what they need but no more.
2. *Accuracy.* No matter how careful and painstaking you may have been in conducting your research, compiling your notes, and creating your outline, you could easily have made errors when transferring your thoughts from the outline to the rough draft. Look for contradictory facts that may have crept into your draft.
3. *Unity and coherence.* If a paragraph has unity, all its sentences and ideas are closely tied together and contribute directly to the main idea expressed in the topic sentence of the paragraph. Writing that is coherent flows smoothly from one point to another, from one sentence to another, and from one paragraph to another. Where transition is missing, provide it; where transition is weak, strengthen it.
4. *Consistent labeling.* Make sure, for example, that you have not called the same item a "routine" on one page and a "program" on another.
5. *Conciseness.* Tighten your writing so that it says exactly what you mean by pruning unnecessary words, phrases, sentences, and even paragraphs.
6. *Awkwardness.* Look especially for passive voice constructions and excess words.
7. *Word choice.* Delete or replace vague or pretentious words and unnecessary intensifiers. Check for sexist language, especially in pronoun references.
8. *Jargon.* If you have any doubt that *all* your readers will understand any jargon you may have used, eliminate it.
9. *Clichés.* Replace clichés with fresh figures of speech or direct statements.
10. *Grammar.* Check your draft for possible grammatical errors.
11. *Proofreading.* Finally, check your final draft for typographical errors by proofreading it.

The following list directs you to further discussion of concepts in the revision checklist.

Entry	Tab
awkwardness	Style and Clarity
clichés	Style and Clarity
conciseness/wordiness	Style and Clarity

Entry	Tab
figures of speech	Style and Clarity
grammar	Grammar
introductions	Business Writing Forms and Elements
jargon	Style and Clarity
openings	The Business Writing Process
proofreading	The Business Writing Process
transition	The Business Writing Process
voice	Grammar
word choice	Style and Clarity

scope

If you know your reader and the purpose of your writing project, you will know the type and amount of detail to include in your document. Scope may be defined as the depth and breadth of necessary detail to cover your subject. If you do not determine your scope of coverage in the planning stage of your writing project, you will not know how much or what kind of information to include. Your scope should be designed to satisfy the needs of your purpose and your reader.

sentence construction

Subjects, verbs, and complements (which include direct and indirect objects) are the main elements of a sentence. A sentence that progresses quickly from subject to verb to complement is clear and easy to understand. The basic sentence patterns in English are the following:

EXAMPLES   The cable snapped. (subject-verb)

Generators produce electricity. (subject-verb-direct object)

The test results gave us confidence. (subject-verb-indirect object-direct object)

Repairs made the equipment operational. (subject-verb-direct object-objective complement)

The metal was aluminum. (subject-linking verb-subjective complement)

Most sentences follow the subject-verb-object pattern. In "The company dismissed Joe," we know the subject and the object by their positions relative to the verb. The knowledge that the usual sentence order is subject-verb-object helps readers interpret what they read.

An inverted sentence places the elements in other than normal order.

EXAMPLES   A better job I never had. (direct object-subject-verb)

More optimistic I have never been. (subjective complement- subject-linking verb)

Inverted sentence order may be used in questions and exclamations and also to achieve emphasis.

EXAMPLES   Have you a pencil? (verb-subject-complement)

A sorry sight we presented! (complement-subject-verb)

CONSTRUCTING CLEAR SENTENCES

Use uncomplicated sentences to state complex ideas. If readers must cope with a complicated sentence in addition to a complex idea, they are likely to become confused.

CHANGE   When you are purchasing parts, remember that although an increase in the cost of aluminum forces all the vendors to increase their prices, some vendors will have a supply of aluminum purchased at the old price, and they may be willing to sell parts to you at the old price in order to get your business.

TO   Although an increase in the cost of aluminum forces all vendors to increase their prices, some vendors will have a supply of aluminum purchased at the old price. When you are purchasing aluminum parts, remember that these vendors may be willing to sell you the parts at the old price in order to get your business.

Just as simpler sentences make complex ideas more digestible, a complex sentence construction makes a series of simple ideas more palatable.

CHANGE   The computer is a calculating device. It was once known as a mechanical brain. It has revolutionized industry.

TO   The computer, a calculating device once known as a mechanical brain, has revolutionized industry.

Do not string together a number of thoughts that should be written as separate sentences or some of which should be subordinated to others. Sentences carelessly tacked together this way are monotonous and hard to read because all ideas seem to be of equal importance.

CHANGE   We started the program three years ago, there were only three members on the staff, and each member was responsible for a separate state, but it was not an efficient operation.

TO   When we started the program three years ago, there were only three members on the staff, each having responsibility for a separate state; however, that arrangement was not efficient.

Constructing Parallel Sentences

Express coordinate ideas in similar form. The very construction of the sentence helps the reader grasp the similarity of its components. (See the **parallel structure** entry on the STYLE AND CLARITY tab.)

EXAMPLE Similarly, atoms come and go in a molecule, but the molecule remains; molecules come and go in a cell, but the cell remains; cells come and go in a body, but the body remains; persons come and go in an organization, but the organization remains.

—Kenneth Boulding, *Beyond Economics* (Ann Arbor: U of Michigan P, 1968) 131.

Constructing Sentences to Achieve Emphasis

Subordinate your minor ideas to emphasize your more important ideas. (See the **emphasis** and **subordination** entries in this tabbed section.)

CHANGE We all had arrived, and we began the meeting early.

TO Since we all had arrived, we began the meeting early.

The most emphatic positions within a sentence are at the beginning and the end. Do not waste them by tacking on phrases and clauses almost as an afterthought or by burying the main point in the middle of a sentence between less important points. For example, consider the following original and revised versions of a statement written for a company's annual report to its stockholders:

CHANGE Sales declined by 3 percent in 19--, but nevertheless the company had the most profitable year in its history, thanks to cost savings that resulted from design improvements in several of our major products; and we expect 19-- to be even better, since further design improvements are being made.

TO Cost savings from design improvements in several major products not only offset a 3-percent sales decline but made 19-- the most profitable year in the company's history. Further design improvements now in progress promise to make 19-- even more profitable.

The following list directs you to other entries that relate to constructing sentences.

Entry	Tab
complements	Grammar
conjunctions	Grammar
emphasis	The Business Writing Process
expletives	Style and Clarity

Entry	*Tab*
objects	Grammar
parallel structure	Style and Clarity
subjects of sentences	Grammar
subordination	The Business Writing Process
verbs	Grammar

subordination

Subordination is a technique used by writers to show, in the structure of a sentence, the appropriate relationship between ideas of unequal importance by subordinating the less important ideas to the more important ideas.

> CHANGE Beta Corp. now employs 500 people. It was founded just three years ago.
>
> TO Beta Corp., *which now employs 500 people,* was founded just three years ago.
>
> OR Beta Corp., *which was founded just three years ago,* now employs 500 people.

Effective subordination can be used to achieve sentence variety, conciseness, and emphasis. For example, consider the sentence, "The city manager's report was carefully illustrated, and it covered five typed pages." See how it might be rewritten, using subordination, in any of the following ways:

> EXAMPLES The city manager's report, *which covered five typed pages,* was carefully illustrated. (dependent clause)
>
> The city manager's report, *covering five typed pages,* was carefully illustrated. (phrase)
>
> The city manager's *five-page* report was carefully illustrated. (single modifier)

We sometimes use a coordinating conjunction to concede that an opposite or balancing fact is true; however, a subordination connective can often make the point more smoothly.

> CHANGE Their bank has a lower interest rate on loans, *but* ours provides a fuller range of essential services.
>
> TO *Although* their bank has a lower interest rate on loans, ours provides a fuller range of essential services.

The relationship between a conditional statement and a statement of consequences will be clearer if the condition is expressed as a subordinate clause.

CHANGE The bill was incorrect, *and* the customer was angry.

TO The customer was angry *because* the bill was incorrect.

Subordinating connectives *(such as, because, if, while, when, though)* achieve subordination effectively.

EXAMPLE A buildup of deposits is impossible *because* the apex seals are constantly sweeping the inside chrome surface of the rotor housing.

Relative pronouns *(who, whom, which, that)* can be used effectively to combine related ideas that would be stated less smoothly as independent clauses or sentences.

CHANGE The generator is the most common source of electric current. It uses mechanical energy to produce electricity.

TO The generator, *which* is the most common source of electric current, uses mechanical energy to produce electricity.

Avoid overlapping subordinate constructions, with each depending on the last. Often the relationship between a relative pronoun and its antecedent will not be clear in such a construction.

CHANGE Shock, *which* often accompanies severe injuries, severe infections, hemorrhages, burns, heat exhaustion, heart attacks, food or chemical poisoning, and some strokes, is a failure of the circulation, *which* is marked by a fall in blood pressure *that* initially affects the skin (*which* explains pallor) and later the vital organs of kidneys and brain; there is a marked fall in blood pressure.

TO Shock often accompanies severe injuries, severe infections, hemorrhages, burns, heat exhaustion, heart attacks, food or chemical poisoning, and some strokes. It is a failure of the circulation, initially to the skin (this explains pallor) and later to the vital organs of kidneys and brain; there is a marked fall in blood pressure.

tone

Tone is the writer's attitude toward the subject and his or her readers. The tone may be casual or serious, enthusiastic or skeptical, friendly or hostile. In business writing, the tone in correspondence and reports may range widely—depending on the purpose, situation, and context. For example, in a memo read only by an associate who is also a friend, your tone might be casual and friendly.

EXAMPLE I think your proposal to Smith and Sons is great. If we get the contract, I owe you a lunch! I've marked a couple of places where we could cover ourselves on the schedule. See what you think.

In a memo to a superior, however, your tone might be quite different.

EXAMPLE   I think your proposal to Smith and Sons is excellent. I have marked
a couple of places for your consideration where we could ensure that
we are not committing ourselves to a schedule we might not be able
to keep. If I can help in any other way, please let me know.

In a memo that serves as a report to numerous readers, the tone would again
be different.

EXAMPLE   The Smith and Sons proposal appears complete and thorough, based
on our department's evaluation. Several small revisions, however,
would ensure that the company is not committing itself to an un-
realistic schedule. These are marked on the copy of the report being
circulated.

Your choice of words, your introduction or opening, and even your title
contribute to the overall tone of your document. For instance, a title such
as "Some Observations on the Diminishing Oil Reserves in Wyoming"
clearly sets a different tone from "What Happens When We've Pumped
Wyoming Dry?" The first title would be appropriate for a report; the second
title would be appropriate for a newsletter article or a popular magazine
article. The important thing is to make sure that your tone is the one best
suited to your purpose/objective and your reader.

In business correspondence, tone is particularly important because the
letter represents direct communication between two people. Moreover,
good business letters establish rapport between your organization and the
public, and a positive and considerate tone is essential.

topic selection

On the job, the topic of a writing project is usually determined by need. In
a college writing course, you may have to select your own topic. If you do,
keep the following points in mind:

1. Select a topic that interests you.
2. Select a topic that you can research adequately with the facilities available to you.
3. Limit your topic so that its scope is small enough to handle within the
   time you are given. A topic like "Air Pollution," for example, would be
   too broad. On the other hand, keep the topic broad enough so that you
   will have enough to write about.
4. Select a topic for which you can make adequate preparation to ensure
   a good final report.

topic sentences

A topic sentence states the controlling idea of a paragraph; the rest of the
paragraph supports and develops that statement with carefully related
details.

The topic sentence is often the first sentence because it states the subject.

EXAMPLE *The arithmetic of searching for oil is stark.* For all his scientific methods of detection, the only way the oil driller can actually know for sure that there is oil in the ground is to drill a well. The average cost of drilling an oil well is over $300,000, and drilling a single well may cost over $8,000,000. And once the well is drilled, the odds against its containing any oil at all are 8 to 1! Even after a field has been discovered, one out of every four holes drilled in developing the field is a dry hole because of the uncertainty of defining the limits of the producing formation. The oil driller can never know what Mark Twain once called "the calm confidence of a Christian with four aces in his hand."

On rare occasions, the topic sentence logically falls in the middle of a paragraph.

EXAMPLE It is perhaps natural that psychologists should awaken only slowly to the possibility that behavioral processes may be directly observed, or that they should only gradually put the older statistical and theoretical techniques in their proper perspective. But it is time to insist that science does not progress by carefully designed steps called "experiments," each of which has a well-defined beginning and end. *Science is a continuous and often a disorderly and accidental process.* We shall not do the young psychologist any favor if we agree to reconstruct our practices to fit the pattern demanded by current scientific methodology. What the statistician means by the design of experiments is design which yields the kind of data to which *his* techniques are applicable. He does not mean the behavior of the scientist in his laboratory devising research for his own immediate and possibly inscrutable purposes.

—B. F. Skinner, "A Case History in Scientific Method," *American Psychologist* 2 (May 1956): 232.

Although the topic sentence is usually most effective early in the paragraph, a paragraph can lead up to the topic sentence; this is sometimes done to achieve emphasis. When a topic sentence concludes a paragraph, it can also serve as a summary or conclusion based on the details that were designed to lead up to it.

EXAMPLE Energy does far more than simply make our daily lives more comfortable and convenient. Suppose you wanted to stop—and reverse—the economic progress of this nation. What would be the surest and quickest way to do it? Find a way to cut off the nation's oil resources! Industrial plants would shut down; public utilities would stand idle; all forms of transportation would halt. The economy would plummet into the abyss of national economic ruin. *Our economy, in short, is energy-based.*

—*The Baker World* (Los Angeles: Baker Oil Tools).

transition

Transition is the means of achieving a smooth flow of ideas from sentence to sentence, paragraph to paragraph, and subject to subject. Transition is a two-way indicator of what has been said and what will be said; that is, it provides a means of linking ideas to clarify the relationship between them. You can achieve transition with a word, a phrase, a sentence, or even a paragraph. Without the guideposts of transition, readers can lose their way.

Transition can be quite obvious.

> **EXAMPLE** Having considered the economic feasibility of this business process, we turn now to the problem of inadequate supply.

Or it can be more subtle.

> **EXAMPLE** Even if this business process is economically feasible, there still remains the problem of inadequate supply.

Either way, you now have your reader's attention fastened on the problem of inadequate supply, exactly what you set out to do.

Certain words and phrases are inherently transitional. Consider the following terms and their functions:

> **RESULT** *therefore, as a result, consequently, thus, hence*
>
> **EXAMPLE** *for example, for instance, specifically, as an illustration*
>
> **COMPARISON** *similarly, likewise*
>
> **CONTRAST** *but, yet, still, however, nevertheless, on the other hand*
>
> **ADDITION** *moreover, furthermore, also, too, besides, in addition*
>
> **TIME** *now, later, meanwhile, since then, after that, before that time*
>
> **SEQUENCE** *first, second, third, then, next, finally*

Within a paragraph, such transitional expressions clarify and smooth the movement from idea to idea. Conversely, the lack of transitional devices can make the going bumpy for the reader. Consider first the following passage, which lacks adequate transition:

> **EXAMPLE** People had always hoped to fly. Until 1903 it was only a dream. It was thought by some that human beings were not meant to fly. The Wright brothers launched the world's first heavier-than-air flying machine. The airplane has become a part of our everyday life.

Now read the same passage with words and phrases of transition added (in italics), and notice how much more smoothly the thoughts flow.

> **EXAMPLE** People had always hoped to fly, *but* until 1903 it was only a dream. *Before that time,* it was thought by some that human beings were not meant to fly. *However,* in 1903 the Wright brothers launched the world's first heavier-than-air flying machine. *Since then* the airplane has become a part of our everyday life.

Transition between Sentences

In addition to using transitional words and phrases such as those shown above, the writer may achieve effective transition between sentences by repeating key words or ideas from preceding sentences and by using pronouns that refer to antecedents in previous sentences. Consider the following short paragraph, in which all these means are employed.

EXAMPLE Representative of many American university towns is Millville. *This midwestern town,* formerly a *sleepy farming community,* is today the home of a large and bustling *academic community.* Attracting students from all over the Midwest, *this university* has grown very rapidly in the last ten years. *This same decade* has seen a physical expansion of the campus. The state, recognizing *this expansion,* has provided additional funds for the acquisition of land adjacent to the university.

Another device for achieving transition is enumeration:

EXAMPLE The recommendation rests upon *three conditions. First,* the department staff must be expanded to a sufficient size to handle the increased work load. *Second,* sufficient time must be provided for the training of the new members of the staff. *Third,* a sufficient number of qualified applicants must be available.

Transition between Paragraphs

All the means discussed above for achieving transition between sentences may also be effective for transition between paragraphs. For paragraphs, however, longer transitional elements are often required. One technique is to use an opening sentence that summarizes the preceding paragraph and then to move ahead to the business of the new paragraph.

EXAMPLE One property of material considered for manufacturing processes is hardness. Hardness is the internal resistance of the material to the forcing apart or closing together of its molecules. Another property is ductility, the characteristic of material that permits it to be drawn into a wire. The smaller the diameter of the wire into which the material can be drawn, the greater the ductility. Material also may possess malleability, the property that makes it capable of being rolled or hammered into thin sheets of various shapes. Engineers, in selecting materials to employ in manufacturing, must consider these properties before deciding on the most desirable for use in production.

The requirements of hardness, ductility, and malleability account for the high cost of such materials. . . .

You may ask a question at the end of one paragraph and answer it at the beginning of the next.

EXAMPLE   Automation has become an ugly word in the American vocabulary because it has at times displaced some jobs. But the all-important fact that is often overlooked is that it invariably creates many more jobs than it eliminates. (The vast number of people employed in the great American automobile industry as compared with the number of people that had been employed in the harness-and-carriage-making business is a classic example.) Almost always, the jobs that have been eliminated by automation have been menial, unskilled jobs, and those who have been displaced have been forced to increase their skills, which resulted in better and higher-paying jobs for them. *In view of these facts, is automation really bad?*
Certainly automation has made our country the most technologically advanced nation the world has ever known. . . .

A purely transitional paragraph may be inserted to aid readability.

EXAMPLE: . . . that marred the progress of the company.
There were two other setbacks to the company's fortunes that year that also marked the turning of the tide: the loss of many skilled workers through the early retirement program and the intensification of the devastating rate of inflation.
The early retirement program . . .

unity

Unity is singleness of purpose and treatment, the cohesive element that holds a document together; it means that everything in an article or paper is essentially about one thing or idea.

To achieve unity, the writer must select one topic and then treat it with singleness of purpose—without digressing into unrelated paths. The prime contributors to unity are a good outline and effective transition. After you have completed your outline, check it to see that each part relates to your subject. Be certain that your transitional terms make clear the relationship of each part to what precedes it.

Transition dovetails sentences and paragraphs like the joints of a well-made drawer. Notice, for example, how neatly the sentences in the following paragraph are made to fit together by the italicized words and phases of transition:

EXAMPLE   Any company that operates internationally today faces a host of difficulties. Inflation is worldwide. Most countries are struggling with other economic problems *as well. In addition,* many monetary uncertainties and growing economic nationalism are working against multinational companies. *Yet* ample business is available in most developed countries if you have the right products, services, and marketing organization. To maintain the growth Data Corporation has achieved overseas, we recently restructured our international

> operations into four major trading areas. *This* reorganization will improve the services and support that the corporation can provide to its subsidiaries around the world. *At the same time,* the reorganization establishes firm management control, ensuring consistent policies around the world. *So* you might say the problems of doing business abroad will be more difficult this year, but we are better organized to meet those problems.

The logical sequence provided by a good outline is essential to achieving unity. An outline enables the writer to lay out the most direct route from introduction to conclusion without digressing into side issues that are not related, or that are only loosely related, to the subject. Without establishing and following such a direct route, a writer cannot achieve unity.

word processing

The word processor is obviously a powerful tool that can help you record your ideas quickly, improve your writing and revising skills, and create well-designed documents. But remember that good writing is still the result of careful planning, constant practice, and thoughtful revision. In some cases, word-processing technology can initially intrude on the writing process and impose certain limitations that many beginners overlook. The ease of making minor, sentence-level changes and the limitation of a 24-line viewing screen, for example, may focus your attention too narrowly on surface problems of the text so that you lose sight of larger problems of scope and organization. Or the fluid and rapid movement of the text on the screen, together with last-minute editing changes, may allow undetectable errors to creep into the text. Also, as you master the software and become familiar with its powerful revision capabilities, you may begin to "overwrite" your documents. Inserting phrases and rewriting sentences becomes so easy that you may find yourself generating more text and rewriting more extensively but ultimately saying less. The following tips will help you avoid these initial pitfalls and develop writing strategies that take full advantage of the great benefits offered by word-processing technology.

TIPS ON USING THE WORD PROCESSOR TO IMPROVE WRITING SKILLS

1. Avoid the temptation of writing first drafts on the computer *without any planning or outlining*. Plan your document carefully by identifying your objective, readers, and scope and by completing your research and preparing an outline before you begin writing the draft on the computer.
2. Use the word processor's outline feature to brainstorm and organize an initial outline for your topic.

3. When you're ready to begin writing, you can overcome "writer's block" by practicing free writing on the computer. *Free writing* means typing your thoughts as quickly as possible from an outline without stopping to correct mistakes or to complete sentences—saving these steps for the revision phase.

4. Use the search command to find and delete wordy phrases such as *that is, there are, the fact that,* and *to be,* and unnecessary helping verbs such as "will."

5. Use a spellchecker and other specialized programs to identify and correct typographical errors, misspellings, and grammar and diction problems. Maintain a file of your most frequently misspelled or misused words and use the search command to check for them in your documents.

6. Avoid excessive editing and rewriting on the screen. Print out a complete paper copy of your drafts periodically for major revisions and reorganizations.

7. Always proofread your final copy on paper, since the fluidity of the viewing screen makes it difficult to catch all the errors in your manuscript. Print out an extra copy of your document for your peers to comment on before making final revisions.

8. When writing a single document for multiple readers, use the search command to find technical terms and other data that may need further explanation for secondary readers, either in the text or in a glossary.

9. Use the computer for effective document design by emphasizing major headings and subheadings with bold print, by using the copy command to create and duplicate parallel headings throughout your text, and by inserting blank lines (carriage returns) and tab key spaces in your text to create extra white space around examples and illustrations.

10. Keep the standard version of certain documents, such as your résumé and application letters, on file so you can revise them to meet specific needs.

11. Frequently "save" (store your text on disk) during long writing sessions if your computer does not have an automatic storage backup feature. Routinely create an extra, or "backup," copy of your documents on duplicate disks for safekeeping.

writing a draft

You are well prepared to write a rough draft when you have established your purpose, readers' needs, and scope and when you have done adequate research and outlining. Writing a rough draft is simply transcribing and expanding the notes from your outline into paragraphs, without worrying about grammar, refinements of language, or such mechanical aspects of writing as spelling. Refinement will come with revision.

Write a rough draft as though you were explaining your subject to someone across the desk from you. Don't worry about a good opening. Just start. There is no need in a rough draft to be concerned about an introduction or transitions unless they come easily—concentrate on ideas. Keep writing quickly to achieve unity and coherence.

Even with good preparation, however, writing a draft remains a chore and an obstacle for many writers. Experienced writers use the following tactics to get started and keep moving. Discover which ones are the most helpful to you.

TIPS FOR WRITING THE ROUGH DRAFT

Following is a list of tips you can use to help you write better rough drafts.

- Set up your writing areas with the equipment and materials (paper, dictionary, source books, etc.) you will need to keep going once you get started. Then hang out the "Do Not Disturb" sign.
- Use whatever writing tools, separately or in combination, that are most comfortable for you: pencil, felt-tip pen, typewriter, word processor, etc.
- Remind yourself that you are beginning a version of your writing project that *no one else* will read.
- Remember the writing projects you have finished in the past—you *have* completed something before and you *will* this time.
- Start with the section that seems easiest to you. Your reader will neither know nor care that you first wrote a section in the middle.
- Give yourself a time limit (ten or fifteen minutes, for example) in which you write continually, regardless of how good or bad your writing seems to you. The point is to *keep moving.*
- Don't let anything stop you when you are rolling along easily—if you stop and come back, you may not regain the momentum.
- Stop writing before you're completely exhausted; when you begin again, you may be able to regain the momentum.
- Give yourself a small reward—a short walk, a soft drink, a short chat with a friend, an easy task—after you have finished a section.
- Reread what you have written when you return to your writing. Often, seeing what you have written will trigger the frame of mind that was productive.

The most effective way to start and keep going, however, is to use a good outline as a springboard and map for your writing. Your outline notes can become the topic sentences for paragraphs in your draft, as shown below. For example, notice that items III.A. and III.B. in the following topic outline become the topic sentences of the succeeding two paragraphs and that the subordinate items in the outline become sentences in the two paragraphs.

Outline

III. Advantages of Chicago as Location for New Plant
    A. Outstanding Transport Facilities
        1. Rail
        2. Air
        3. Truck
        4. Sea (except in winter)
    B. Ample Labor Supply
        1. Engineering and scientific personnel
           a. Many similar companies in the area
           b. Several major universities
        2. Technical and manufacturing personnel
           a. Existing programs in community colleges
           b. Possible special programs designed for us

Resulting Paragraphs

Probably the greatest advantage of Chicago as a location for our new plant is its excellent transport facilities. The city is served by three major railroads. Both domestic and international air cargo service is available at O'Hare International Airport; Midway Airport's convenient location adds flexibility for domestic air cargo service. Chicago is a major hub of the trucking industry, and most of the nation's large freight carriers have terminals there. Finally, except in the winter months when the Great Lakes are frozen, Chicago is a seaport, accessible through the St. Lawrence Seaway.

A second advantage of Chicago is that it offers a large labor force. An ample supply of engineering and scientific personnel is assured not only by the presence of many companies engaged in activities similar to ours but also by the presence of several major universities in the metropolitan area. Similarly, technicians and manufacturing personnel are in abundant supply. The colleges in the Chicago City College system, as well as half a dozen other two-year colleges in the outlying areas, produce graduates with associate degrees in a wide variety of technical specialties appropriate to our needs. Moreover, three of the outlying colleges have expressed an interest in establishing courses attuned specifically to our requirements.

Remember that your function as a writer is to communicate certain information to your readers. Don't try to impress them with a fancy writing style. Write in a plain and direct style that is comfortable and natural for both you and your reader—and remember that the first rule of good writing is to help the reader.

As you write your rough draft, keep in mind your reader's level of knowledge of the subject. Doing so will not only help you write directly to your reader, it will also tell you which terms you must define.

When you come to something difficult to explain, try to relate the new concept to something with which the reader is already familiar. Although figures of speech are not used extensively in business writing, they can be very useful in explaining a complex process. In the rough draft, a figure of speech might be just the tool you need to keep moving when you encounter a complex concept that must be explained or described.

Above all, don't wait for inspiration to write your rough draft—treat writing a draft as you would any on-the-job task.

you viewpoint

The "you viewpoint" (or "you attitude") is a writing technique that places the readers' interest foremost in your writing. It is based on the principle that your readers are more concerned about their own needs than they are about yours. The "you viewpoint" often, but not always, means using the words *you* and *your* rather than *we, our, I* and *mine*. Consider the following sentence that focuses on the writer's, rather than the reader's, needs.

> EXAMPLE   *We must receive* your receipt with the merchandise before *we can process* your refund.

Even though the sentence uses *your* twice, the words in italics suggest that the point of view centers on the writer's need to process the refund. You can make the request more politely, as in the following example.

> EXAMPLE   Please enclose the sales receipt with the merchandise so we can process your refund promptly.

Although the tone is now more polite and friendly (which is important in most correspondence), this version still emphasizes the writer's need to get the receipt. But what is the reader's interest? The reader is not interested in helping the business process its paperwork. He or she simply wants the refund—and by emphasizing that need the writer encourages the reader to act quickly. Consider the following revision, written with the you viewpoint.

> EXAMPLE   So you can receive your refund promptly, please enclose the sales receipt with the merchandise.

In this example, the reader's benefit is stressed as the reason the reader should enclose the receipt. The writer using this sentence, therefore, is more likely to accomplish his or her purpose: to get the reader to act.

Obviously, using the you viewpoint means more than just using the pronouns *you* and *your*. It means seeing a situation from the reader's viewpoint and writing accordingly. (See also **persuasion** in this tabbed section.)

OVERVIEW

For business writing, the term "format" has at least two distinct, but related, meanings: it can refer (1) to the sequence in which information is presented in a document, and (2) to the physical arrangement of information on the page and the general physical appearance of the finished document. The first meaning applies to the standard arrangement of information in many of the forms of business writing discussed in this tabbed section: feasibility reports, progress and activity reports, proposals, trip reports, and so on. These documents are characterized by conventions that govern where each section is placed. In formal reports, for example, the table of contents normally precedes the foreword but follows the title page and abstract.

This tab contains entries on complete documents (like formal reports), parts of documents (like executive summaries and introductions), and methods of gathering information (like note taking and library research).

Types of letters and memos, as well as résumés, are covered on the CORRESPONDENCE AND JOB APPLICATION tab. Entries related to the second meaning of "format" (physical appearance) and the use of visual material such as drawings and illustrations appear on the FORMAT AND VISUAL AIDS tab.

abstracts

An abstract highlights the major points of a document to enable readers to decide whether they need to read the work in full. Abstracts vary in the amount of information they provide, depending on whether they are *descriptive abstracts* or *informative abstracts.*

DESCRIPTIVE ABSTRACTS

A descriptive abstract includes information about the purpose and scope of the document, as well as any methods used to arrive at the findings. It is almost an expanded table of contents in sentence form. A descriptive abstract need not be longer than several sentences.

The following descriptive abstract comes from a 30-page report that describes how a select group of countries provide engineering expertise to their control-room operators for round-the-clock shift work at nuclear power plants:

ABSTRACT

Purpose and   This report describes the practices of selected countries for pro-
scope   viding engineering expertise on shift in nuclear power plants. The
report discusses the extent to which engineering expertise is made
available and the alternative models of providing such expertise. The
implications of foreign practices for U.S. consideration are discussed, with particular reference to the shift adviser position and to
a proposed shift engineer position. The relevant information for this
Methods used   methods study came from the open literature, interviews with utility
staff and officials, and governmental and nuclear utility reports.

INFORMATIVE ABSTRACTS

The informative abstract is an expanded version of the descriptive abstract.
In addition to information about the purpose, scope, and methods of the
report, the informative abstract includes the results, conclusions, and any
recommendations.

The following informative abstract expands the scope of the sample
descriptive abstract by including the report's findings, conclusions, and
recommendation:

ABSTRACT

Purpose and   This report describes the practices of selected countries for pro-
scope   viding engineering expertise on shift in nuclear power plants. The
report discusses the extent to which engineering expertise is made
available and the alternative models for providing such expertise.
The implications of foreign practices for U.S. consideration are
discussed, with particular reference to the shift adviser position and
Methods used   to a proposed shift engineer position. The relevant information for
this study came from the open literature, interviews with utility staff
and officials, and governmental and nuclear utility reports.

Finding   The countries studied used two approaches to provide engineering expertise on shift: (1) employing a graduate engineer in a line
management operations position and (2) creating a specific engi-
General   neering position to provide expertise to the operations staff. The
conclusions   comparison of these two models did not indicate that one system
inherently functions more effectively than does the other for safe
operations. However, the alternative modes are likely to affect crew
relationships and performance; labor supply, recruitment, and re-
tention; and system implementation. Of the two systems, the non-
Recommendation   supervisory engineering position seems more advantageous within
the context of current recruitment and career-path practices.

LENGTH OF ABSTRACTS

A long abstract defeats the purpose of an abstract. For this reason, informative abstracts are usually no longer than 200 to 250 words, and descriptive
abstracts may be considerably shorter.

Do not include the following kinds of information in an abstract:

- the background of the study
- a detailed discussion or explanation of the methods used
- administrative details about how the study was undertaken, who funded it, who worked on it, and the like
- figures, tables, charts, maps, and bibliographic references
- any reference to tables or illustrations in the report (abstracts may be published independently).

(For guidance about the location of an abstract in a report, see the **formal reports** entry in this tabbed section.)

appendixes

An appendix, located at the end of a formal report, supplements or clarifies the information in the body of the document. (The plural form of the word may be either *appendixes* or *appendices.*)

An appendix can be useful for explanations that are too long for notes but could be helpful to the reader seeking further assistance or a clarification of points made in the report. Information can be placed in an appendix because it is too detailed or voluminous to appear in the text without impeding the orderly presentation of ideas for the primary reader. However, don't use an appendix for miscellaneous bits and pieces of information you were unable to work into the text.

Generally, each appendix contains only one type of information. When the report contains more than one appendix, arrange them in the order to which they are referred in the text. Begin each appendix on a new page, and identify each with a title and a head. If you have only one appendix, title it "Appendix." If you have more then one, title them alphabetically, beginning with the letter *A:*

Appendix A
Sample Questionnaire

List the titles and beginning page numbers of the appendixes in the table of contents of the report in which they appear.

bibliography

A bibliography is a list of the books, articles, and other source materials consulted in the preparation of a paper, report, or article. It provides a convenient alphabetical listing of these sources in a standardized form for readers interested in getting further information on the topic or in assessing the scope of the research.

Works consulted for background information in addition to those actually cited in the text should be included in a bibliography. The entries in a bibliography are listed alphabetically by the author's last name. If the author is unknown, the entry is alphabetized by the first word in the title (following *a, an,* or *the*). Entries may also be arranged into subject categories and then by alphabetical order within these categories.

An annotated bibliography includes complete bibliographic information about a work (author, title, publisher) followed by a brief description or evaluation of what the work contains.

documenting sources

By documenting sources, writers identify where they obtained the facts, ideas, quotations, and paraphrases used in preparing a document. The information can come from books, manuals, correspondence, interviews, software documentation, reference works, and many other sources.

This entry describes and provides examples of the three principal methods of documenting sources: (1) *parenthetical documentation*—putting brief citations in parentheses in the text and providing full information in a list of "Works Cited"; (2) *reference documentation*—referring to sources with numbers in parentheses or by superscripts in the text and providing full information in a "References" section where the entries are listed numerically in the order of their first citation in the text; and (3) *notational documentation*—using superscript numbers in the text to refer to notes either at the bottom of the page (footnotes) or at the end of the paper, article, or chapter (endnotes). Many professional organizations and journals publish style manuals that describe their own formats for documenting sources. If you are writing for publication in a professional field, consult the manual for the particular field or the style sheet for the journal to which you are submitting your article, and follow it exactly.

Use the following directory to this entry to locate information quickly. Samples of each format appear at the end of each discussion. Parenthetical samples begin on page 61; reference samples begin on page 65; and notational samples begin on page 68.

PARENTHETICAL DOCUMENTATION

The parenthetical method that follows is recommended by the Modern Language Association of America (MLA) in the *MLA Handbook for Writers of Research Papers,* Fourth Edition. This method gives an abbreviated reference to a source parenthetically in the text and lists full information about the source in a separate section called "Works Cited."

When documenting sources in text, include only the author and page number in parentheses. If the author's name is mentioned in the text, include only the page number of the source. The parenthetical citation should include no more information than is necessary to enable the reader to relate it to the corresponding entry in the list of "Works Cited." When referring to an entire work rather than to a particular page in a work, mention the author's name in the text, and omit the parenthetical citation.

The following passages contain sample parenthetical citations.

EXAMPLES

Steve Wozniak's first computer was the so-called Cream Soda Computer, which he and a friend built in 1971, staying up all night and drinking cream soda (Freiberger and Swaine 205).

According to Freiberger and Swaine, the development of the BASIC programming language by two Dartmouth professors in 1964 gave ordinary people the means of using the computing power put in their hands by microprocessor technology and its commercial exploitation (140).

When placing parenthetical citations in text, insert them between the closing quotation mark or the last word of the sentence (or clause) and the period or other punctuation. Use the spacing shown above. If the parenthetical citation follows an extended quotation or paraphrase, however, place it outside the last sentence of the quotation or paraphrase, with two spaces between the period and the first parenthesis. Within the citation itself, allow one space (no punctuation) between the name of the author and the page number. Don't use the word *page* or its abbreviation.

If you are citing a page or pages of a multivolume work, give the volume number, followed by a colon, space, and page number: (Jones 2: 53). If the entire volume is being cited, identify the author and volume as follows: (Smith, vol. 3).

If your list of "Works Cited" includes more than one work by the same author, include the title of the work (or a shortened version if the title is long) in the parenthetical citation, unless you mention it in the text. If, for example, your list of "Works Cited" included more than one work by David Landes, a proper parenthetical citation for his book *Revolution in Time: Clocks and the Making of the Modern World* would appear as in the following sample:

> The tremendous success of Timex watches in the 1950s is attributable to drastic simplification of design; standardization of parts, making them interchangeable even between plants; and thorough-going automation of the manufacturing process (Landes, Revolution in Time 340).

Use only one space between the title and the page number. The works cited in the sample passages given would be listed alphabetically, as follows, in a "Works Cited" section:

> Hirshfield, Alan, and Roger W. Sinnott, eds. Sky Catalogue 2000.0. 2 vols. Cambridge, MA: Sky, 1982.
>
> von Auw, Alvin. Heritage and Destiny: Reflections of the Bell System in Transition. New York: Praeger, 1983.
>
> Landes, David S. Revolution in Time: Clocks and the Making of the Modern World. Cambridge, MA: Belknap-Harvard UP, 1983.

CITATION FORMAT FOR WORKS CITED

The list of "Works Cited" should begin on the first new page following the end of the text. Each new entry should begin at the left margin, with the second and subsequent lines within an entry indented five spaces. Double-space within and between entries.

AUTHOR

Entries appear in alphabetical order by the author's last name (by the last name of the first author if the work has more than one author). Works by the same author should be alphabetized by the first major word of the title (following *a, an* or *the*). If the author is a corporation, the entry should be alphabetized by the name of the corporation; if the author is a government agency, entries are alphabetized by the government, followed by the agency (for example, "United States. Dept. of Health and Human Services."). Some sources require more than one agency name (for example, "United States. Dept. of Labor. Bureau of Labor Statistics."). If no author is given, the entry should begin with the title and be alphabetized by the first significant word in the title.

After the first listing for an author, put three hyphens and a period in place of the name for subsequent entries with the same author. An editor's name is followed by the abbreviation, "ed."

McNeill, William H. The Pursuit of Power. Chicago: U of Chicago P, 1982.

———. The Rise of the West. Chicago: U of Chicago P, 1963.

TITLE

The second element is the title of the work. Capitalize the first word and each significant word thereafter. Underline the title of a book or pamphlet. Place quotation marks around the title of an article in a periodical, an essay in a collection, and a paper in a proceedings. Each title should be followed by a period.

PERIODICALS

For an article in a periodical (journal, magazine, or newspaper), the volume number, date (for a magazine or newspaper, simply the date), and the page numbers should immediately follow the title of the periodical.

SERIES OR MULTIVOLUME WORKS

For works in a series and multivolume works, the name of the series and the series number of the work in question, or the number of volumes, should follow the title. If the edition used is not the first, the edition should be specified.

PUBLISHING INFORMATION

The final elements of the entry for a book, pamphlet, or conference proceedings are the place of publication, publisher, and date of publication. Use a shortened form of the publisher's name (for example, *St. Martin's* for St. Martin's Press, Inc., *Random* for Random House, *Oxford UP* for Oxford University Press). If any of these cannot be found in the work, use the abbreviations n.p. (no publication place), n.p. (no publisher), and n.d. (no date), respectively. For familiar reference works, list only the edition and year of publication.

SAMPLE ENTRIES (MLA STYLE)

BOOK, ONE AUTHOR

Landes, David S. Revolution in Time: Clocks and the Making of the Modern World. Cambridge, MA: Belknap-Harvard UP, 1983.

BOOK, TWO OR MORE AUTHORS

Freiberger, Paul, and Michael Swaine. Fire in the Valley: The Making of the Personal Computer. Berkeley: Osborne/McGraw, 1984.

BOOK, CORPORATE AUTHOR

CompuServe Incorporated. CompuServe Information Service: User's Guide. Columbus, OH: CompuServe, 1985.

WORK IN AN EDITED COLLECTION

Gibson, Ralph. "High Contrast Printing." Darkroom. Ed. Eleanor Lewis. N.p.: Lustrum, 1977. 63–76.

BOOK EDITION, IF NOT THE FIRST

Gibson, H. Lou. Photography by Infrared: Its Principles and Applications. 3rd ed. New York: Wiley, 1978.

TRANSLATED WORK

Texereau, Jean. How to Make a Telescope. Trans. Allen Strickler. 2nd English ed. Richmond, VA: Willmann-Bell, 1984.

MULTIVOLUME WORK

Hirshfield, Alan, and Roger W. Sinnott, eds. Sky Catalogue 2000.0. 2 vols. Cambridge, MA: Sky, 1982.

WORK IN A SERIES

Armstrong, Joe E., and Willis W. Harman. Strategies for Conducting Technology Assessments. Westview Special Studies in Science, Technology, and Public Policy. Boulder, CO: 1980.

REPORT

Gould, John D. Composing Letters with Computer-Based Text Editors. IBM Computer Science Research Report RC 8446 (#36750). Yorktown Heights, NY: 1980.

THESIS OR DISSERTATION

Ross, Brant Arnold. "Flexible Engineering Software: An Integrated Workstation Approach to Finite Element Analysis." Diss. Brigham Young U. 1985.

ENCYCLOPEDIA ARTICLE

Heginbotham, Wilfred Brooks. "Robot Devices." Encyclopaedia Britannica: Macropaedia. 15th ed. 1982.

PROCEEDINGS

Crawford, David L. Instrumentation in Astronomy IV. Proc. of the Society of Photo-Optical Instrumentation Engineers. 8–10 March, 1982. Tucson, AZ. Bellingham, WA: SPIE, 1982.

PAPER IN A PROCEEDINGS

Carr, Marilyn. "Appropriate Technology: Theory, Policy and Practice." Fundamental Aspects of Appropriate Technology. Proc. of the International

Workshop on Appropriate Technology. 4–7 Sept. 1980. Ed. J. de Schutter and G. Bemer. Delft, Neth.: Delft UP, 1980. 145–53.

Paper Presented at a Conference

Madson, Elizabeth Ann. "Use of Writer's Workbench Software." Midwest MLA Annual Meeting, Bloomington, IN, 3 Nov. 1984.

Journal Article

MacDonald, Nina H., Lawrence T. Frase, Patricia S. Gingrich, and Stacey A. Keenan. "The Writer's Workbench: Computer Aids for Text Analysis." IEEE Transactions on Communications 30(1982): 105–10.

Magazine Article

Sinfelt, John H. "Bimetallic Catalysts." Scientific American Sept. 1985: 90–98.

Anonymous Article (in Weekly Periodical)

"T&W Systems Adds Relational Database." Infoworld 20 Jan. 1986: 49.

Newspaper Article

Schmeck, Harold M., Jr. "Gene-Spliced Hormone for Growth is Cleared." New York Times 19 Oct. 1985, national ed.: 8.

Letter from One Official to Another

Brown, Charles L. Letter to retired members of Bell System Presidents' Conference. 8 Jan. 1982.

Letter Personally Received

Harris, Robert S. Letter to the author. 3 Dec. 1985.

Personal Interview

Denlinger, Virgil, Assistant Chief of Police, Alexandria, VA. Personal interview. 15 Dec. 1984.

Computer Software

PowerEdit. Vers. 1.0. Computer software. Artificial Linguistics, 1991. IBM MS-DOS 3.0 or higher, 470K RAM.

Reference Documentation

The reference system of documenting sources lists the numbered references at the end of the work. The references on the list are identified by numbers in the text that correspond to the numbered items in the list. The reference list cites only those works referred to in text.

The styles for references vary. The style described here is recommended by the American National Standards Institute (ANSI) in *American National Standard for Bibliographic References*, Z39.29-1977.

The citations in a reference list are arranged in numerical sequence (1, 2, 3), according to the order in which they are first mentioned in the text. The most common method for directing readers from your text to specific references is to place the reference number in parentheses after the work cited. Thus in the text, the number one in parentheses (1) after a reference to a book, article, or other work refers the reader to the first citation in the reference list. The number five in parentheses (5) refers the reader to the fifth citation in the reference list. A second number in the parentheses, separated from the first by a colon (3:27), refers to the page number of the source from which the information was taken.

There are several other common methods for directing readers from your text to specific references. You can place the word *Reference,* or the abbreviation *Ref.,* within parentheses with the numbers: (Reference 1) or (Ref. 1). Or you can write the reference number as a superscript: text[1]. Sometimes you may cite your sources within a sentence in the text; then you should spell out the word *Reference:* "The data in Reference 3 include. . . ." For subsequent references in the text, simply repeat the reference number of the first citation.

CITATION FORMAT FOR REFERENCES

In the numbered reference list, the number begins at the left margin, followed by a period. Then leave two spaces and begin the entry, indenting the second and subsequent lines to be even with the first. Single-space within entries, and double-space between them.

The recommended order for information groupings within an entry and for punctuation within and between these groups are shown in the samples beginning on page 65. In general, put a period between groups and at the end of the entry, a semicolon between elements within a group, and a comma between subelements or closely related elements.

AUTHOR

Authors' names should be given with the last name first. If a work has two authors, both names should be given, with the last name first, separated by a semicolon. If a work has more than two authors, the first author should be cited, last name first, followed by "and others" in square brackets. For an edited work (if you are listing the whole work, not just an article in it) begin the entry with the editor(s), giving the names as described for the authors, followed by a comma and the abbreviation, "ed."

TITLE

Only the first word and any proper nouns should be capitalized in a book or article title. The title of an article, followed by a period, should precede the title of the journal or book in which it appears. In journal or magazine titles, abbreviations may be used, and all significant words (or abbreviations for them) should be capitalized.

In an entry for an article or paper in an edited collection, the authorship group and title group for the article are followed by the editors and title group for the collection.

Publishing Information

For a book, the publishing information consists of the place of publication followed by a colon, the publisher followed by a semicolon, and the year of publication followed by a period. For a journal or magazine, the date (in year–month–day order) may either precede or follow the volume number, issue number, and pages, separated from them by a semicolon. The volume number is followed by the issue number in parentheses, a colon after the closing parenthesis, and then the pages of the article.

Sample References (ANSI Style)

The following examples will acquaint you with the ANSI style. If you need to list a source for which no example is given, follow the pattern from the examples that are most like it. If you are uncertain whether to include a piece of information about the source, include it.

Book, One Author

1. Landes, David S. Revolution in time: clocks and the making of the modern world. Cambridge, MA: Belknap/Harvard Univ. Press; 1983.

Book, Two Authors

2. Inose, Hiroshi; Pierce, John R. Information technology and civilization. New York: W. H. Freeman; 1984.

Book, Corporate Author

3. CompuServe Incorporated. CompuServe Information Service: user's guide. Columbus, OH: CompuServe Inc.; 1985.

Work in an Edited Collection

4. Broadhead, Glenn J. Style in business writing. In: Moran, Michael G.; Journet, Debra, eds. Research in business communication: a bibliographic sourcebook. Westport, CT: Greenwood Press; 1985: 217–252.

Book Edition, If Not the First

5. Gibson, H. Lou. Photography by infrared: its principles and applications. 3rd ed. New York: Wiley; 1978.

Multivolume Work

6. Hirshfield, Alan; Sinnott, Roger W., ed. Sky catalogue 2000.0. Cambridge, MA: Sky Publishing; 1982. 2v.

BOOK IN A SERIES

7. Osborne, D. J.; Gruneberg, M. M. The physical environment at work. Chichester, Eng.: John Wiley and Sons; 1983. (Wiley series in psychology and productivity at work.)

REPORT

8. Zombeck, Martin V. High energy astrophysics handbook. Cambridge, MA: Smithsonian Astrophysical Observatory; 1980; Research in Space Science SAO Special Report 386.

THESIS OR DISSERTATION

9. Weitz, Rob Roy. Nostradamus: an expert system for guiding the selection and use of appropriate forecasting techniques. Boston: Univ. of Massachusetts; 1985. 146 p. Dissertation.

PAPER IN A CONFERENCE PROCEEDINGS

10. Cochran, William D.; Smith, Harlan J.; Smith, William Hayden. Ultrahigh precision radial velocity spectrometer. Crawford, David L., ed. Instrumentation in astronomy IV. Proceedings of the Society of Photo-Optical Instrumentation Engineers; 1982 March 8–10; Tucson, AZ. Bellingham, WA: SPIE 315–320.

UNPUBLISHED PAPER

11. Madson, Elizabeth Ann. Use of Writer's Workbench software. 1984. Unpublished draft supplied to author by Elizabeth Ann Madson.

JOURNAL ARTICLE

12. Winn, William. Color in document design. IEEE Transactions on Professional Communications. 1991 September; 34(3): 180–185.

COMPUTER SOFTWARE

13. PowerEdit. vers. 1.0. (Computer software). Dallas, TX: Artificial Linguistics, 1991. IBM MS-DOS 3.0 or higher, 470K RAM, 1MB extended memory, 12MB available disk space.

NOTATIONAL DOCUMENTATION

Notes in publications have two uses: (1) to provide background information in publications or explanations that would interrupt the flow of thought in the text and (2) to provide documentation references.

EXPLANATORY FOOTNOTES

Explanatory or content notes are useful when the basis for an assumption should be made explicit but spelling it out in the text might make readers lose the flow of an argument. Because explanatory or content notes can be distracting, however, they should be kept to a minimum.

DOCUMENTATION NOTES

Notes that document sources can appear as either endnotes or footnotes. Endnotes are placed in a separate section at the end of a report, article, chapter, or book; footnotes (including explanatory notes) are placed at the bottom of a text page.

Use superscript numbers in the text to refer readers to notes, and number them consecutively from the beginning of the report, article, or chapter to the end. Place each superscript number at the end of a sentence, clause, or phrase, at a natural pause point like this,[1] right after the period, comma, or other punctuation mark (except a dash, which the number should precede[2]—as here).

FOOTNOTE FORMAT

To type footnotes, leave two line spaces beneath the text on a page, and indent the first line of each footnote five spaces. Begin each note with the appropriate superscript number, and skip one space between the number and the text of the footnote. If the footnote runs longer than one line, the second and subsequent lines should begin at the left margin. Single-space within each footnote, and double-space between footnotes.

EXAMPLE

Assume that this is the last line of text on a page.

[1]Begin the first footnote at this position. When it runs longer than one line, begin the second and all following lines at the left margin.

[2]The second footnote follows the same spacing as the first. Single-space within footnotes, and double-space between them.

ENDNOTE FORMAT

Endnotes should begin on a separate page entitled "Works Cited" or "References" after the end of the text. The individual notes should be typed as for footnotes. Double-space within and between endnotes.

DOCUMENTATION NOTE STYLE

The following guidelines for documentation note style are based on those provided in the Modern Language Association's *MLA Handbook for Writers of Research Papers,* Fourth Edition.

Documentation notes give the author's full name, title, and publication information for the source, including the page or pages from which material was taken. This information is given in full in the first note for the source, and the second and subsequent notes give abbreviated author and title information.

In a footnote or endnote, the information is given in a somewhat different order and uses somewhat different punctuation than in a bibliography or a list of "References" or "Works Cited." The author's name is given in normal order (Jane F. Smith) rather than last name first; the elements of the entry are separated by commas rather than periods; and the publication information for a book is enclosed in parentheses. The first reference to a book appears as follows:

[1]David S. Landes, Revolution in Time: Clocks and the Making of the Modern World (Cambridge, MA: Belknap-Harvard UP, 1983) 340.

There is no punctuation mark between the title and the opening parenthesis or between the closing parenthesis and the page number, and the page number is not preceded by the word page or its abbreviation. Compare this sample note with how the same book would be listed in a bibliography or list of "Works Cited":

Landes, David S. Revolution in Time: Clocks and the Making of the Modern World. Cambridge, MA: Belknap-Harvard UP, 1983.

SAMPLE ENTRIES (MLA STYLE)

The following sample notes for first references are based on the format style of the *MLA Handbook:*

BOOK WITH A CORPORATE AUTHOR

[2]Borland International, Turbo Pascal Version 2.0 Reference Manual (Scotts Valley, CA: Borland, 1984) 157.

WORK IN AN EDITED COLLECTION

[3]Ralph Gibson, "High Contrast Printing," Darkroom, ed. Eleanor Lewis (N.p.: Lustrum, 1977) 74.

REPORT

[4]Martin V. Zombeck, High Energy Astrophysics Handbook, Research in Space Science SAO Special Report No. 386 (Cambridge, MA: Smithsonian Astrophysical Observatory, 1980) 123.

PAPER PRESENTED AT A CONFERENCE

[5]Elizabeth Ann Madson, "Use of Writer's Workbench Software," Midwest MLA Annual Meeting, 3 Nov. 1984.

JOURNAL ARTICLE

[6]William Winn, "Color in Document Design," IEEE Transactions in Professional Communications 34 (1991): 180.

MAGAZINE ARTICLE

[7]John H. Sinfelt, "Bimetallic Catalysts," Scientific American Sept. 1985: 95.

THESIS OR DISSERTATION

[8]Arnold Brant Ross, "Flexible Engineering Software: An Integrated Workstation Approach to Finite Element Analysis," diss., Brigham Young U, 1985, 96.

For periodicals, the date (enclosed in parentheses if the periodical is a journal) is followed by a colon.

SECOND AND SUBSEQUENT REFERENCES

Notes for second and subsequent references to works should contain only enough information to allow the reader to relate it to the note for the first reference. Generally, the author's name and page number will suffice:

[9]Landes 343.

Even if the second reference immediately follows the first, put the author's last name and the page number as shown.

If two or more works by the same author are being cited, include a shortened version of the title in the second and subsequent notes. Insert a comma between the author's name and the title, with no punctuation between the title and the page number.

BIBLIOGRAPHY FORMAT (MLA STYLE)

The following list shows how each of the works cited in the sample notes would appear in a bibliography:

BOOK WITH A CORPORATE AUTHOR

Borland International. Turbo Pascal Version 2.0 Reference Manual. Scotts Valley, CA: Borland, 1984.

WORK IN AN EDITED COLLECTION

Gibson, Ralph. "High Contrast Printing." Darkroom. Ed. Eleanor Lewis. N.p.: Lustrum, 1977.

REPORT

Zombeck, Martin V. High Energy Astrophysics Handbook. Research in Space Science SAO Special Report No. 386. Cambridge, MA: Smithsonian Astrophysical Observatory, 1980.

PAPER PRESENTED AT A CONFERENCE

Madson, Elizabeth Ann. "Use of Writer's Workbench Software." Midwest MLA Annual Meeting, 3 Nov. 1984.

JOURNAL ARTICLE

Winn, William. "Color in Document Design." IEEE Transactions in Professional Communications 34 (1991): 180–85.

MAGAZINE ARTICLE

Sinfelt, John H. "Bimetallic Catalysts." <u>Scientific American</u> Sept. 1985: 90–98.

THESIS OR DISSERTATION

Ross, Arnold Brant. "Flexible Engineering Software: An Integrated Workstation Approach to Finite Element Analysis." Diss. Brigham Young U, 1985.

STYLE MANUALS

Many professional societies, publishing companies, and other organizations publish manuals that prescribe bibliographic reference formats for their publications or publications in their fields.

Following is a selected list of style manuals for various fields:

BIOLOGY

Council of Biology Editors. *CBE style manual: a guide for authors, editors, and publishers in the biological sciences.* 5th ed. Bethesda: Council of Biology Editors, 1983.

CHEMISTRY

American Chemical Society. *ACS style guide: a manual for authors and editors.* Washington, DC: American Chemical Soc., 1986.

GEOLOGY

U. S. Geological Survey. *Suggestions to authors of the reports of the United States Geological Survey.* 7th ed. Washington, DC: U.S. GPO, 1991.

MATHEMATICS

American Mathematical Society. *A manual for authors of mathematical papers.* Providence, RI: American Mathematical Soc., 1990.

MEDICINE

International Steering Committee of Medical Editors. *Uniform requirements for manuscripts submitted to biomedical journals.* Annals of Internal Medicine. 90 (Jan. 1978): 95–99.

PHYSICS

American Institute of Physics, Publications Board. *AIP style manual.* 4th ed. New York: American Institute of Physics, 1990.

PSYCHOLOGY

American Psychological Association. *Publication manual of the American Psychological Association.* 4th ed. Washington, DC: American Psychological Assn., 1995.

GENERAL

American national standard for bibliographic references. New York: American National Standards Institute, 1977. ANSI Z39.29—1977.

The Chicago manual of style. 14th ed. Chicago: U of Chicago P, 1993.

Gibaldi, Joseph. *MLA handbook for writers of research papers.* 4th ed. New York: Modern Language Assn. of America, 1995.

National Information Standards Organization. *Scientific and technical reports: organization, preparation, and production.* New York: National Information Standards Org., 1987. ANSI Z39.18—1987.

Skillin, M. E., and Gay, R. M. *Words into type.* 3rd ed. Englewood Cliffs, NJ: Prentice, 1974.

Turabian, K. L. *A manual for writers of term papers, theses, and dissertations.* 4th ed. Chicago: U of Chicago P, 1973.

United States Government Printing Office style manual. Washington, DC: U.S. GPO, 1984.

executive summaries

The purpose of an executive summary is to consolidate the principal points of a report in one place. It must cover the information in the report in enough detail to reflect accurately its contents but concisely enough to permit an executive to digest the significance of the report without having to read it in full. Because they are comprehensive, executive summaries tend to be proportional in length to the larger work they summarize. The typical summary is about 10 percent of the length of the report and is usually organized according to the sequence of the report it summarizes.

The executive summary should be written so that it can be read independently of the report. It must not refer by number to figures, tables, or references contained elsewhere in the report. Executive summaries may occasionally contain a figure, table, or footnote if that information is integral to the summary. Because executive summaries are frequently read in place of the full report, all uncommon symbols, abbreviations, and acronyms must be spelled out.

The sample executive summary in Figure 1 is adapted from a report on the social responsiblities of business corporations. (For guidance about the location of an executive summary, see the **formal reports** entry in this tabbed section.)

EXECUTIVE SUMMARY

Background and purpose

Many recent business reports and academic papers have suggested that businesses like ours must alter our marketing approaches to benefit society as well as business. They advocate that our marketing decisions should consider not only the profitability of new products but also the value of those products to society. As in most companies, Blyco Corporation has seldom given much consideration to the societal value of new products. In practice, our overriding concern has always been profitability and the competitive position of our firm in the marketplace. This report

Findings

says that this attitude will change, but slowly and only with strong pressures from both consumers and lawmakers, and concludes that the change will occur because our nation will eventually have to make more efficient use of our resources. Today we may still be able to ask only "Will it sell?" Tomorrow we will be forced to ask also "Do we need it?"

Producers of frivolous products will disappear because their markets will evaporate. Producers of marginally useful goods will face shrinking markets. The firms that survive will do so only by making major shifts in both direction and emphasis.

Scope

For business to make this change, however, government must put profit in the area of social responsibility. Only by so doing can government assure the maximum response from the business community. If government does not take this necessary step, it will have to resort to laws and regulations to force business to make the needed adjustments.

Blyco can take a lead in meeting this challenge by working with government to ensure that we become partners rather than adversaries. We can take the following specific steps to establish this relationship:

Recommendations

- Include on our board of directors a representative of a responsible consumer group and a person with legislative experience.
- Employ a person to act as a legislative liaison with congressional committees concerned with consumer issues.
- Implement a policy of considering the social impact of new products as we make marketing decisions.
- Publicize our willingness to cooperate with the government and responsible consumer groups in this area.

Taking these steps will not mean that we must abandon our traditional concern for profitability; rather it will help us gain new respect from consumers and will place us in a better position as legislative bodies scrutinize the marketing practices of large corporations in the years to come.

Figure 1 *Executive Summary*

feasibility reports

When the managers of an organization plan to undertake a new project (a move, the development of a new product, an expansion, or the purchase of new equipment) they try to determine the project's chances for success. A feasibility report documents the study conducted to help them make this determination. This report presents evidence about the practicality of the proposed project: How much will it cost? Is sufficient personnel available? Are any legal or other special requirements necessary? Based on the evidence, the writer of the feasibility report recommends whether or not the project should be carried out. Management then considers the recommendation and makes the decision.

Before beginning to write a feasibility report, state clearly and concisely the purpose of the study.

> EXAMPLE   This study will determine which of three possible sites should be selected for our new warehouse.

In a feasibility report, the scope should include the alternatives for accomplishing the purpose and the criteria by which each alternative will be examined. An organization that needs to upgrade its word-processing software, for example, might conduct a feasibility study to determine which software would best suit its requirements. The organization's requirements would establish the criteria by which each alternative is evaluated. The following example shows how the preliminary topic outline for such a study might be organized:

I. Purpose: To determine which word-processing software would best serve our office needs.
II. Alternatives: List of software provided by various vendors.
III. Criteria:
  A. Current task requirements
    1. Memos and letters—100 per month
    2. Brief interoffice reports—8–10 per month
    3. One or two 30- to 50-page reports per month
    4. Numerous financial tables: need to link data between spreadsheet programs and text tables
    5. Occasional need to create and edit business graphics—bar and pie charts
  B. Compatibility with present hardware
    1. Need to upgrade hard-disk memory?
    2. Need to upgrade printers and purchase font cartridges?
  C. Costs
    1. Purchase of new software or upgrade of present software?
    2. Installation and transfer of existing working files
    3. Training of professional and secretarial staffs

In writing a feasibility report, you must first identify the alternatives and then evaluate each against your established criteria. After completing these analyses, summarize them in a conclusion. This summary of relative strengths and weaknesses usually points to one alternative as the best, or most feasible. Make your recommendation on the basis of this conclusion.

Every feasibility report should contain the following sections: (1) an introduction, (2) a body, (3) a conclusion, and (4) a recommendation.

INTRODUCTION

The introduction should state the purpose of the report, describe the problems that led to the report, and include any pertinent background information. You *may* also discuss the scope or extent of the report in the introduction and any procedures or methods used in the analyses of alternatives. Any limitations on the study should be noted here as well.

BODY

The body of the report should present a detailed evaluation of all alternatives under consideration. Evaluate each alternative according to your established criteria. Ordinarily, each evaluation would comprise a separate section of the body of the report.

CONCLUSION

The conclusion should summarize the evaluation of alternatives, usually in the order in which they are discussed in the body of the report.

RECOMMENDATION

This section presents the alternative that best meets the criteria.

The sample feasibility report shown in Figure 1 opens with an introduction that states the purpose of the report, the problem that prompted the study, the alternatives that were examined, and the criteria used. The body presents a detailed discussion of each alternative, particularly in terms of the criteria stated in the introduction. The conclusion draws together and summarizes the details in the body of the study. The recommendation section suggests the course of action that the company should take.

INTRODUCTION
The purpose of this report is to determine which of two proposed computer processors would best enable the Jonesville Engineering and Manufacturing Branch to increase its data-processing capacity and thus to meet its expanding production requirements.

Problem
In October 19-- the Information Systems and Support Group at Jonesville put the MISSION System into operation. Since then the volume of processing transactions has increased fivefold (from 1,000 to 5,000 updates per day). This increase has severely impaired system response time from less than 10 seconds in 1988 to 120 seconds on average at present. Degraded performance is also apparent in the backlog of batch-processing transactions. During a recent

---

Figure 1 *Feasibility Report*

check 70 real-time and approximately 2,000 secondary transactions were backlogged. In addition, the ARC 98 Processor that runs MISSION is nine years old and frequently breaks down. Downtime caused by these repairs must be made up in overtime. In a recent 10-day period in January, processor downtime averaged 25 percent during working hours (7:30 a.m. to 6:00 p.m.). In February the system was down often enough that the entire plant production schedule was endangered.

Finally, because the ARC 98 cannot keep up with the current workload, the following new systems, all essential to increased plant efficiency and productivity, cannot be implemented: shipping and billing, labor collection, master scheduling, and capacity planning.

Scope
Two alternative solutions to provide increased processing capacity have been investigated: (1) purchase of a new ARC 98 Processor to supplement the first, and (2) purchase of a Landmark I Processor to replace the current ARC 98. The two alternatives will be evaluated primarily according to cost and, to a lesser extent, according to expanded capacity for future operations.

PURCHASING A SECOND ARC 98 PROCESSOR
This alternative would require additional annual maintenance costs, salary for an additional computer operator, increased energy costs, and a one-time construction cost for a new facility to house the processor.

Annual maintenance costs	$ 45,000
Annual salary for computer operator	28,000
Annual increased energy costs	7,500
Annual operating costs	$ 80,500
Facility cost (one-time)	$ 50,000
Total first-year cost	$130,500

These costs for the installation and operation of another ARC 98 Processor are expected to produce the following anticipated savings in hardware reliability and system readiness.

Hardware Reliability
A second ARC 98 would reduce current downtime periods from four to two per week. Downtime recovery averages 30 minutes and affects 40 users. Assuming that 50 percent of users require the system at a given time, we determined that the following reliability savings would result:

2 downtimes × 0.5 hours × 40 users × 50% × $12.00/
hour overtime × 52 weeks = $12,480 (annual savings)

Figure 1 *Feasibility Report (continued)*

System Readiness
Currently, an average of one day of batch processing per week cannot be completed. This gap prevents online system readiness when users report to work and affects all users at least one hour per week. Improved productivity would yield these savings:

> 40 users × 1 hour/week × $9.00/hour average wage rate
> × 52 weeks = $18,720 (annual savings)

Summary of Savings

Hardware reliability	$12,480
System readiness	18,720
Total annual savings	$31,200

Costs and Savings for ARC 98 Processor

Costs

Annual	$ 80,500
One-time	50,000
First-year total	$130,500
	–50,000
Annual total	$ 80,500

Savings

Hardware reliability	$ 12,480
System readiness	18,720
Total annual savings	$ 31,200

Annual Costs Less Savings

Annual costs	$ 80,500
Annual savings	–31,200
Net additional annual operating cost	$ 49,300

ARC 98 Capacity
By adding a second ARC 98 processor, current capacity will be doubled. Each processor could process 2,500 transactions per day while cutting response time from 120 seconds to 60 seconds. However, if new systems essential to increased plant productivity are added to the MISSION System, efficiency could be degraded to its present level in the next three to five years. This estimate is based on the assumption that the new systems will add between 250 and 500 transactions per day immediately. These figures could increase tenfold in the next several years if current rates of expansion continue.

Figure 1 *Feasibility Report (continued)*

PURCHASING A LANDMARK I PROCESSOR

This alternative will require additional annual maintenance costs, increased energy costs, and a one-time facility adaptation cost.

Annual maintenance costs	$ 75,000
Annual energy costs	9,000
Annual operating costs	$ 84,000
Cost of adapting existing facility	$ 24,500
Total first-year cost	$108,500

These costs for installation of the Landmark I Processor are expected to produce the following anticipated savings in hardware reliability, system readiness, and staffing for the Information Systems and Services Department.

Hardware Reliability
Annual savings will be the same as those for the ARC 98 Processor: $12,480.

System Readiness
Annual savings will be the same as those for the ARC 98 Processor: $18,720.

Wages for the Information Systems and Services Department
New system efficiencies would permit the following wage reductions in the department:

One computer operator	
(wages and fringe benefits)	$28,000
One-shift overtime premium	
(at $200/week × 52 weeks)	10,400
Total annual wage savings	$38,400

Summary of Savings

Hardware reliability	$12,480
System readiness	18,720
Wages	38,400
Total annual savings	$69,600

Cost and Savings for Landmark I Processor

Costs	
Annual	$ 84,000
One-time	24,500
First-year total	$108,500
	−24,500
Annual total	$ 84,000

Figure 1 *Feasibility Report (continued)*

Savings	
Hardware reliability	$ 12,480
System readiness	18,720
Wages	38,400
Total annual savings	$ 69,600

Annual Costs Less Savings	
Annual costs	$ 84,000
Annual savings	−69,600
Net additional annual operating cost	$ 14,400

Landmark I Capacity

The Landmark I processor can process 5,000 transactions per day with an average response time of 10 seconds per transaction. Should the volume of future transactions double, the Landmark I could process 10,000 transactions per day without exceeding 20 seconds per transaction on average. This increase in capacity over the present system would permit implementation of plans to add four new systems to MISSION.

CONCLUSION

A comparison of costs for both systems indicates that the Landmark I would cost $60,400 less in first-year costs.

ARC 98 Costs	
Net additional operating	$49,300
One-time facility	50,000
First-year total	$99,300

Landmark I Costs	
Net additional operating	$14,400
One-time facility	24,500
First-year total	$38,900

Installation of a second ARC 98 Processor will permit the present information-processing systems to operate relatively smoothly and efficiently. It will not, however, provide the expanded processing capacity that the Landmark I Processor would for implementing new subsystems essential to improved production and record keeping.

RECOMMENDATION

The Landmark I Processor should be purchased because of the initital and long-term savings and because its expanded capacity will allow the addition of essential systems.

Figure 1 *Feasibility Report (continued)*

foreword/preface

The terms *foreword* and *preface* are usually differentiated.

A foreword is an optional introductory statement about a book or formal report written by someone other than the author. The writer of the foreword is usually an authority in the field or an executive of the company, whose name and affiliation (as well as the date the foreword was written) appear at its end. The foreword generally provides background information about the study's significance or places the study in the context of other works written in the field. The foreword precedes the preface when a work has both.

The preface, an optional introductory statement to a book or formal report, is written by the author. The preface may announce the purpose, background, and scope of the work. Typically, it highlights the relationship of the work to a given project or program and discusses any special circumstances leading to the study. A preface may also specify the audience for whom the work is intended, and it may contain acknowledgments of help received during the course of the project or in the preparation of the publication. Finally, a preface may cite permission obtained for the use of copyrighted works.

formal reports

Formal reports are written accounts of major projects. Most formal reports are divided into three major parts—front matter, body, and back matter—each of which contains a number of elements. The number and arrangement of the elements may vary, depending on the subject, the length of the report, and the kinds of material covered.

ORDER OF ELEMENTS IN A FORMAL REPORT

Many companies and other organizations have a preferred style for formal reports and furnish guidelines that staff members must follow. If your employer does not, you may use the format recommended in this entry. The following list includes most of the elements a formal report might contain, in the order of their appearance in the report.

Front Matter

Title page
Abstract
Table of contents
List of figures
List of tables
Foreword
Preface
List of abbreviations and symbols

Body

Executive summary
Introduction
Text (including headings)
Conclusions
Recommendations
References

Back Matter

Bibliography
Appendixes
Glossary
Index

FRONT MATTER

The front matter serves several purposes: it gives the reader a general idea of the author's purpose in writing the report; it indicates whether the report contains the kind of information the reader is looking for; and it lists where in the report the reader can find specific information. Not all formal reports require every element of front matter. A title page and table of contents are usually mandatory, but whether the other elements are used depends on the scope of the report and its intended audience. The front matter pages are numbered with lower case Roman numerals *(i, ii, iii . . .)* and the body of the report begins with Arabic number 1. Throughout the report, page numbers should be centered near the bottom of each page.

Title Page. The formats of title pages for formal reports vary, but the page should include the following information:

1. *The full title of the report.* The title should imply the topic, scope, and purpose of the report to the extent possible. Follow these guidelines when creating the title:
   - Do not use "Report on . . .," or "XYZ Corporation Report on . . .," in the title, since the fact that the information appears in a report will be self-evident to your reader.
   - Do not use abbreviations in the title. Use acronyms only when the report is intended for an audience familiar enough with the topic that the acronym will not confuse them.
   - Do not include the period covered by a report in the title; include that information in a subtitle:

     EFFECTS OF PROPOSED HIGHWAY
     CONSTRUCTION ON PROPERTY VALUES
     Annual Report, 19--

2. *The name of the writer, principal investigator, or compiler.* Sometimes contributors identify themselves by their job title in the organization

(Jane R. Doe, Cost Analyst; Jack T. Doe, Head, Research and Development). Sometimes contributors identify themselves by their tasks in contributing to the report (Jane R. Doe, Compiler; Jack T. Doe, Principal Investigator).

3. *The date or dates of the report.* For one-time reports, list the date when the report is to be distributed. For periodic reports, which may be issued monthly or quarterly, list in a subtitle the time period that the present report covers. Elsewhere on the title page, list the date when the report is to be distributed.

4. *The name of the organization for which the writer works.*

5. *The name of the organization to which the report is being submitted,* if the work is being done for a customer or client.

The title page, although unnumbered, is considered page i (small Roman numeral *i*). The back of the title page, which is blank and unnumbered, is considered page ii, and the abstract falls on page iii so that it appears on a right-hand (odd-numbered) page. New sections and chapters of reports typically begin on a new right-hand page. Reports with printing on only one side of each sheet can be numbered consecutively regardless of where new sections begin.

Abstract. An abstract, which normally follows the title page, highlights the major points of the report, enabling the prospective reader to decide whether to read the entire report. (For a complete discussion of abstracts, supported with samples, see the **abstracts** entry in this tabbed section.)

Table of Contents. A table of contents lists all the major headings or sections of the report in their order of appearance, along with their page numbers. (For a complete discussion of the table of contents, see the **tables of contents** entry in this tabbed section.)

List of Figures. Figures include all illustrations—drawings, photographs, maps, charts, and graphs—contained in the report. When a report contains more than five figures, they should be listed, along with their page numbers, in a separate section immediately following the table of contents. The section should begin on a new page. The figures are numbered consecutively with Arabic numbers.

List of Tables. When a report contains more than five tables, they should be listed, along with their titles and page numbers, in a separate section immediately following the list of figures (if there is one). Tables are numbered consecutively with Arabic numbers. For a complete discussion of tables, see the **tables** entry on the FORMAT AND VISUAL AIDS tab.

Foreword. A foreword is an optional introductory statement written by someone other than the author. (See the **foreword/preface** entry in this tabbed section.)

Preface. The preface is an optional introductory statement written by the author that announces the purpose, background, and scope of the report. (See the **foreword/preface** entry in this tabbed section.)

List of Abbreviations and Symbols. When the abbreviations and symbols used in the report are numerous and there is a chance that readers will not be able to interpret them, the front matter should include a list of all symbols and abbreviations (including acronyms) and what they stand for.

BODY (TEXT)

The body is that portion of the report in which the author describes in detail the methods and procedures used in the study, demonstrates how results were obtained, and draws conclusions on which any recommendations are based.

Executive Summary. The body of the report begins with an executive summary that provides a more complete overview of the report than an abstract does. (For a more detailed discussion, see the **executive summaries** entry in this tabbed section.)

Introduction. The purpose of an introduction is to give the readers any general information they must have in order to understand the detailed information in the rest of the report. (For a detailed discussion of introductions, see the **introductions** entry in this tabbed section.)

Text. The text (or body) presents the details of how the topic was investigated, how the problem was solved, how the best choice from among alternatives was selected, or whatever your situation may be. This information is often clarified and further developed by the use of illustrations and tables and may be supported by references to other studies.

Conclusions. The conclusion section pulls together the results of your study in one place. (See the **conclusions** entry on THE BUSINESS WRITING PROCESS tab.)

Recommendations. Recommendations, which are sometimes combined with the conclusions section, state what course of action should be taken based on the results of the study. Of the three possible locations for a new warehouse, for example, which is the best? The recommendations section says, in effect, "I think we should purchase this, or do that, or hire them."

References. If in your report you refer to material in, or quote directly from, a published work or other research source, you must provide a list of references in a separate section. If your employer has a preferred reference style, follow it; otherwise, use the guidelines provided in the **documenting sources** entry in this tabbed section. For a relatively short report, the references should go at the end of the body of the report. For a report with a number of sections or chapters, the reference section should fall at the end of each major section or chapter. In either case, every reference section should be labeled as such and should start on a new page. If a particular reference appears in more than one section or chapter, it should be repeated in full in each appropriate reference section.

BACK MATTER

The back matter of a formal report contains supplemental information, such as where to find additional information about the topic (bibliography) and how the information in the report can be easily located (index), clarified (glossary), and explained in more detail (appendix).

Bibliography. A bibliography is an alphabetical list of all sources that were consulted in researching the report but are not cited in the text. A bibliography is not necessary if the reference listing contains a complete list of sources. (For detailed information about creating a bibliography, see the **bibliography** entry in this tabbed section.)

Appendixes. An appendix contains information that clarifies or supplements the text. (For a detailed discussion, see the **appendixes** entry in this tabbed section.)

Glossary. A glossary is an alphabetical list of definitions of selected technical terms used in the report. (See the **glossaries** entry in this tabbed section for a more detailed discussion.)

Index. An index is an alphabetical list of all the major topics discussed in the report. It cites the pages where each topic can be found and thus allows readers to find information on topics quickly and easily. The index is always the final section of the report.

glossaries

A glossary is an alphabetical list of definitions of terms used in a report.

If you are writing a report that will go to people who are not familiar with many of your technical terms, you may want to include a glossary. If you do, keep the entries concise and be sure they are so clear that any reader can understand the definitions.

> EXAMPLES   *Amplitude Modulations:* Varying the amplitude of a carrier current with an audio-frequency signal.
>
> *Carbon Microphone:* A microphone that uses carbon granules as a means of varying resistance with sound waves.

interviewing

A discussion of interviewing can be divided into three parts: (1) determining the proper person to interview, (2) preparing for the interview, and (3) conducting the interview.

DETERMINING THE PROPER PERSON TO INTERVIEW

Many times your subject, or your purpose in writing about the subject, logically points to the proper person to interview. If you were writing about the use of a freeway onramp metering device on Highway 103, for example, you would want to interview the Director of the Traffic Engineering Department. Other sources available to help you determine the appropriate person to interview are (1) the city directory in the library, (2) professional societies, (3) the yellow pages in the local telephone directory, or (4) a local firm that is involved with all or some aspects of your subject.

PREPARING FOR THE INTERVIEW

After determining the name of the person you want to interview, you must request the interview by telephone or by letter, although a letter may be too slow to allow you to meet your deadline.

Learn as much as possible about the person you are going to interview and about the company or agency for which he or she works. When you make contact with your interviewee, whether by letter or by telephone, explain (1) who you are, (2) why you are contacting him, (3) why you chose him for the interview, (4) the subject of the interview, (5) that you would like to arrange an interview at his convenience, and (6) that you will allow him to review your draft.

Prepare a list of specific questions to ask your interviewee. The natural temptation for the untrained writer is to ask general questions rather than specific ones. "What are you doing about air pollution?" for example, may be too general to elicit specific and useful information. "Residents in the east end of town complain about the black smoke that pours from your east-end plant; are you doing anything to relieve the problem?" is a more specific question. Analyze your questions to be certain that they are specific and to the point.

CONDUCTING THE INTERVIEW

When you arrive for the interview, be prepared to guide the discussion. The following list of points should help you do so.

1. Be pleasant, but purposeful. You are there to get information, so don't be timid about asking leading questions on the subject.
2. Use the list of questions you have prepared, starting with the less controversial aspects of the topic to get the conversation started and then going on to the more controversial aspects.
3. Let your interviewee do the talking. Don't try to impress him or her with your own knowledge of the subject.
4. Be objective. Don't offer your opinions on the subject. You are there to get information, not to debate.
5. Some answers prompt additional questions; ask them. If you do not ask these questions as they arise, you may find later that you have forgotten to ask them at all.
6. When the interviewee gets off the subject, be ready with a specific and direct question to guide him or her back onto the track.
7. Take only memory-jogging notes that will help you recall the conversation later. Do not ask your interviewee to slow down so you can take detailed notes. To do so would not only be an undue imposition on the interviewee's time but might also disturb or destroy his or her train of thought.
8. The use of a tape recorder is often unwise, since it often puts people on edge and requires tedious transcription after the interview. On the

other hand, a tape recorder does allow you to listen more intently instead of taking notes. If you do use one, do not let it lure you into relaxing so that you neglect to ask crucial questions.

Immediately after leaving the interview, use your memory-jogging notes to help you mentally review the interview and record your detailed notes. Do not postpone this step. No matter how good your memory is, you will forget some important points if you do not do this at once.

introductions

The purpose of an introduction is to give your readers enough general information about your topic to enable them to understand the detailed information in the body of your document.

In your introduction, you need to state the subject, the purpose of your document, its scope, and the way you plan to develop the topic.

Stating the Subject. In addition to stating the subject, you may need to define it if it is one with which some of your readers may be unfamiliar.

Stating the Purpose. The statement of purpose should make your readers aware of your goal as they read your document. It should also tell them why you are writing about the subject and whether your material provides a new perspective or clarifies an existing perspective.

Stating the Scope. Stating the scope of your article or report tells your readers how much or how little detail to expect.

Stating the Development of the Subject. In a larger work, it may be helpful to your reader if you state how you plan to develop the subject. Providing such information makes it easier for your readers to anticipate how the subject will be presented, and it gives them a basis for evaluating how you arrived at your conclusions or recommendations.

The following introduction is from a journal article:

	The steady increase in incoming orders over the past eighteen months represents a significant increase in the corporation's percentage of the market for office furniture, and the market survey conducted by a consulting firm indicates that the increase is permanent. Therefore, at its September meeting, the corporation's board of directors
Subject	approved the construction of a new manufacturing plant to increase our manufacturing capacity to accommodate the present increase in demand and the anticipated increase indicated by the market survey.
	A committee was appointed by the president of the corporation to investigate various potential sites for the new manufacturing plant. The committee was to investigate all potential building sites and select several of the best alternative sites for manufacturing office furniture. These selections were to be made on the basis of
Purpose and scope	such considerations as the availability of transportation, the local tax structure, the availability of labor, and the local living conditions.

The purpose of this report is to submit the results of that investigation. The report offers first a brief background, or summary, of the committee's complete investigation; then it presents, in complete detail, the results of the studies conducted on the three most promising building sites for the new manufacturing plant.

Background   The committee initially considered thirty possible locations for the proposed new factory. Of these, twenty were eliminated almost immediately for one reason or another (unfavorable tax structure, inadequate labor supply, and the like). Of the remaining ten locations, the committee selected for intensive study the three that seemed the most promising: Chicago, Minneapolis, and Salt Lake City. The committee then visited these three cities, and its observations on each of them are contained in the body of this report.

Development   The report presents the significant details of each city in the following sequence: (1) the location of the city, (2) the availability of air, highway, and rail transportation, (3) the availability of labor, (4) the local tax structure, and (5) the local living conditions (housing, education, recreation, and climate).

CHICAGO

Body of report   Of the three cities, Chicago presently seems to the committee to offer the greatest advantages. . . .

Not every document needs an introduction. When your readers are already familiar with the major elements of your topic, you can save them time and hold their interest better by getting on to the details. If you do not need a full-scale introduction, turn to the entry on **openings** on THE BUSINESS WRITING PROCESS tab for a variety of interesting ways to begin without an introduction.

Consider writing the introduction last. Many writers find this helpful because they feel that only then do they have a full enough perspective on the writing to introduce it adequately.

investigative reports

When a person investigates a particular topic, he or she might document the results in an investigative report (for example, such a report might summarize the findings of a product evaluation). An investigative report gives a precise analysis of its topic and then offers the writer's conclusions and recommendations.

Open the report with a statement of its purpose. In the body of the report, define the scope of your investigation first. If the report is on a survey of opinions, for example, you might need to indicate the number of people and the geographical areas surveyed as well as the income categories, the occupations, the age groups, and possibly even the racial groups of those surveyed. Include any information that is pertinent in defining the extent of

MEMORANDUM

To: Noreen Rinaldo, Training Manager
From: Charles Lapinski, Senior Instructor C𝐼
Date: February 14, 19--

Subject: Addison Corporation's Basic English Program

Purpose

    As you requested, I have investigated Addison's program to determine whether we might also adopt such a program. The purpose of the Addison Basic English course is to teach foreign mechanics who do not speak or read English to understand repair manuals written in a special 800-word vocabulary called "Basic English," and thus eliminate the need for Addison to translate its manuals into a number of different languages. The Basic English Program does not attempt to teach the mechanics to be fluent in English but, rather, to recognize the 800 basic words that appear in the repair manuals.

    The course does not train mechanics. Students must know, in their own language, what a word like <u>torque</u> means; the course simply teaches them the English term for it. As prerequisites for the course, students must have a basic knowledge of their trade, must be able to identify a part in an illustrated parts book, must have served as a mechanic on Addison products for at least one year, and must be able to read and write in their own language.

Scope

    Students are given the specially prepared instruction manual, an illustrated book of parts and their English names, and a pocket reference containing all 800 words of the Basic English vocabulary plus the English names of parts (students can write the corresponding word in their language beside the English words and then use the pocket reference as a bilingual dictionary). The course consists of thirty two-hour lessons, each lesson introducing approximately 27 words. No effort is made to teach pronunciation; the course teaches only recognition of the 800 words, which include 450 nouns, 70 verbs, 180 adjectives and adverbs, and 100 articles, prepositions, conjunctions, and pronouns.

    The 800-word vocabulary enables the writers of the manuals to provide mechanics with any information that might be required, because the area of communication is strictly limited to maintenance, inspection, troubleshooting, safety, and the operation of Addison equipment. All nonessential words (such as <u>apple</u>, <u>father</u>, <u>mountain</u>, and so on) have been eliminated, as have most synonyms (for example <u>under</u> appears, but <u>beneath</u> does not).

<u>Conclusions</u>

I see three possible ways in which we might be able to use some or all of the elements of the Basic English Program: (1) in the preparation of all our student manuals, (2) in the preparation of student manuals for the international students in our service school, or (3) as Addison uses the program.

    I think it would be unnecessary to use the Basic English methods in the preparation of student manuals for <u>all</u> our students. Most of our students are English-speaking people to whom an unrestricted vocabulary presents no problem.

Recommendations

    In conjunction with the preparation of student manuals for international students, the program might have more appeal. Students would take the Basic English course either before coming to this country to attend school or after arriving but before beginning their technical training.

    As for our initiating a Basic English Program similar to Addison's, we could create our own version of the Basic English vocabulary and write our service manuals in it. Since our product lines are much broader than Addison's, however, we would need to create illustrated parts books for each of the different product lines.

Figure 1 *Investigative Report*

the investigation. Then report your findings and, if necessary, discuss their significance. End your report with your conclusions and, if appropriate, any recommendations.

library research

The key tools for doing library research include the card catalog, periodical indexes, bibliographies, computer-search services, reference books, and, increasingly, information stored on compact disks.

THE CARD CATALOG

The card catalog contains a listing of each book a library owns. It is usually found in cabinets near the reference or circulation section, though some larger libraries keep their card catalogs in bound books or on computer terminals. Go to the card catalog to determine whether the library has the book you need and where to find it.

Most books have three types of cards in the catalog—an *author card,* a *title card* (found in the Author/Title Index) and a *subject card* (found in the Subject Index). Cards are arranged alphabetically. Author cards are filed by the author's last name, title cards are filed by the first important word in the title (excluding *a, an,* and *the*), and subject cards are filed by the first word of the general subject. All three cards include the author, the title, the publisher, the date and place of publication, the number of pages, and the major topics covered. They indicate if a book has an index, a bibliography, or any illustrations. At the bottom are subject headings that lead you to more materials on the same topic.

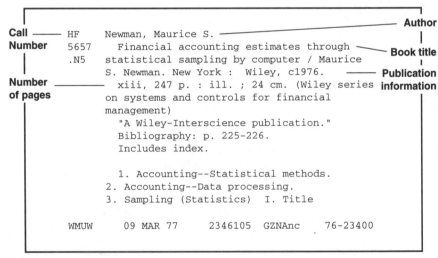

Figure 1 *Author Card*

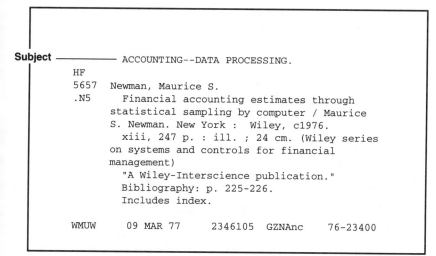

Figure 2 *Subject Card*

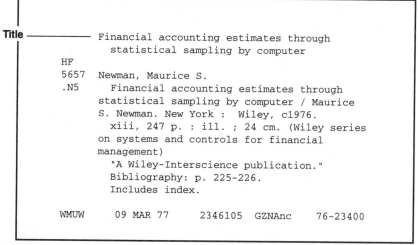

Figure 3 *Title Card*

Each card also includes, in the upper left-hand corner, the *call number,* which indicates where the book is kept in the library. The call number is also written on the book's spine, which enables you to find the book on the shelf. Call numbers are actually the book's classification according to the Dewey Decimal System, the Library of Congress System, or the library's own system.

A card catalog also contains *see* cards and *see also* cards. *See* cards indicate that the heading you are looking under is not the one used for your topic and refer you instead to another heading. For example, if you looked up *letter writing,* a *see* card might refer you to *correspondence. See also* cards list additional headings related to the topic. Under *word processing,* for example, a *see also* card might refer you to *computers.*

BIBLIOGRAPHIES AND PERIODICAL INDEXES

Bibliographies list books, periodicals, and other research materials published in specific subject areas. The following is a list of basic guides to bibliographies:

> Besterman, Theodore. *A World Bibliography of Bibliographies*
> *Bibliographic Index: A Cumulative Bibliography of Bibliographies,*
>   *1937–* (updated three times annually)
> Sheehy, Eugene P. *Guide to Reference Books*

Periodical indexes list journal, magazine, and newspaper articles. (Periodicals are publications that are issued regularly—daily, weekly, monthly, and so on.) The following indexes are useful for locating business topics:

> *Accountant's Index, 1920–*
> *Business Education Index, 1941–* (annual)
> *Business Periodicals Index, 1958–*
> *Index to U.S. Government Periodicals, 1851–* (bimonthly)
> *Wall Street Journal Index, 1958–* (monthly)
> *New York Times Index, 1851–* (every two weeks)
> *Readers' Guide to Periodical Literature, 1900–* (every two weeks)
> *Ulrich's International Periodicals Directory: A Classified Guide to Current Periodicals, Foreign and Domestic* (annually)

Instructions for using these periodical indexes are found in the front of each volume (or the first volume of a series). There you also find a list of the specific topics covered and, for periodical indexes, a list of which newspapers, magazines, and journals are included. A number of these indexes are available on CD-ROM, described later in this entry.

Libraries generally keep periodicals in a separate room or area. Current issues are often in one area, back issues (which are bound in volumes) in another. Back issues of some journals and most newspapers are generally in microform, descriptions of which appear at the end of this entry. If your library does not have the periodicals you need, you can get them through interlibrary loan, a service that permits you to borrow books and buy photocopied periodical articles from other libraries. Consult your librarian for specific details of the system.

COMPUTER-SEARCH SERVICES AND INDEXES

Most academic, industrial, and medical libraries now offer computer-search services. Such services can provide you with a computer printout of a list of citations, some with abstracts, appropriate to your subject. Databases are available in medicine, business, psychology, biology, management, engineering, environmental studies, and many other subjects. Ordinarily there is a charge for this service, but the cost is relatively low when the speed and convenience of the search are taken into account.

Computer-search services are usually located in the reference section of the library. The reference staff can provide information about the range of subjects in the database, the types and cost of search services, and procedures for using the service. After completing the search, the librarian can help you evaluate the citations for their relevance to your project and can also assist you in finding them.

REFERENCE WORKS

Additional sources of information include abstracts, biographical guides, book guides, book reviews, commercial guides, directories, encyclopedias, government publications, specialized dictionaries, handbooks and manuals, statistical sources, and atlases.

Abstracts. Abstracting services provide lists of articles with abstracts of usually 100–250 words. The following are typical:

> *Accountant's Digest,* 1935– (quarterly)
> *Accounting and Data Processing Abstracts,* 1970– (eight times per year)
> *Accounting Articles,* 1963– (monthly)
> *American Statistics Index* (ASI), 1974– (monthly) (index and abstracts of government publications containing statistics)
> *Dissertation Abstracts International,* 1938– (monthly)
> *Human Resources Abstracts,* 1966– (quarterly)
> *Management Literature in Brief,* 1968– (monthly)
> *Organizational Communication Abstracts: Analysis and Overview,* 1976– (six times per year)
> *Personnel and Training Abstracts,* 1971– (eight times per year)
> *Personnel Management Abstracts,* 1955– (quarterly)
> *Work Related Abstracts,* 1951– (monthly)

Biographical Guides. A number of sources are available that provide information on individuals. The following are typical:

> *Ancient to Modern Times: Biographies and Portraits*
> *Biography Index,* 1946– (quarterly)
> *Current Biography,* 1940– (monthly)
> *Who's Who in America,* 1899– (updated every two years)
> *Who's Who in Banking: The Directory of the Banking Profession*
> *Who's Who in Finance and Industry,* 1936– (every two years)
> *Who's Who in Labor*

Book Guides. Sources are available that provide general information on published books:

Books in Print (issued annually—lists author, title, publication data, edition, and price)

Business Books and Serials in Print, 1977– (annual)

Cumulative Book Index, 1928– (lists all books published in English, with author, title, and subject listings; issued annually with monthly supplements)

Book Reviews. A number of guides are available that provide reviews of published books:

Book Review Digest, 1905–

Current Book Review Citations, 1976–

The Wall Street Review of Books, 1973– (quarterly)

Commercial Guides. The following guides provide information on associations and commercial resources:

Encyclopedia of Associations

MacRae's Blue Book

National Trade and Professional Associations of the United States and Canada and Labor Unions, 1966–

Thomas Register of American Manufacturers, 1905–

Directories. The following sources provide information on specific businesses and corporations:

Consumer Protection Directory

Directory of Business and Financial Services

Directory of Corporate Affiliations, 1967– (annual "Who Owns Whom" of industry)

Encyclopedia of Associations (annual, with a quarterly supplement, *New Associations and Projects*)

Million Dollar Directory

Standard and Poor's Register of Corporations, Directors and Executives, United States and Canada, 1928– (annual)

Standard Directory of Advertising Agencies, 1907– (three times per year)

Encyclopedias. Encyclopedias—alphabetically arranged collections of articles—are often illustrated and usually published in multivolume sets. Some encyclopedias cover a wide range of general subjects, and others specialize in a particular subject. General encyclopedias are useful sources of background information and can be especially helpful in defining the terminology essential for understanding the subject. The following are three major general encyclopedias:

Encyclopedia Americana (30 volumes)

Encyclopedia Britannica (24 volumes)

New Columbia Encyclopedia (1 volume)

Specialized encyclopedias provide detailed information on a particular field of knowledge. Their treatment of a subject is thorough, so the researcher ought to have some background information on the subject in order to use the encyclopedia's information to full advantage. There are specialized encyclopedias on many subjects, examples of which follow:

Encyclopedia of Accounting Systems
Graham Irwin. *Encyclopedia of Advertising*
Heyel, Carl, ed. *The Encyclopedia of Management*
International Encyclopedia of Statistics
Munn, Glenn G. Munn's *Encyclopedia of Banking and Finance*

Government publications. The following are guides to federal and state publications:

Government Reports Announcements (GRA), 1946– (twice-monthly listing of federally sponsored research reports arranged by subject with abstracts)
Monthly Catalog of United States Government Publications, 1895–
Monthly Checklist of State Publications, 1940– (government publications arranged by state)
Schmeckebier, Laurance F., and Roy B. Eastin. *Government Publications and Their Use* (guide to government publications)

Dictionaries. Dictionaries—alphabetical arrangements of words with information about their forms, pronunciations, origins, meanings, and uses—are essential to all writers. The following is a list of major abridged and unabridged dictionaries:

The Random House College Dictionary. Rev. ed. New York: Random.
The American Heritage Dictionary of the English Language. Boston: Houghton.
Funk & Wagnalls Standard College Dictionary. New, updated ed. New York: Funk.
Webster's New World Dictionary of the American Language. Cleveland: World.
Webster's Tenth New Collegiate Dictionary. Springfield, MA: Merriam.

Unabridged dictionaries provide complete and authoritative linguistic information, but they are impractical for desk use because of their size and expense.

Webster's Third New International Dictionary of the English Language, Unabridged (Springfield, MA: Merriam, 1981) contains over 450,000 entries. Since word meanings are listed in historical order, the current meaning is given last. This dictionary does not list personal and geographical names, nor does it include usage information.
The Random House Dictionary of the English Language, 2nd ed. (New York: Random, 1987) contains nearly 300,000 entries, a 31-page color atlas, a manual of style, a chart of the chemical elements, and quick translating dictionaries of French, German, Spanish, and Italian. It

gives a word's widely used current meaning first, and includes personal and geographic names.

The following unabridged dictionary attempts to be exhaustive:

The Oxford English Dictionary, 2nd ed. (Oxford, England: Clarendon, 1991) is the standard historical dictionary of the English language, with definitions of over 500,000 terms. It follows the chronological development of the terms defined, beginning about the year 1000, providing numerous examples of usage and sources. The 20-volume second edition integrates the original dictionary, published in 1928, with the four supplemental volumes published between 1972 and 1986, into one alphabetical sequence. The OED is now available in CD-ROM.

Specialized dictionaries define terms used in a particular field, such as computers, architecture, economics. Their definitions are generally more complete and are more likely to be current, as in the following:

Ammer, Christine, and Dean S. Ammer. *Dictionary of Business and Economics*

Handbooks and Manuals. Compilations of frequently used information in a particular field of knowledge, handbooks and manuals are usually single volumes that generally provide such information as brief definitions of terms or concepts and explanations and details about particular organizations. Handbooks and manuals are most valuable for someone with a basic knowledge of the topic. Every field has its own handbook or manual; the following are typical:

Sabin, William A. *The Gregg Reference Manual*
Environmental Regulation Handbook
Merritt, F. S., ed. *Building Construction Handbook*
United States Government Printing Office Style Manual

Statistical Sources. Collections of numerical data, these are the best sources for such information as the height of the Washington Monument; the population of Boise, Idaho; the cost of living in Aspen, Colorado; and the annual number of motorcycle fatalities in the United States. The answers to such questions are most likely to be found in works devoted exclusively to statistical data, a selection of which follows:

American Statistics Index, 1978– (with monthly accumulations, quarterly, and annual supplements. Lists and abstracts all statistical publications issued by agencies of the U.S. government, including periodicals, reports, special surveys, and pamphlets.)
The Budget in Brief (a condensed version of the annual U.S. federal budget)
Demographic Yearbook, 1979– (annual U.N. collection of information on world economics and trade)

Facts on File, 1974– (weekly digest of world news, collected annually)

Johnson, Otto T., et al. *Information Please Almanac; Atlas Yearbook*

U.S. Bureau of the Census. *County and City Data Book,* 1952– (issued every five years. Includes a variety of data from cities, counties, metropolitan areas, and the like. Arranged by geographic and political areas, it covers such topics as climate, dwellings, population characteristics, school districts, employment, and city finances.)

U.S. Bureau of the Census. *Statistical Abstract of the United States,* 1979– (annual. Includes statistics on the U.S. social, political, and economic condition and covers broad topics such as population, education, public land, and vital statistics.)

U.S. Bureau of Labor Statistics. *Occupational Outlook Handbook,* 1949– (annual, updated by *Occupational Outlook Quarterly*)

Atlases. Collections of maps, atlases are classified into two categories—general atlases show physical and political boundaries, and thematic atlases give special information, such as climate, population, natural resources, or agricultural products. The following atlases are typical:

Business Atlas of Western Europe
Hammond Medallion World Atlas
Oxford Economic Atlas of the World
Rand McNally Commercial Atlas and Marketing Guide
Rand McNally New Cosmopolitan World Atlas
Times Atlas of the World: Comprehensive Edition
U.S. Geological Survey. *National Atlas of the United States of America*

Other sources. The following are general guides to information about business subjects:

Corman, Edwin, ed. *Sources of Business Information*
Brownstone, David M., and Gorton Carruth. *Where to Find Business Information: A Worldwide Guide for Everyone Who Needs the Answers to Business Questions*
Daniells, Lorna M. *Business Information Sources*

COMPACT DISK/READ ONLY MEMORY (CD-ROM)

Libraries increasingly make reference materials available that use CD-ROM technology. CD-ROM (compact disk—read-only memory) refers to an optical (rather than magnetic) medium for the storage and retrieval of information. The major benefit of this medium is its enormous storage capacity. Each disk can store approximately 275,000 pages. CD-ROM technology also permits full-text subject searches. Every word in a text (except conjunctions, prepositions, and articles) is indexed, thereby simplifying and greatly expanding the user's search capabilities compared with a manual search.

MICROFORMS

Some library source materials may require you to use microforms. Reduced photographic images of printed pages, microforms are used by many libraries for storing magazines, newspapers, and other materials. Because they are reduced, microforms must be magnified by machines called microreaders in order to be read. The most common kinds of microforms are microfilm and microfiche.

Microfilm. Rolls of 35-millimeter film, usually with four printed pages per frame, microfilm must be read on manually or electrically operated machines that advance the roll, frame by frame, for viewing.

Microfiche. A flat sheet of film, usually 4 × 6 inches, that can contain as many as 98 pages, microfiche is read on a microreader, where it can be moved horizontally or vertically from frame to frame for viewing.

TIPS FOR DOING LIBRARY RESEARCH

Once you find sources with the information you need and actually get your hands on those sources, you must be conscientious about keeping track of them. Besides taking careful notes of any information they contain, you should methodically note certain information about the sources themselves.

When you get the book, magazine, or microform, there are certain shortcuts that can help you decide quickly whether it has information that will be useful to your research. In a book it is best to start by looking over the table of contents and then by reading the introductions, conclusions, and summaries.

Does the book have an index or a bibliography? For a magazine article, it helps first to scan the heads, to get an idea of its major topics. With microforms, you can quickly flip through the text also looking for major topics. No matter what form your source takes, always consider its date: How current is the information? Timeliness is important in any research; you don't want to use out-of-date information.

Prepare a 3 × 5-inch note card for any source that you include in your research. The card should include the source's call number, author, and publication information (publisher, city, year). Then, when you compile your bibliography, you will have all necessary information on these cards. Figures 1 and 2 are examples of bibliography cards.

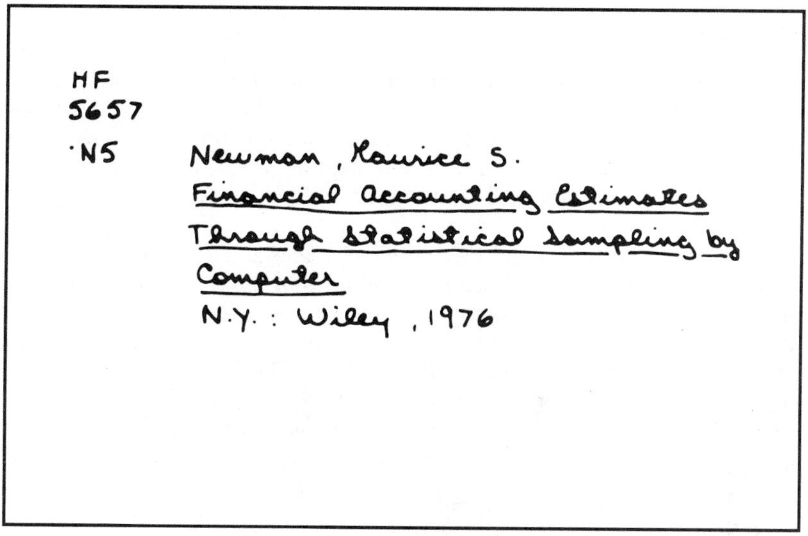

HF
5657
·N5   Newman, Maurice S.
      <u>Financial accounting estimates</u>
      <u>Through statistical sampling by</u>
      <u>Computer</u>
      N.Y. : Wiley , 1976

Figure 1 *Bibliography Card for a Book*

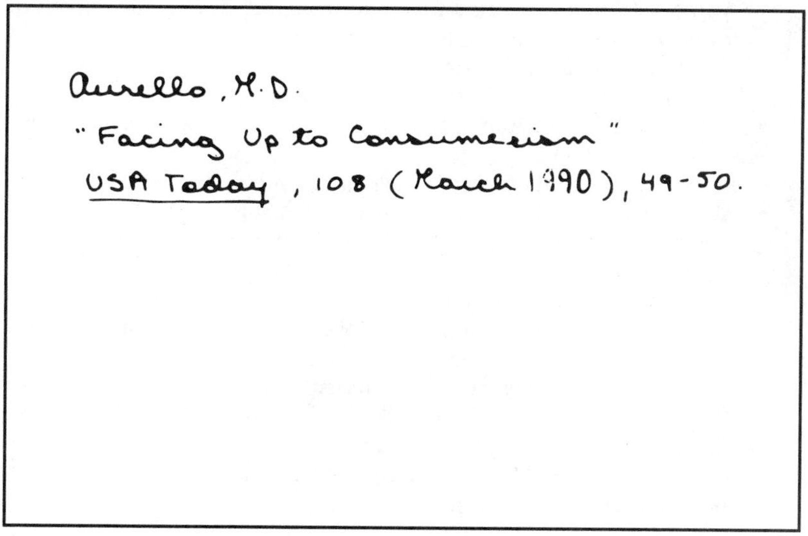

Aurello, M.D.
"Facing Up to Consumerism"
<u>USA Today</u> , 108 (March 1990), 49-50.

Figure 2 *Bibliography Card for a Periodical*

minutes of meetings

Organizations keep official records of their meetings; such records are known as *minutes*. If you attend many business-related meetings, you may be asked to write and distribute the minutes of a meeting. Most businesses do not have continuing committees, and meetings are somewhat ad hoc and minutes are issued after each meeting even though the group conducting the meeting may not meet again or may meet only a specified number of times. For continuing committees, which hospitals and educational and government organizations often have, the minutes of the previous meeting are usually read aloud if printed copies of the minutes were not distributed to the members beforehand; the group then votes to accept the minutes as prepared or to revise or clarify specific items. The bylaws or policies and procedures of such organizations may specify what must be included in your minutes of meetings. As a general guide, *Robert's Rules of Order* recommends that the minutes of meetings include the following:

- Name of the group or committee holding the meeting.
- Place, time, and date of the meeting.
- Kind of meeting (a regular meeting or a special meeting called to discuss a specific subject or problem).
- Number of members present and, for committees or boards of ten or fewer members, their names.
- A statement that the chairperson and the secretary were present, or the names of any substitutes.
- A statement that the minutes of the previous meeting were approved, revised, or not read.
- A list of any reports that were read and approved.
- All the main motions that were made, with statements as to whether they were carried, defeated, or tabled (vote postponed) and the names of those who made and seconded the motions (motions that were withdrawn are not mentioned).
- A full description of resolutions that were adopted and a simple statement of any that were rejected.
- A record of all ballots with the number of votes cast for and against.
- The time the meeting was adjourned (officially ended) and the place, time, and date of the next meeting.
- The recording secretary's signature and typed name and, if desired, the signature of the chairperson.

Except for recording motions, which must be transcribed word for word, summarize what occurs and paraphrase discussions.

Since minutes are often used to settle disputes, they must be accurate, complete, and clear. When approved, minutes of meetings are official and can be used as evidence in legal proceedings.

Keep your minutes brief and to the point. Give complete information on each topic, but do not ramble—consider the topic and go on to the next one.

MINUTES OF MEETING

Group: Training Committee at Bruxler Corporation and Sales
Consultants from Business Communications Consultants

Place: Bruxler's Training Center at Canton, Ohio

Date: November 14, 19--   Time: 11:00 a.m.

TOPIC: BRUXLER'S TRAINING STRUCTURE

Discussion: They train field engineers, systems engineers, sales force, and managers. They also offer training in employee development.

Action: The decision was made to concentrate only on management training and employee development in 19--.

TOPIC: TRAINING NEEDS FOR THEIR MANAGEMENT TRAINING AND EMPLOYEE DEVELOPMENT PROGRAMS

Discussion: They know they have a need for improved writing skills, listening skills, and presentation skills.

Action: We are to teach those three courses for them in February.

TOPIC: NEEDS ANALYSIS

Discussion: They would like to do a needs analysis to determine the extent of their need for our Conducting Productive Meetings Workshop.

Action: We will provide them with the tools to do a needs analysis. They will administer the needs analysis and get back to us on the results.

Figure 1 *Sample Set of Minutes*

Following a set format will help you keep the minutes concise. You might, for example, use the heading TOPIC, followed by the subheadings Discussion and Action Taken, for each major point discussed.

Avoid abstractions and generalities; always be specific. If you are referring to a nursing station on the second floor of a hospital, write "the nursing station on the second floor" or "the second-floor nursing station," not just "the second floor."

Be especially specific when referring to people. Avoid using titles (the chief of the Records Department) in favor of names and titles (Ms. Florence Johnson, head of the Records Department). And be consistent in the way you refer to people. Do not call one person Mr. Jarrel and another Janet Wilson. It may be unintentional, but a lack of consistency in titles or names may reveal a deference to one person at the expense of another. Avoid adjectives and adverbs that suggest either good or bad qualities, as in "Mr. Sturgess's *capable* assistant read the *comprehensive* report to the subcommittee." Minutes should always be objective and impartial.

If a member of the committee is to follow up on something and report back to the committee at its next meeting, state clearly the person's name and the responsibility he or she has accepted.

When assigned to take the minutes at a meeting, be prepared. Bring more than one pen and plenty of paper. If convenient, you may bring a tape recorder as a backup to your notes (although some people are reluctant to talk in the presence of a tape recorder). Have any material you may need ready. If you do not know shorthand, take memory-jogging notes during the meeting and then expand them with the appropriate details immediately after the meeting.

Figure 1 (see p. 99) is a sample set of minutes.

note taking

The purpose of note taking is to summarize and record the information you extract from your research material. The great challenge in taking notes is to condense another's thoughts in your own words without distorting the original thinking.

When taking notes on abstract ideas, as opposed to factual data, be careful not to sacrifice clarity for brevity. You can be brief—if you are accurate—with statistics, but notes expressing concepts can lose their meaning if they are too brief. The critical test of a note is whether after a week has passed, you will still know what the note means and from it be able to recall the significant ideas of the passage. If you are in doubt about whether or not to take a note, take it—it is much easier to discard a note you don't need than to find the source again if it is needed.

As you extract information, be guided by the purpose of your writing and by what you know about your readers. (How much do they know about your subject? What are their needs?)

Resist the temptation to copy your source word for word as you take notes. Paraphrase the author's idea or concept in your own words. But don't just change a few words in the original passage; you will be guilty of plagiarism. On occasion, when your source concisely sums up a great deal of information or points to a trend or development important to your subject, you are justified in quoting it verbatim and then incorporating that quotation into your paper. As a general rule, you will rarely need to quote anything longer than a paragraph.

If a note is copied word for word from your source, be certain to enclose it in quotation marks so that you will know later that it is a direct quotation. In your finished writing, be certain to give the source of your quotation; otherwise, you will be guilty of plagiarism.

The mechanics of note taking are simple and, if followed conscientiously, can save you much unnecessary work. The following guidelines may help you take notes more effectively:

1. Don't try to write down everything. Pick out the most important ideas and concepts to record as notes.
2. Create your own shorthand. Common words can be indicated by symbols. For example, you can use *&* for *and,* + for *plus, w* for *with,* and so on.
3. Use numbers (5, 10, 20) for numerical terms instead of writing *five, ten,* and *twenty.*
4. Leave out vowels when you can do so and still keep the word recognizable, as in *vwl* for vowel.
5. Be sure to record all vital names, dates, and definitions.
6. Mark any notes you need to question. You might put an asterisk beside any note you don't fully understand or think you might need to pursue further.
7. Check your notes for accuracy against the printed material before leaving it.

Consider the information in the following paragraph:

The arithmetic of searching for oil is stark. For all his scientific methods of detection, the only way the oilman can actually know that there is oil in the ground is to drill a well. The average cost of drilling a well is over $300,000, and drilling a single well may cost over $8,000,000. And once the well is drilled, the odds against its containing enough oil to be commercially profitable are 49 to 1. The odds against its containing any oil at all are 8 to 1! Even after a field has been discovered, one out of every four holes drilled in developing the field is a dry hole because of the uncertainty of defining the limits of the producing formation. The oilman can never know what Mark Twain once called "the calm confidence of a Christian with four aces in his hand."

The paragraph says essentially the following things:

1. Many scientific methods of detection.
2. Only sure way to know is to drill a well.
3. Average cost of drilling a well over $300,000; actual cost can go over $8,000,000.
4. Odds against profitable well: 49 to 1.
5. Odds against any oil: 8 to 1.
6. If existence of oil is known, 1 in 4 wells still dry because limits of field unknown.

If your readers' needs and your purpose involved only questions of cost and profit, you might take notes 3 and 4; if they involved only the technical process of oil drilling, you might take 1, 2, and 6. However, if there is any doubt about whether you should take a note, *take it.*

So that you will give proper credit when you incorporate your notes into your writing, be sure to include the following with the first note taken from a book: author, title, publisher, place and date of publication, and page number. (On subsequent notes from the same book, you will need to include only the author and page number.)

Figures 1 and 2 are examples of a first and a subsequent note taken from the paragraph on oil drilling.

If you do not have time to take careful notes in the library, you may want to check out a book or books to review at home. If you need to take more information from periodical articles (which cannot be checked out) than can be conveniently committed to notes, you may want to make a photographic copy at the library to take home for fuller evaluation.

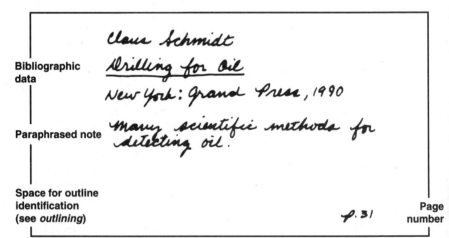

Figure 1 *First Note from a Source*

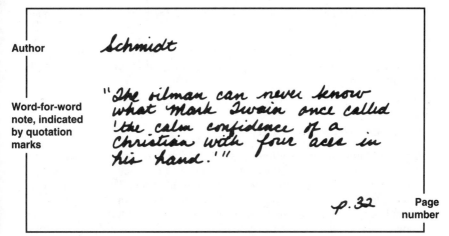

Author *Schmidt*

Word-for-word note, indicated by quotation marks "The oilman can never know what Mark Twain once called 'the calm confidence of a Christian with four aces in his hand.'"

p. 32 **Page number**

Figure 2 *Subsequent Note from a Source*

paraphrasing

When you paraphrase a written passage, you rewrite it to state the essential ideas in your own words. Because you do not quote your source word for word when paraphrasing, it is unnecessary to enclose the paraphrased material in quotation marks. However, paraphrased material should be footnoted because the ideas are taken from someone else whether or not the words are identical.

Original Material

One of the major visual cues used by pilots in maintaining precision ground reference during low-level flight is that of object blur. We are acquainted with the object-blur phenomenon experienced when driving an automobile. Objects in the foreground appear to be rushing toward us while objects in the background appear to recede slightly. There is a point in the observer's line of sight, however, at which objects appear to stand still for a moment, before once again rushing toward him with increasing angular velocity. The distance from the observer to this point where objects appear stationary is sometimes referred to as the "blur threshold" range.

Paraphrased

Object blur refers to the phenomenon by which observers in a moving vehicle look out and see the foreground objects appear to rush at them, while background objects appear to recede. But objects at some point appear temporarily stationary. The distance separating observers from this point is sometimes called the "blur threshold" range.

Note that the paraphrased version includes only the essential information from the original passage. Strive to put the original ideas into your words without distorting them.

policies and procedures

A policy states an organization's posture, or stand, on a subject, whereas a procedure provides instructions for carrying out the policy. Policies and procedures, therefore, are often written at the same time. They usually originate at top- or middle-management levels and are always subjected to a careful review process—mainly because they are considered a "bible" for management. Policies and procedures thus require extraordinarily careful thought and planning. Language and word choices must be as precise as possible so that policies and procedures are clear and understandable—with no ambiguity.

POLICIES

A statement of policy is often preceded by an explanation of the policy's purpose or rationale, as in the following policy regarding company tuition refunds:

1.0 GENERAL

1.1 The purpose of the Blaylock Tuition Refund Plan is to encourage the development of employees through college-level academic training consistent with their abilities and interests and consistent with the needs of the company.

1.2 Financial assistance is offered through the Tuition Refund Plan to encourage college-level work. The plan supports graduate and undergraduate courses and degree programs when the education is appropriately related to department or division objectives.

Such general statements are then followed by the specific details of the policy—in this case, who is eligible, when the tuition refund is appropriate, and so on.

2.0 POLICY

2.1.1 The Blaylock Tuition Refund Plan is intended for full-time personnel classified in supervisory, managerial, professional, sales, administrative, technical, and administrative support jobs.

2.1.2 An individual must be in the employ of the company at the time of enrollment and the completion of the course in order to receive a refund. Should an individual's employment be terminated because of a reduction in force, fees will be refunded for currently approved courses upon satisfactory completion (the last class meeting having been held and a grade one level above passing having been earned). When courses are not satisfactorily completed, reimbursement may be deferred for those individuals having degree approval if, upon completion of the degree, the individual obtains an accumulative grade average of at least "C" (or "B" for most graduate-degree programs).

Sections of a policy are usually numbered (as in the preceding example) and kept in loose-leaf binders, so they can be easily referred to and updated as the need arises.

PROCEDURES

A statement of procedures provides a step-by-step explanation of how to carry out a policy. It provides instructions not only for employees directly involved in the procedure but also for management, who must ensure that the policy is carried out properly.

As preparation for writing procedures, keep track of who is doing what. An easy and effective way is to draw a line vertically down the page of a note pad, an inch or so to the left of center. Then write the word *actor* at the top of the left column and the word *directions* at the top of the right column. Under *directions* describe each step of the procedure; under *actor* write who is performing the action in each step. Make sure your list describes each step of the procedure fully and in the correct sequence. In effect, this technique serves as an outline. The following is an example of the chart you might prepare to write a degree-approval procedure:

ACTOR	DIRECTIONS
Employee	Determines his or her eligibility for degree program, gains approval of manager, and submits request to Personnel Resources Department.
Personnel Resources	Reviews request and, if reason is not obvious, asks manager to justify, in writing, the benefits of approving the degree program.
Employee	Completes Sections I and II of Form F-6970.
Personnel Resources	Sends form to each of two levels of management above employee for approval.

The following might be the draft created from the preceding chart:

1.0 PROCEDURE

1.1 *Degree Approval*

1.1.1 Individuals who meet school requirements and are interested in receiving tuition refunds should gain the approval of their management and Personnel Resources. Personnel Resources may request a manager to justify, in writing, the benefits of approving a degree request if the reason is not obvious.

1.1.2 After agreement is reached, the employee should complete Sections I and II of Form F-6970. After two levels of management approval have been gained, the form should be forwarded to Personnel Resources. Approval must be given by the "staff" manager before degree approval can be granted. Copies of Form F-6970 will then be returned to the student and the manager.

1.1.3 The employee who has been granted degree approval must complete Sections I and II of Form F-6970 when registering for each course required for the degree, whether or not reimbursement will be granted upon completion of a course or deferred until completion of the degree.

progress and activity reports

Progress reports and activity reports differ because progress reports are submitted by a vendor to a client company, and activity reports are submitted by an employee to a superior.

PROGRESS REPORTS

A progress report provides information about a project—its current status, whether it is on schedule, whether it is within the budget, and so on. Progress reports are often submitted by a contracting company to a client company. They are issued at regular intervals throughout the life of a project and state what has been done in a specified interval and what has yet to be done before the project can be completed. The progress report is used primarily with projects that involve many steps over a period of weeks, months, or even years. Progress reports help keep projects running smoothly by allowing management to assign workers, adjust schedules, allocate budgets, or schedule supplies and equipment, as necessary.

All reports in a series of progress reports should have the same format. Since progress reports are normally sent outside the company, they are often written in letter format.

The introduction to the first progress report should identify the project, any methods and necessary materials, and the date by which the project is to be completed. Subsequent reports should then summarize the progress since the first report.

The body of the progress report should describe the project's present status, including such details as schedules and costs.

The report should end with conclusions and recommendations about changes in the schedule, materials, techniques, and so on. The conclusion may also include a statement of the work done and an estimate of future progress.

The example shown in Figure 1 is the first progress report submitted by an electrical contractor (REMCON) to a client (the Arena Committee).

─────── **REMCON ELECTRIC** ───────
5099 Seventh Street, St. Paul, Minnesota 55101 (612) 555-1212

August 20, 19--

Arena Committee
Minnesota Sports
708 N. Case St.
St. Paul, MN 55101

Subject: Arena Rewiring Progress Report

Introduction identifies project and completion date

This report, as agreed to in our contract, covers the progress on the rewiring program at the Sports Arena from May 5 to August 15 of 19--. Although the costs of certain equipment are higher than our original bid indicated, we expect to complete the project by December 23, without going over cost; the speed with which the project is being completed will save labor costs.

Work Completed

On August 15, we finished installing the circuit-breaker panels and meters of Level I service outlets and of all subfloor rewiring. Lighting fixture replacement, Level II service outlets, and the upgrading of stage lighting equipment are in the preliminary stages (meaning that the wiring has been completed but installation of the fixtures has not yet begun).

Body details schedules and costs

Costs

Equipment used up to this point has cost $10,800, and labor has cost $31,500 (including some subcontracted plumbing). My estimate for the rest of the equipment, based on discussions with your lighting consultant, is $11,500; additional labor costs should not exceed $25,000.

Work Schedule

I have scheduled the upgrading of stage lighting equipment from August 16 to October 5, the completion of Level II service outlets from October 6 to November 12, and the replacement of lighting fixtures from November 15 to December 17.

Conclusion indicates pertinent changes

Conclusion

Although my original estimate on equipment ($20,000) has been exceeded by $2,300, my original labor estimate ($60,000) has been reduced by $3,500; so I will easily stay within the limits of my original bid. In addition, I see no difficulty in having the arena finished for the Christmas program on December 23.

Sincerely,

John Remcon

John Remcon
President and Owner

ics

Figure 1 *Progress Report*

ACTIVITY REPORTS

Within an organization, professional employees often submit reports on the progress and current status of all ongoing projects assigned to them by their managers. The managers combine these activity reports (also called *status reports*) into larger activity reports that they, in turn, submit to their managers. Activity reports help keep all levels of management aware of the progress and status of projects within an organization.

An activity report includes information about the status of all current projects, including any problems, the action currently being taken to resolve any problems, and the writer's plans for the coming month. A manager's activity report should also indicate the current number of employees.

Because the activity report is issued periodically (often monthly) and contains material familiar to its readers, it normally needs no introduction or conclusion. The format of an activity report may vary from company to company, or even among different parts of the same company. The following sections are typical and would be adequate for most situations:

Current Projects
This section lists every project assigned to the employee or manager and summarizes its current status.

Current Problems
This section details any problems confronting the employee or manager and explains the steps being taken to resolve them.

Plans for the Next Period
This section projects what the writer expects to achieve on each project during the next month or reporting period.

Current Staffing Level
This section, included by managers and project leaders, lists the number of subordinates assigned to the writer and correlates that number with the staffing level considered necessary for the projects assigned.

The activity report shown in Figure 2, using a memorandum form, was submitted by a manager of software development (Wayne Tribinski) who supervises 11 employees. The reader of the report (Kathryn Hunter), Tribinski's manager, is the director of engineering.

proposals

A proposal is a document written to persuade someone to follow a plan or course of action. It may be internal to an organization, or it may be sent outside the organization to a potential client.

Since proposals offer plans to fill a need, your readers will evaluate your plan according to how well your written presentation answers their questions about what you are proposing to do, how you plan to do it, when you plan to do it, and how much it is going to cost.

To answer these questions satisfactorily, make certain that your proposal is written at your reader's level of knowledge. If you have more than one reader—and proposals often require more than one level of approval—take into account all your readers. For example, if your immediate reader is an expert on your subject but the next higher level of management (which must

INTEROFFICE MEMORANDUM

```
Date:        June 5, 19--
To:          Kathryn Hunter, Director of Engineering
From:        Wayne Tribinski, Manager, Software Development  ω.T.

Subject:     Activity Report for May, 19--
```

Projects

Status of current projects

1. The Problem-Tracking System now contains both software and hardware problem-tracking capabilities. The system upgrade took place over the weekend of May 11 and 12 and was placed online on the 13th.
2. For the Software Training Mailing Campaign, we anticipate producing a set of labels for mailing software-training information to customers by June 10.
3. The Search Project is on hold until the PL/I training has been completed, probably by the end of June.
4. The project to provide a data base for the Information Management System has been expanded in scope to provide a data base for all training activities. We are in the process of rescheduling the project to take the new scope into account.
5. The Metering Reports project is part of a larger project called "Reporting Upgrade." We have completed the Final Project Requirements and sent it out for review. The Resource Requirements estimate has also been completed, and Phase Three is scheduled for completion by June 17.

Problems

Existing problems

The Information Management System has been delayed. The original schedule was based on the assumption that a systems analyst who was familiar with the system would work on this project. Instead, the project was assigned to a newly hired systems analyst who was inexperienced and required much more learning time than expected.

Bill Michaels, whose activity report is attached, is correcting a problem in the CNG Software. This correction may take a week.

The Beta Project was delayed for approximately one week because of two problems: interfacing and link handling. The interfacing problem was resolved rather easily. The link-handling problem, however, was more severe, and Debra Mann has gone to the customer's site in France to resolve it.

Plans for Next Month

Plans for the coming months

• Complete the Software Training Mailing Campaign.
• Resume the Search Project.
• Restart the project to provide a data base on information management with a schedule that reflects its new scope
• Complete the Phase Three project.
• Write a report to justify the addition of two software engineers to my department.
• Congratulate publicly the recipients of Meritorious Achievement Awards: Bill Thomasson and Nancy O'Rourke.

Current Staffing Level

```
Current staff: 11
Open requisitions: 0

ja
Enclosure
```

Figure 2 *Activity Report*

also approve the proposal) is not, provide an executive summary written in language that is as nontechnical as possible. You might also include a glossary of terms used in the body of the proposal, or an appendix that explains highly detailed information in nontechnical language. On the other hand, if your immediate reader is not an expert but the person at the next level is, write the proposal with the nonexpert in mind and include an appendix that contains the details.

Proposals consist of an introduction, a body, and a conclusion. The introduction should summarize the problem you are proposing to solve and your solution to the problem. It may also summarize the benefits your reader will receive from your solution and its total cost if there are reasons to include them. The body should explain in detail (1) how the job will be done, (2) what methods will be used to do it, (3) when work will begin, (4) when the job will be completed, and (5) a cost breakdown for the entire job. The conclusion should emphasize the benefits for the reader and should urge him or her to take action. Your conclusion should have an encouraging, confident, and reasonably assertive tone.

INTERNAL PROPOSALS

The purpose of an internal proposal is to suggest a change or an improvement within an organization. For example, one might be written to propose initiating a new management reporting system, expanding the cafeteria service, or changing a policy. An internal proposal, usually in memo format, is prepared by a person or a department and is sent to a higher-ranking person who has the authority to accept or reject the proposal. In the opening of a proposal, you must establish that a problem exists that needs a solution. If the person who is to judge the proposal is not convinced that there is a problem, your proposal will have no chance of success. Notice how the following opening to a proposal states its problem directly:

> Date: December 5, 19--
> To: Harriet Sullivan
> From: Christine Thomas
> Subject: Advantages of Expanding HVS Computing Facilities
>
> As we discussed earlier, because our computing facilities currently operate at maximum capacity, we are turning new customers away in growing numbers and will soon have to deny present customers computer time for emergencies or overload backups. By purchasing a new VT-8000 minicomputer and expanding our staff, we could respond to new service requests, provide better service to valued customers, and attract new customers who would not have previously considered using our service.

The body of a proposal should offer a practical solution to the problem. In building a case for a solution, be as specific as possible. When it is appropriate, include (1) a breakdown of costs; (2) information about equipment, material, and personnel requirements; and (3) a schedule for completing the task. Consider the following example, which continues the proposal introduced above:

> Last month we turned away 21 new service requests. At least six of these requests were equal to the largest accounts we currently serve. Furthermore, since our aging mainframe computer cannot handle the latest software available from ABC Systems, we can neither offer improved, faster services to our most profitable accounts (such as First International Savings and Loan) nor attract the new customers who are eager to take advantage of the most recent advances in computer technology.
>
> The VT-8000 is a very fast, reasonably priced minicomputer with massive peripheral memory capacity in the form of removable disk packs. This machine would triple our current processing capacity and enable us to use the full range of new VRX software now available. The following details show how purchasing the VT-8000 system would triple our number of customers and pay for itself within two years.
>
> *Cost of New Equipment*
>
> | | |
> |---|---|
> | VT-8000 minicomputer | $12,500 |
> | Two 3033 disks and disk drives | 1,800 |
> | One VT80 computer terminal | 980 |
> | New VRX software | 1,050 |
> | Total cost of equipment | $16,330 |
>
> *Increases in Annual Operating Budget*
>
> | | |
> |---|---|
> | Salaries: Computer operator | $19,000 |
> | Data entry technician | 12,000 |
> | Total increase in annual operating budget | $31,000 |
>
> *Total Costs*
>
> | | |
> |---|---|
> | First year | $47,330 |
> | Second year | 26,200 |
> | Two-year total cost | $73,530 |
>
> *Increased Income Generated by Expansion*
>
> | | |
> |---|---|
> | First-year estimate (45 new customers) | $37,010 |
> | Second-year estimate (50 new customers) plus the 45 of the first year | $64,400 |
> | Total | $101,410 |

Since the purchase of the VT-8000 system is a one-time investment a profit of $27,880 will be generated by the end of the second year.

The estimates are based on the $751 average annual value of accounts over the past two years.

Because this system is reliable, easy to install, and easy to operate, we could have it running in three weeks with little disturbance of our normal office routine. More importantly, buying the VT-8000 will provide a cost-effective solution to the current problem of overburdened computing resources and will clear the way for meeting the demands of a growing base of customers. Although the VT-8000 printer is somewhat noisier than the VT-3400 printer, soundproofing the computer room is something that we had planned to do anyway.

The conclusion should be brief but must tie everything together. It is a good idea to restate recommendations here. Be careful, of course, to conclude in a spirit of cooperation, offering to set up a meeting, supply further facts and figures, or provide any other assistance that might solve the problem, as is done in the following example:

> On the basis of these details, I recommend that we expand HVS services by purchasing the VT-8000 system. An enclosed brochure describes the system in more detail. I will be happy to provide additional information about the system at your request.

quotations

When you have borrowed words, facts, or ideas from someone else's work, acknowledge your debt by giving your source credit in a footnote. Otherwise, you will be guilty of plagiarism. Also be sure that you have represented the original material honestly and accurately.

DIRECT QUOTATIONS

Direct word-for-word quotations are enclosed in quotation marks and separated from the rest of the sentence by a comma or colon.

EXAMPLES
The noted economist says, "If monopolies could be made to behave as if they were perfectly competitive, we would be able to enjoy the benefits both of large-scale efficiency and of the perfectly working price mechanism."

The noted economist pointed out: "There are three options available when technical conditions make a monopoly the natural outcome of competitive market forces: private monopoly, public monopoly, or public regulation."

INDIRECT QUOTATIONS

Indirect quotations, which are essentially paraphrased and are usually introduced by *that*, are not set off from the rest of the sentence by punctuation marks.

DIRECT
He said in a recent interview, "Regulation cannot supply the dynamic stimulus that in other industries is supplied by competition."

INDIRECT
In a recent interview he said that regulation does not stimulate the industry as well as competition does.

When a quotation is divided, the material that interrupts the quotation is set off, before and after, by commas, and quotation marks are used around each part of the quotation.

> EXAMPLE "Regulation," he said in a recent interview, "cannot supply the dynamic stimulus that in other industries is supplied by competition."

DELETIONS OR OMISSIONS

Deletions or omissions from quoted material are indicated by three ellipsis dots within a sentence and four ellipsis dots at the end of a sentence.

> EXAMPLE "If monopolies could be made to behave . . . we would be able to enjoy the benefits of . . . large-scale efficiency. . . ."

When a quoted passage begins in the middle of a sentence rather than at the beginning, however, ellipsis dots are not necessary; the fact that the first letter of the quoted material is not capitalized tells the reader that the quotation begins in midsentence.

> CHANGE He goes on to conclude that ". . . coordination may lessen competition within a region."

> TO He goes on to conclude that "coordination may lessen competition within a region."

When quoted material is worked into a sentence, be sure that it is related logically, grammatically, and syntactically to the rest of the sentence.

INSERTING MATERIAL INTO QUOTATIONS

When it is necessary to insert a clarifying comment within quoted material, use brackets.

> EXAMPLE "The industry is organized as a relatively large, integrated system serving an extensive [geographic] area, with smaller systems existing as islands within the larger system's sphere of influence."

When quoted material contains an obvious error, or might in some other way be questioned, the expression *sic,* enclosed in brackets, follows the questionable material to indicate that the writer has quoted the material exactly as it appeared in the original.

> EXAMPLE In *Basic Astronomy,* Professor Jones noted that the "earth does not revolve around the son [*sic*] at a constant rate."

INCORPORATING QUOTATIONS INTO TEXT

Depending on the length, there are two mechanical methods of incorporating quotations into your text.

Quotations of four or fewer lines are incorporated into your text and enclosed in quotation marks. (Many writers use this method regardless of length. When this method is used with multiple paragraphs, quotation marks appear at the beginning of each new paragraph, but at the end of only the last paragraph.)

Material longer than five lines is usually inset; that is, it is set off from the body of the text by being indented five spaces from the left margin and by triple-spacing above and below the quotation. The quoted passage is single-spaced and not enclosed in quotation marks.

OVERQUOTING

Do not rely too heavily on the use of quotations in the final version of your report or paper. If you do, your work will appear merely derivative. The temptation to overquote during the note-taking phase of your research can be avoided if you concentrate on summarizing what you read. Quote word for word only when your source concisely sums up a great deal of information or points to a trend or development important to your subject. As a rule of thumb, avoid quoting anything over one paragraph.

reports

A report is an organized presentation of factual information that answers a request by supplying the results of an investigation, a trip, a test, a research project, and the like. All reports can be divided into two broad categories: *formal* and *informal.*

Formal reports present the results of projects that may require months of work and involve large sums of money. These projects may be done either for one's own organization or as a contractual requirement for an outside organization. Formal reports generally follow a stringent format and include some or all of the report elements discussed in the entry on **formal reports** in this tabbed section.

Informal reports normally run from a few paragraphs to a few pages and include only the essential elements of a report: introduction, body, conclusion, and recommendations. Because of their brevity, informal reports are customarily written as a letter (if the report is to be sent to someone outside the organization) or as a memorandum (if it is to be sent to someone inside the organization).

The introduction serves several functions: it announces the subject of the report, states its purpose, and, when appropriate, gives essential background information. The introducton should also summarize any conclusions, findings, or recommendations made in the report. Managers, supervisors, and clients find a concise summary useful because it gives them the essential information at a glance and helps focus their thinking as they read the rest of the report.

The body of the report should present a clearly organized account of the report's subject—the results of a test carried out, the status of a construction project, and so on. The amount of detail to include depends on the complexity of the subject and on your reader's familiarity with it.

The conclusion should summarize your findings and tell the reader what you think their significance may be. In some reports, a final section gives recommendations. (Sometimes the conclusions and recommendations sections are combined.) In this section, you make suggestions for a course of action based on the data you have pressented.

tables of contents

A table of contents is a list of heads in a report or chapters in a book. It lists them in their order of appearance and cites their page numbers. Appearing at the front of a work, a table of contents permits readers to preview what is in the work and assess the work's value to them. It also aids readers who may want to read only certain sections.

The length of your report should determine whether it needs a table of contents. If it does, use the major heads and subheads of your outline (exactly as they appear in the text) to create your table of contents, as shown in Figure 1.

To punctuate a table of contents, place a series of periods, called "leaders," between the head and the page number on which the head appears. For guidance on the placement of the table of contents in a report, see the **formal reports** entry in this tabbed section.

Table of Contents

Abstract ii
Foreword iii
Executive Summary 1
Part I: A Condensed Report of Observations 3
  Publications 4
  Organization 6
  Operation 8
  Personnel 10
Part II: Conclusions and Recommendations 12
Appendix A: Observations in Detail 14
  Publications 15
  Organization 23
  Operation 41
  Personnel 56
Appendix B: Individual Reports 85
  Memorandum from the Chairman 86
  Report by Walter Browser 88
  Report by Gerald Watson 92
  Report by Gunther Brown 96
  Report by Robert Helms 99

Figure 1 *Sample Table of Contents*

titles

The title of a document should indicate its topic and, when possible, indicate its scope and purpose.

To create accurate titles, keep the following guidelines in mind:

1. *Be specific.* Do not use general or vague terms when specific ones will pinpoint the topic and its scope. Although the title "Electric Fields and Living Organisms" announces the topic of a report, it leaves the reader with important unanswered questions: What is the relationship between electric fields and living organisms? What stage in the organism's life cycle does it discuss? The addition of details identifies not only the topic but its scope and purpose as well: *Effects of 60-Hz Electric Fields on Embryo and Chick Development, Growth, and Behavior.*

2. *Be concise,* but don't make your title short just for the sake of being short. As the example above indicates, making a title accurate may mean adding a few terms. Conciseness, instead, means eliminating words that do not contribute to accuracy. Avoid titles that begin "Notes on . . .," "Studies on . . .," "A Report on . . .," or "Observations on. . . ." These notions are self-evident to the reader. On the other hand, certain works, like annual reports or feasibility studies, should be identified as such in the title because this information helps define the purpose and scope.

3. *Do not indicate dates* in the title of a periodic or progress report, but put them in a subtitle:

The Effects of Acid Rain on Red Spruce
in the White Mountains
Quarterly Report
January-March 19--

4. *Avoid using abbreviations, acronyms and initialisms, chemical formulas,* and the like unless the work is addressed exclusively to specialists in the field.

5. *Do not put titles in sentence form.*

> CHANGE How Residential Passive Solar Heating Could Affect Seven Electric Utilities
>
> TO Potential Effects of Residential Passive Solar Heating on Seven Utilities

6. *For multivolume publications, repeat the title on each volume.* The distinction between the volumes is made by the volume number (Volume 1, 2, 3, and so on), and sometimes each volume has a different subtitle. For example, Volume 1 could be an executive summary; Volume 2 could be the main report; and any subsequent volumes could be lengthy appendixes.

trip reports

Many companies require or encourage reports of the business trips their employees take. A trip report both (1) provides a permanent record of a business trip and its accomplishments and (2) enables many employees to benefit from the information that one employee has gained.

A trip report should normally be in the format of a memorandum, addressed to your immediate superior. On the subject line give the destination and dates of the trip. The body of the report will explain why you made the trip, whom you visited, and what you accomplished. The report should devote a brief section to each major event and many include a head for each

---

MEMORANDUM

To: Manuel Cruz, Manager, Customer Relations
From: Isoroku Somoto, Field Service Engineer
Date: May 31, 19--
Subject: Trip to Inspect New Power Unit Installations, May 26–30

The purpose of this trip was to inspect the installation of Taylor Auxilliary Power Units in five hospitals and to train the maintenance staffs at those hospitals to operate the units during a commercial power failure. I visited the New Orleans General Hospital on the 26th, Our Lady of Mercy Hospital in San Antonio on the 27th, Dallas Presbyterian Hospital on the 28th, St. Elizabeth Hospital in Oklahoma City on the 29th, and the Jefferson Davis Memorial Hospital in Atlanta on the 30th.

At each site, I found that the installation of the equipment had been done properly. I made arrangements, in each hospital, with the administrative office and then placed the hospital on auxilliary power for one hour as a trial run. In every location, the transfer from commercial power to auxilliary power was made without problems.

After inspecting the equipment and its installation, I held a brief training session with the maintenance staff. The training consisted of instruction in starting the unit's engine, in operating the generator's controls to produce 220 volts of electricity at 60 Hertz, and in activating the operating unit in the event of a commercial power failure.

In all five hospitals, both the administrative and maintenance staffs appeared to have a favorable opinion of the Taylor Power Equipment Company, its product, and its field personnel. Our sales staff and installers seem to be doing a good job.

IS/bb

Figure 1 *Trip Report*

section (you needn't give equal space to each event, but instead, elaborate on the more important events). Follow the body of the report with any appropriate conclusions and recommendations. The trip report shown in Figure 1 (see p. 117) is typical.

trouble reports

The trouble report is used to report an accident, an equipment failure, an unplanned work stoppage, and so on. The report enables the management of an organization to determine the cause of the problem and to make any changes necessary to prevent its recurrence. The trouble report normally follows a simple format (often a memorandum), since it is an internal document and is not large enough in either size or scope to require the format of a formal report.

In the subject line of the memorandum, state the precise problem you are reporting. Then begin your description of the problem in the body of your report. What happened? Where did it occur? When did it occur? Was anybody hurt? Was there any property damage? Was there a work stoppage? Since insurance claims, worker's compensation awards, and, in some instances, lawsuits may hinge on the information contained in a trouble report, be sure to include precise times, dates, locations, treatment of injuries, names of any witnesses, and any other crucial information. Give a detailed analysis of what caused the problem. Be thorough and accurate in your analysis, and support any judgments or conclusions with facts. Be careful about your tone; avoid any condemnation or blame. If you speculate about the cause of the problem, make it clear to your reader that you are speculating.

In your conclusion, state what has been done, what is being done, or what will be done to correct the conditions that led to the problem. This may include training in safety practices, better or improved equipment, protective clothing (for example, shoes or goggles), and so on.

The report shown in Figure 1, about an accident involving personal injury, was written by the foreman of a group of punch press operators for the plant's safety officer, at the safety officer's request. Since there were no witnesses, the foreman obtained the information for the report by talking to the plant nurse, hospital personnel, and the victim—and by inspecting the equipment used by the victim at the time of the accident.

MEMORANDUM

```
To:       James K. Arburg, Safety Officer
From:     Lawrence T. Baker, Foreman of Section A-40  LTB
Date:     November 30, 19--

Subject:  Personal-Injury Accident in Section A-40
          October 10, 19--
```

On October 10, 19--, at 10:15 p.m., Jim Hollander, operating
punch press #16, accidentally brushed the knee switch of his
punch press with his right knee as he swung a metal sheet over
the punching surface. The switch activated the punching unit,
which severed Hollander's left thumb between the first and
second joints as his hand passed through the punch station.
While an ambulance was being summoned, Margaret Wilson, R.N.,
administered first aid at the plant dispensary. There were no
witnesses to the accident.

The ambulance arrived from Mercy Hospital at 10:45 p.m.,
and Hollander was admitted to the emergency room at the
hospital at 11:00 p.m. He was treated and kept overnight for
observation, then released the next morning.

Hollander returned to work one week later, on October 17.
He has been given temporary duties in the tool room until his
injury heals.

Conclusions About the Cause of the Accident

The Maxwell punch press on which Hollander was working has two
switches, a hand switch and a knee switch, and both must be
pressed to activate the punch mechanism. The hand switch must
be pressed first, and then the knee switch, to trip the punch
mechanism. The purpose of the knee switch is to leave the
operator's hands free to hold the panel being punched. The
hand switch, in contrast, is a safety feature. Because the
knee switch cannot activate the press until the hand switch has
been pressed, the operator cannot trip the punching mechanism
by touching the knee switch accidentally.

Inspection of the punch press that Hollander was operating
at the time of the accident made it clear that Hollander had
taped the hand switch of his machine in the ON position,
effectively eliminating its safety function. He could then
pick up a panel, swing it onto the machine's punching surface,
press the knee switch, stack the newly punched panel, and grab
the next unpunched panel, all in one continuous motion--
eliminating the need to let go of the panel, after placing it
on the punching surface, in order to press the hand switch.

To prevent a recurrence of this accident, I have conducted
a brief safety session with all punch press operators, at which
I described Hollander's experience and cautioned them against
tampering with the safety features of their machines.

mo

Figure 1 *Trouble Report*

OVERVIEW

The process of writing letters and memorandums involves many of the same steps that go into most other on-the-job tasks. So before using the entries in this section, consider reviewing the overview to THE BUSINESS WRITING PROCESS tab.

One very important element in business letters is that they are more personal than reports or other forms of business writing. Since letters vary in style, tone, and strategy, you may wish to review the **correspondence** entry before reading such specific entries as **complaint letters, inquiry letters and responses, sales letters,** or **refusal letters.**

Memorandums provide a record of decisions made and virtually all actions taken within an organization. Effective managers also use memos to keep employees informed and motivate them. Many of the types of business writing described in the BUSINESS WRITING FORMS AND ELEMENTS tab are written in memo format. In addition to typical letters and memos, this tab includes entries on **electronic mail** and **international correspondence.**

Finally, this tab includes entries on two of the most crucial writing tasks in anyone's career—**application letters** and **résumés.** Preparing them will help you assess your specific skills and goals—knowledge that is essential to a successful job search and to preparation for a job interview.

acceptance letters

When you have received an offer of a job that you want to accept, begin by accepting, with pleasure, the job you have been offered. Identify the job you are accepting, and state the salary so there is no confusion on these two important points.

The second paragraph might go into detail about moving dates and reporting for work—the details will vary depending on what occurred during your job interview. Complete the letter with a statement that you are looking forward to working for your new employer.

Figure 1 is an example of an acceptance letter.

2647 Patterson Road
Beechwood, OH   45432
March 6, 19--

Mr. F. E. Cummins
Personnel Manager
Calcutex Industries, Inc.
3275 Commercial Park Drive
Bintonville, MI   49474

Dear Mr. Cummins:

State the job and salary you are accepting.

I

Specify the date on which you will report to work.

I

State your pleasure at joining the firm.

I am pleased to accept your offer of a position as assistant personnel manager at a salary of $X,XXX per month.

Since graduation is August 30, I plan to leave Dayton on Tuesday, September 2. I should be able to locate suitable living accommodations within a few days and be ready to report for work on the following Monday, September 8. Please let me know if this date is satisfactory to you.

I look forward to a rewarding future with Calcutex.

Sincerely,

Craig Adderly

Craig Adderly

Figure 1 *Acceptance Letter*

acknowledgment letters

It is sometimes necessary (and always considerate) to let someone know that you have received something sent to you. An acknowledgment letter serves such a function. It should usually be a short, polite note that mentions when the item arrived and expresses thanks. See the **correspondence** entry in this tabbed section for general advice on letter writing, and study Figure 1 to get an idea of how to phrase an acknowledgment letter.

Energy Savings Systems
501 North Springfield
Phoenix, AZ 85302

November 8, 19--

Ms. Wanda Evans, Consultant
936 East Avenue
Phoenix, AZ 85301

Dear Ms. Evans:

I received your report today; it appears to be complete and well done. Thank you for sending it so promptly.

When I finish studying the report, I will send you our cost estimate for the installation of the Mark II Energy-Saving System.

Sincerely,

Robert A. Martinez

Robert A. Martinez
Administrative Assistant

RAM/mo

Figure 1 *Acknowledgment Letter*

adjustment letters

An adjustment letter is written in response to a complaint letter and tells the customer what your organization intends to do about his or her complaint. You should settle claims quickly and courteously, trying always to satisfy the customer at a reasonable cost to your company.

Although it is sent in response to a problem, an adjustment letter actually provides an excellent opportunity to build goodwill for your company. An effective adjustment letter both repairs the damage that has been done and restores the customer's confidence in your firm.

Grant adjustments graciously, for a settlement made grudgingly will do more harm than good. Tone is critical (see the **correspondence** entry in this tabbed section for a discussion of tone). No matter how unpleasant or unreasonable the complaint letter, your response should remain positive and respectful. Avoid emphasizing the unfortunate situation at hand; put your emphasis instead on what you are doing to correct it. Not only must you be gracious, but also you must admit your error in such a way that the buyer will not lose confidence in your company or organization.

Before granting an adjustment to a claim for which your company is at fault, you must investigate what happened and decide what you can do to satisfy the customer. Be certain that you know your company's policy regarding adjustments before you attempt to write an adjustment letter. Also, be careful about how you put certain words together; for example, "we have just received your letter of May 7 about our *defective product*" could be ruled in a court of law as an admission that the product is in fact defective. Treat every claim individually, and lean toward giving the customer the benefit of the doubt.

Use the following guidelines to help you write adjustment letters:

1. Open with whatever you believe the reader will consider good news:
   - *Grant the adjustment,* if appropriate, for uncomplicated situations ("Enclosed is a replacement for the damaged part").
   - *Reveal that you intend to grant the adjustment* by admitting that the customer was right ("Yes, you were incorrectly billed for the oil delivery"). Then later explain the specific details of the adjustment. This method is good for adjustments that require detailed explanations.
   - *Apologize for the error* ("Please accept our apologies for not acting sooner to correct your account"). This method is effective when the customer's inconvenience is as much an issue as money.
   - *Use a combination of these techniques.* Often, situations requiring an adjustment are unique and do not fit a single pattern.
2. If such an explanation will help restore your reader's confidence or goodwill, explain what caused the problem.
3. Explain specifically how you intend to make the adjustment, if it is not obvious in your opening.
4. Express appreciation to the customer for calling your attention to the situation, explaining that this helps your firm keep the quality of its product or service high.

5. Point out any steps you may be taking to prevent a recurrence of whatever went wrong, giving the customer as much credit as the facts allow.
6. Close pleasantly—looking forward, not back. Avoid recalling the problem in your closing ("Again, we apologize . . ."). Figure 1 is a typical adjustment letter.

ELECTRONIC Parts Inc.
One South Park Avenue
Columbia, AL 36319

January 17, 19--

Mr. Paul E. Denlinger
Denlinger Television Services, Inc.
4873 Wenton Way
Birmingham, AL 35214

Dear Mr. Denlinger:

We have received your letter regarding your order for nine TR-5771-3 tuners and have shipped the correct tuners by United Parcel. You should receive them shortly after you receive this letter. I have also instructed our Billing Department to charge you our preferred-customer rate--normally reserved for orders of more than $2000. Please accept our apologies for not sending the proper tuners and for incorrectly billing you.

Evidently, when your package arrived at our loading docks, a dock worker failed to see your letter in the container. We set the box aside with several boxes of parts destined for our Rebuilt Parts Department; therefore, your note did not come to the attention of our parts manager.

We appreciate your business and hope we have resolved your problem to your satisfaction.

Sincerely,

Jonathan L. Pennington

Jonathan L. Pennington
Office Manager

JLP/jq

Figure 1 *Adjustment Letter Granting the Claim*

Sometimes you may decide to grant a partial adjustment, even though the claim is not really justified, as in Figure 2. You would do this only to regain the lost goodwill of the customer.

You may sometimes need to educate your reader about the use of your product or service. Customers sometimes submit claims that are not justified, even though they honestly believe them to be (for example, a problem resulting from a customer not following prescribed maintenance instruc-

---

General Television, Inc.
5521 West 23rd Street
New York, NY 10062

Customer Relations
(212) 574-3894

September 28, 19--

Mr. Fred J. Swesky
7811 Ranchero Drive
Tucson, AZ 85761

Dear Mr. Swesky:

We have received your letter regarding the replacement of your KL-71 television set and have investigated the situation.

You stated in your letter that you used the set on an uncovered patio. As our local service representative pointed out, this model is not designed to operate in extreme heat conditions. As the instruction manual accompanying your new set stated, such exposure can produce irreparable damage to this model. Since your set was used in such extreme heat conditions, therefore, we cannot honor the two-year replacement warranty.

However, we are enclosing a certificate entitling you to a trade-in allowance equal to your local GTI dealer's markup for the set. This certificate will enable you to purchase a new set from the dealer at the wholesale price when you return the original set to your local dealer.

Sincerely yours,

Susan Siegel

Susan Siegel
Assistant Director

SS/mr

Figure 2 *Adjustment Letter Granting Partial Adjustment*

tions properly). You would grant such a claim only to build goodwill. When you write a letter of adjustment in such a situation, it is wise to give the explanation before granting the claim—otherwise, your reader may never get to the explanation. If your explanation establishes customer responsibility, be sure to do so tactfully. Examine the example of such an educational adjustment letter in Figure 3.

SWELCO Coffee Maker, Inc. _____
9025 North Main Street
Butte, MT 59702

August 26, 19--

Mr. Carlos Ortiz
638 McSwaney Drive
Butte, MT 59702

Dear Mr. Ortiz:

Enclosed is your SWELCO Coffee Maker, which you sent to us on August 17.

In various parts of the country, tap water may contain a high mineral content. If you fill your SWELCO Coffee Maker with water for breakfast coffee before going to bed, a mineral scale will build up on the inner wall of the water tube--as explained on page 2 of your SWELCO Instruction Booklet.

We have removed the mineral scale from the water tube of your coffee maker and thoroughly cleaned the entire unit. To ensure the best service from your coffee maker in the future, clean it once a month by operating it with four ounces of white vinegar and eight cups of water. To rinse out the vinegar taste, operate the unit twice with clear water.

With proper care, your SWELCO Coffee Maker will serve you faithfully and well for many years to come.

Sincerely,

Helen Upham

Helen Upham
Customer Services

HU/mo
Enclosure

Figure 3 *Educational Adjustment Letter*

application letters

The letter of application is essentially a sales letter. You are marketing your skills, abilities, and knowledge. Remember that you may be competing with many other applicants. The immediate objective of an application letter is to get the attention of the person who screens and hires job applicants. Your ultimate goal is to obtain a job interview.

The successful application letter does three things: it catches the reader's favorable attention, it convinces the reader that you are qualified for consideration, and it requests an interview.

A letter of application should provide the following information:

1. Identify an employment area or state a specific job title.
2. Point out your source of information about the job.
3. Summarize your qualifications for the job, specifically education, work experience, and activities showing leadership skills.
4. Refer the reader to your résumé.
5. Ask for an interview, stating where you can be reached and when you will be available for an interview.

If you are applying for a specific job, include any information pertinent to the position that is not included on the more general résumé.

Personnel directors review many letters each week. To save them time, you should state your job objective directly at the beginning of the letter.

> **EXAMPLE** I am seeking a position in an accounting department where I can use my computer science training to solve business problems.

If you have been referred to a prospective employer by one if its employees, a placement counselor, a professor, or someone else, however, you might say so before stating your job objective.

> **EXAMPLE** During the recent NOMAD convention in Washington, D.C., a member of your sales staff, Mr. Dale Jarrett, informed me of a possible opening for a manager in your Dealer Sales Division. My extensive background in the office machine industry, I believe, qualifies me for the position.

In succeeding paragraphs expand upon the qualifications you mentioned in your opening. Add any appropriate details, highlighting the experience listed on your résumé that is especially pertinent to the job you are seeking. Close your letter with a request for an interview.

See the accompanying three sample letters of application. The first one is by a recent college graduate, the second by a college student about to graduate, and the third by a person with many years of work experience. Figure 1 is in response to a local newspaper article about a company's plan to build a new plant. The writer is not applying for a specific job opening,

6819 Locustview Drive
Topeka, Kansas 66614
June 14, 19--

Loudons, Inc.
4619 Drove Lane
Kansas City, Kansas 63511

Dear Personnel Manager:

The Kansas Dispatch recently reported that Loudons is building a
new computer center just north of Kansas City. I would like to apply
for a position as an entry-level programmer at the center.

I understand Loudons produces both in-house and customer documentation. My technical writing skills, as described in the enclosed
résumé, may be particularly useful. I am a recent graduate of Fair-
view Community College in Topeka, with an Associate Degree in
Computer Science. In addition to taking a broad range of courses,
I have served as a computer consultant at the college's computer
center, where I helped train novice computer users.

I will be happy to meet with you at your convenience and discuss
how my education and experience will suit your needs. You can
reach me either at my home address or at (913) 233-1552.

Sincerely,

David B. Edwards

David B. Edwards

Enclosure: Résumé

Figure 1 *Sample Application Letter*

but describes the position he is looking for. In Figure 2 the writer does not
specify where she learned of the opening because she does not know
whether a position is actually available. Figure 3 opens with an indication of
where the writer learned of the job vacancy.

273 East Sixth Street
Bloomington, IN 47401
May 29, 19--

Ms. Laura Goldman
Personnel Manager
Acton, Inc.
80 Roseville Road
St. Louis, MO 63130

Dear Ms. Goldman:

I am seeking a responsible position as a financial
research assistant in which I may use my training to
solve financial problems. I would be interested in
exploring the possibility of obtaining such a position
within your firm.

I expect to receive a Bachelor of Business Administration
degree in finance from Indiana University in June. Since
September 19-- I have been participating, through the
university, in the Professional Training Program at
Computer Systems International, in Indianapolis. In the
program I was assigned, on a rotating basis, to several
staff sections in apprentice positions. Most recently
I have been a financial trainee in the Accounting
Department and have gained a great deal of experience.
Details of the academic courses I have taken are
contained in the enclosed resume.

I look forward to meeting you soon in an interview.
I can be contacted at my office (812-866-7000,
ext. 312) or at home (812-256-6320).

Sincerely yours,

Carol Ann Walker

Carol Ann Walker

Enclosure: Resume

Figure 2 *Sample Application Letter*

522 Beethoven Drive
Roanoke, Virginia 24017
November 15, 19--

Ms. Cecilia Smathers
Vice-President, Dealer Sales
Hamilton Office Machines, Inc.
6194 Main Street
Hampton, Virginia 23661

Dear Ms. Smathers:

During the recent NOMAD convention in Washington, a member of your sales staff, Mr. Dale Jarrett, informed me of a possible opening for a Manager in your Dealer Sales Division. My extensive background in the office machine industry, I believe, makes me highly qualified for the position.

I was with the Technology, Inc., Dealer Division from its formation in 1979 to its phaseout last year. During this period, I was involved in all areas of dealer sales, both within Technology, Inc., and through personal contact with a number of independent dealers. Between 1987 and 1990 I served as Assistant to the Dealer Sales Manager as a Special Representative. My education and work experience are contained in the enclosed résumé.

I would like to discuss my qualifications in an interview at your convenience. Please write to me or telephone me at (804) 449-6743 any weekday.

Sincerely,

Gregory Mindukakis

Gregory Mindukakis

Enclosure: Résumé

Figure 3 *Sample Application Letter*

collection letters

Collection letters serve a two-fold purpose of (1) collecting the overdue bill and (2) preserving the customer relationship.

Most companies use a series of collection letters in which the letters become increasingly demanding and urgent. However, collection letters should be polite; you can demonstrate insistence with the letters' frequency and tone.

Shoes Incorporated
905 Broad Street
Columbus, MI 48001

August 5, 19--

Clarence Holland
Purchasing Agent
Columbus Shoe Store
1400 State Street
Columbus, MI 48002

Dear Mr. Holland:

With the new school year about to begin, your shoe store
must be busier than ever as students purchase their
back-to-school footwear. Perhaps in the rush of business
you've overlooked paying your account of $742, which is
now 60 days overdue.

Enclosed is our fall sales list. When you send in your
check for your outstanding account, why not send us your
next order and take advantage of these special prices.

Sincerely,

Helen Ball

Helen Ball
Credit Department

HB/ja
Enclosure

Figure 1 *Collection Letter*

A series of collection letters usually proceeds in three stages, each of which may include several letters. All letters should be courteous and show a genuine interest in the customer as well as concern for whatever problems are preventing prompt payment.

The first stage of collection letters consists of reminders stamped on the invoice, form letters, or brief personal notes. These early reminders should maintain a friendly tone that emphasizes the customer's good credit record

---

Shoes Incorporated
905 Broad Street
Columbus, MI 48001

November 5, 19--

Clarence Holland
Purchasing Agent
Columbus Shoe Store
1400 State Street
Columbus, MI 48002

Dear Mr. Holland:

We are concerned that we have not heard from you about your overdue account of $742, even though we have written 3 times in the past 90 days. Since you have always been one of our best customers, we have to wonder whether some special circumstances have caused the delay; if so, please feel free to discuss the matter with us.

By sending us a check today, you can preserve your excellent credit record. Because you have always paid your account promptly in the past, we are sure that you will want to settle this balance now. If your balance is more than you can pay right now, we will be happy to work out satisfactory payment arrangements.

Please use the enclosed envelope to send in your check, or call (800) 526-1945, toll-free, to discuss your account.

Sincerely,

Helen Ball

Helen Ball
Credit Department

HB/ja
Enclosure

Figure 2 *Collection Letter*

until now. You should remind him or her of the debt and may even solicit additional business by including promotional material for new sales items, as is done in Figure 1 (see p. 134).

In the second stage, the collection letters are more than just reminders. You now assume that some circumstances are preventing payment. Ask directly for payment, and inquire about possible problems, perhaps inviting the customer to discuss the matter with you. If you have a standard optional

---

Shoes Incorporated
905 Broad Street
Columbus, MI 48001

December 5, 19--

Clarence Holland
Purchasing Agent
Columbus Shoe Store
1400 State Street
Columbus, MI 48002

Dear Mr. Holland:

Your account in the amount of $742 is now 120 days overdue. You have already received a generous extension of time, and in fairness to our other customers, we cannot permit a longer delay in payment.

Because you have not responded to any of our letters, we will be forced to turn your account over to our attorney for collection if we do not receive payment immediately. Such action, of course, will damage your previously fine credit rating.

Why not avoid this unpleasant situation by sending your check in the enclosed return envelope within 10 days or by calling (800) 526-1945 to discuss payment.

Sincerely,

Helen Ball

Helen Ball
Credit Department

HB/ja
Enclosure

Figure 3 *Collection Letter*

payment plan, you might suggest it to him or her. Mention the importance of good credit, appealing to his or her pride, self-esteem, and sense of fair play. Remind the customer that he or she has always received good value from you. Make it easy to respond by enclosing a return envelope or by offering a toll-free telephone number. In this stage, your tone should be firmer and more direct than in the early stage, but never rude, sarcastic, or threatening. Notice that Figure 2 (see p. 135) is more direct than the first letter, but no less polite.

The third stage of collection letters reflects a sense of urgency, for the customer has not responded to your previous letters. Although your tone should remain courteous, make your demand for payment explicit. Point out how reasonable you have been, and urge the customer to pay at once to avoid legal action. Again, make it easy to respond by providing a return envelope and a toll-free telephone number, as is done in Figure 3 (see p. 136).

complaint letters

Companies sometimes make mistakes when providing goods and services, and customers write complaint letters asking that such situations be corrected. The tone of such a letter is important; the most effective complaint letters do not sound angry. Do not use a complaint letter to vent your anger; remember that the reader of your letter probably had nothing to do with whatever went wrong, and berating that person is not likely to achieve anything positive. In most cases, you need only state your claim, support it with all the pertinent facts, and then ask for the desired adjustment. Most companies are very willing to correct whatever went wrong.

The opening of your complaint letter should include all identifying data concerning the transaction: item, date of purchase, place of purchase if pertinent, cost, invoice number, and so on.

The body of your letter should explain logically and clearly what happened. You should present any facts that prove the validity of your claim. Be sure of your facts, and present them concisely and objectively, carefully avoiding any overtones of accusation or threat. You may, however, wish to state any inconvenience or loss created by the problem, such as a broken machine stopping an entire assembly line.

Your conclusion should be friendly, and it should request action. State what you would like your reader to do to solve your problem.

Large organizations often have special departments to handle complaints. If you address your letter to one of these departments—for example, to Customer Relations or Consumer Affairs—it should reach someone who can respond to your claim. In smaller organizations you might write to a vice-president in charge of sales or service. For a very small business, write directly to the owner.

Figure 1 is an example of a typical complaint letter. (See also the **adjustment letters** and **refusal letters** entries in this tabbed section.)

BAKER MEMORIAL HOSPITAL | *Television Services*
501 Main Street
Springfield, OH 45321
(513) 683-8100

September 23, 19--

General Television, Inc.
5521 West 23rd Street
New York, NY 10062

Attention: Customer Relations Manager

On July 9th I ordered nine TV tuners for your model MX-15 color receiver. The tuner part number is TR-5771-3.

On August 2nd I received from your Newark, New Jersey, parts warehouse seven tuners, labeled TR-413-7. I immediately returned these tuners with a note indicating the mistake that had been made. However, not only have I failed to receive the tuners I ordered, but I have also been billed repeatedly.

Please either send me the tuners I ordered or cancel my order. I have enclosed a copy of my original order and the most recent bill.

Sincerely,

Paul Denlinger
Manager

PD:sj
Enclosure

Figure 1 *Complaint Letter*

correspondence

The process of writing letters involves many of the same steps that go into most other on-the-job tasks. The following list summarizes these steps:

1. Establish your objective, and determine your reader's attitude and needs.
2. Prepare an outline, even if it is only a list of points to be covered in the order you wish to cover them.
3. Write the first draft (see the entry on **writing a draft** on THE BUSINESS WRITING PROCESS tab).
4. Allow a "cooling" period (time for weaknesses to become obvious).
5. Revise the draft.
6. Use good proofreading techniques.

These guidelines will help you write a clear, well-organized letter or memo (see the entry on **memorandums** in this tabbed section). Keep in mind that one very important element in business letters is the impression they leave on the reader. To convey the right impression—of yourself as well as of your company or organization—you must take particular care with both the tone and the style of your writing.

TONE

Letters are generally written directly to another person who is identified by name. For this reason, letters are always more personal than reports or other forms of business writing. Successful business writers find that it helps to imagine their reader sitting across the desk from them as they write; they then write to the reader as if they were talking to him or her in person. This technique helps them keep their language natural.

As a letter writer addressing yourself directly to your reader, you are in a good position to take into account your reader's needs. If you ask yourself, "How might I feel if I were the recipient of such a letter?" you can gain some insight into the likely needs and feelings of your reader and then tailor your message to fit those needs and feelings. Furthermore, you have a chance to build goodwill for your business. Many companies spend large sums to create a favorable public image. A letter to a customer that sounds impersonal and unfriendly can quickly tarnish that image, but a thoughtful letter that communicates sincerity can greatly enhance it. Suppose, for example, you were a department-store manager who receives a request for a refund from a customer who forgot to enclose the receipt with the request. In a letter to that customer, you might write the following:

> EXAMPLE The sales receipt must be enclosed with the merchandise before we can process a refund.

But if you consider how you might keep the customer's goodwill, you might word the request this way:

EXAMPLE Please enclose the sales receipt with the merchandise so that we can
send your refund promptly.

However, you can put the reader's needs and interests at the center of the
letter by writing from the reader's perspective. Often, although not always,
doing so means using the words *you* and *your* rather than *we, our, I,* and
mine. That is why the technique has been referred to as the *you viewpoint.*
Consider the following revision, which is written with the "you viewpoint":

EXAMPLE So you can receive your refund promptly, please enclose the sales
receipt with the merchandise.

In this example, the reader's benefit and interest are stressed. By emphasizing the reader's needs, the writer will be more likely to accomplish his or her
objective: to get the reader to act.

The following tips will help you achieve a tone that builds goodwill with
the reader:

1. *Be respectful,* not demanding.

   CHANGE Submit your answer in one week.

   TO I would appreciate your answer within one week.

2. *Be modest,* not arrogant.

   CHANGE My report is thorough, and I'm sure that you won't be able to continue without it.

   TO I have tried to be as thorough as possible in my report, and I hope
   you find it useful.

3. *Be polite,* not sarcastic.

   CHANGE I just received the shipment we ordered six months ago. I'm sending
   it back—we can't use it now. Thanks!

   TO I am returning the shipment we ordered on March 12, 19—. Unfortunately, it arrived too late for us to be able to use it.

4. *Be positive and tactful,* not negative and condescending.

   CHANGE Your complaint about our prices is way off target. Our prices are
   definitely not any higher than those of our competitors.

   TO Thank you for your suggestion concerning our prices. We believe,
   however, that our prices are competitive with, and in some cases are
   below, those of our competitors.

DIRECT AND INDIRECT PATTERN

It is generally more effective to present good news directly and bad news
indirectly, because readers form their impressions and attitudes very early in
letters.

Consider the thoughtlessness of the rejection in Figure 1. Although the letter is direct and uses the pronouns *you* and *your*, the writer has apparently not considered how the reader will feel as she reads the letter. There is no expression of regret that Mrs. Mauer is being rejected for the position, nor any appreciation of her efforts in applying for the job. The letter is, in short, rude. The pattern of this letter is (1) bad news, (2) explanation, (3) close.

Southtown Dental Center

3221 Ryan Road   San Diego, CA 92217
(714) 321-1579

November 11, 19--

Mrs. Barbara L. Mauer
157 Beach Drive
San Diego, CA 92113

Dear Mrs. Mauer:

Your application for the position of dental receptionist at Southtown Dental Center has been rejected. We have found someone more qualified than you.

Sincerely,

Mary Hernandez

Mary Hernandez
Office Manager

MH/bt

Figure 1 *Poor "Bad News" Letter*

A better general pattern for "bad news" letters is (1) buffer, (2) bad news, (3) good will. The *buffer* may be either neutral information or an explanation that makes the bad news understandable. Although bad news is never pleasant, information that either puts the bad news in perspective or makes the bad news seem reasonable maintains goodwill between the writer and the reader. Consider, for example, a revision of the rejection letter, as shown in Figure 2. This letter carries the same disappointing news as the first one, but the writer is careful to thank the reader for her time and effort, to explain why she was not accepted for the job, and to offer her encouragement in finding a position in another office.

Presenting good news is, of course, easier. Present good news early—at the outset, if at all possible. The pattern for "good news" letters should be (1) good news, (2) explanation of facts, (3) good will. By presenting the good news first, you increase the likelihood that the reader will pay careful attention to details, and you achieve goodwill from the start. Figure 3 (see p. 144) is a good example of a "good news" letter.

WRITING STYLE

Letter-writing style may vary from informal, in a letter to a close business associate, to formal (or restrained) in a letter to someone you do not know.

> INFORMAL It worked! The new process is better than we had dreamed.

> RESTRAINED You will be pleased to know that the new process is more effective than we had expected.

You will probably find yourself relying on the restrained style more frequently than on the informal one. Do not adopt such a formal style, however, that your letters read like legal contracts.

> CHANGE In response to your query, I wish to state that we no longer have an original copy of the brochure requested. Be advised that a photographic copy is enclosed herewith. Address further correspondence to this office for assistance as required.

> TO Because we are currently out of original copies of our brochure, I am sending you a photocopy of it. If I can help further, please let me know.

Being concise in writing is important, but don't be so concise that you become blunt. If you respond to a written request that you cannot understand with "Your request was unclear" or "I don't understand," you will probably offend your reader. Instead, consider that what you are really doing is asking for more information. Say so.

> EXAMPLE I will need more information before I can answer your request. Specifically, can you give me the title and the date of the report you are looking for?

Although this version is a bit longer, it is more polite and more helpful.

Southtown Dental Center

3221 Ryan Road   San Diego, CA 92217
(714) 321-1579

November 11, 19--

Mrs. Barbara L. Mauer
157 Beach Drive
San Diego, CA 92113

Dear Mrs. Mauer:

Buffer Thank you for your time and effort in applying
for the position of dental receptionist at
Southtown Dental Center.

Bad News Since we need someone who can assume the duties
here with a minimum of training, we have selected
an applicant with over ten years of experience.

Goodwill I am sure that with your excellent college record
you will find a position in another office.

Sincerely,

Mary Hernandez

Mary Hernandez
Office Manager

MH/bt

Figure 2 *Courteous and Effective "Bad News" Letter*

ACCURACY

Since a letter is a written record, it must be accurate. Facts, figures, and
dates that are incorrect or misleading may cost time, money, and goodwill.
Always allow yourself time to review a letter before mailing it.

Southtown Dental Center

3221 Ryan Road   San Diego, CA 92217
(714) 321-1579

November 11, 19--

Mrs. Barbara L. Mauer
157 Beach Drive
San Diego, CA 92113

Dear Mrs. Mauer:

Good News   Please accept our offer for the position of dental receptionist at Southtown Dental Center.

Explanation   If the terms we discussed in the interview are acceptable to you, please come in at 9:30 a.m. on November 15. At that time we will ask you to complete our personnel form, in addition to. . . .

Goodwill   Everyone here at Southtown is looking forward to working with you. We all were very favorably impressed with you during your interview.

Sincerely,

Mary Hernandez

Mary Hernandez
Office Manager

MH/bt

Figure 3 *Effective "Good News" Letter*

APPEARANCE

Center the letter on the page vertically and horizontally—a "picture frame" of blank space should surround the contents. When you use your company's letterhead stationery, consider the bottom of the letterhead as the top edge of the paper.

PARTS OF A BUSINESS LETTER

If your employer recommends or requires a particular format, use it. Otherwise, follow the guidelines provided here, and review the illustrations for placement with full- and modified-block style (pp. 149 and 150).

Heading. Place your full address and the date in the heading. Because your name appears at the end of the letter, it need not be included in the heading. The date usually goes directly beneath the last line of the address (do not abbreviate the name of the month). Spell out words like *street, avenue, first,* or *west* rather than abbreviating them. You may either spell out the name of the state in full or use the U.S. Postal Service abbreviations.

> EXAMPLE   1638 Parkhill Drive East
> Great Falls, MT 59407
> April 8, 19--

Align the heading on the page at the center line. If you are using company letterhead that gives the address, enter only the date, two spaces below the last line of printed copy.

The Inside Address. Include the recipient's full name, title, and address in the inside address, two spaces below the date if the letter is long, or four spaces below it if the letter is quite short. The inside address should be aligned with the left margin—and the left margin should be at least one inch wide.

> EXAMPLE   Ms. Gail Silver
> Production Manager
> Quicksilver Printing Company
> 14 President Street
> Sarasota, FL 33546

The Salutation. Place the salutation, or greeting, two spaces below the inside address, also aligned with the left margin. In most business letters, the salutation contains the recipient's personal title (*Mr., Ms., Dr.,* and so on) and last name, followed by a colon. If you are on a first-name basis with the recipient, use only the first name in the salutation.

> EXAMPLES   Dear Ms. Silver:
> Dear George:

Address women as *Ms.,* whether they are married or unmarried, unless they have expressed a preference for *Miss* or *Mrs.* If you do not know whether the recipient is a man or a woman, use a title appropriate to the context of the letter. The following are examples of the kinds of titles you may find suitable:

> EXAMPLES   Dear Customer: (Letter from a department store)
> Dear Homeowner: (Letter from an insurance agent soliciting business)
> Dear Parts Manager: (Letter to an auto-parts dealer)

In the past, correspondence to large companies or organizations was customarily addressed to "Gentlemen." Today, however, writers who do not know the name or title of the recipient often address the letter to an appropriate department or identify the subject in a "subject line" and use no salutation.

EXAMPLE National Business Systems
501 West National Avenue
Minneapolis, MN 55407

Attention: Customer Relations Department

I am returning three calculators that failed to operate. . . .

EXAMPLE National Business Systems
501 West National Avenue
Minneapolis, MN 55407

Subject: Defective Parts for SL-100 Calculators

I am returning three calculators that failed to operate. . . .

When a person's first name could be either feminine or masculine, one solution is to use both the first and the last name in the salutation.

EXAMPLE Dear Pat Smith:

Avoid "To Whom It May Concern" because it is impersonal and dated.

The Body. The body of the letter should begin two spaces below the salutation. Single-space within paragraphs, and double-space between paragraphs. If a letter is very short and you want to suggest a fuller appearance, you may instead double-space throughout and indicate paragraphs by indenting the first line of each paragraph five spaces from the left. The right margin should be approximately as wide as the left margin. (In very short letters, you may increase both margins to about an inch and a half.)

In your opening, identify your subject to focus its relevance for the reader. Remember that your reader may not immediately recognize or see the importance of your topic—indeed, he or she may be preoccupied with some other business at the moment.

EXAMPLES Yesterday, I received your letter and the defective tuner, number AJ 50172, that you described. I sent the tuner to our laboratory for tests.

Carol Moore, our lead technician, reports that preliminary tests indicate. . . .

Your closing should either let the reader know what he or she should do next, or establish goodwill—or often both.

EXAMPLE Thanks again for the report, and let me know if you want me to send you a printout of the tests.

Because a closing is in a position of emphasis, be especially careful to avoid clichés. Of course, some very commonly used closings are so precise that they are hard to replace even though they may be clichés.

EXAMPLES Thank you for your help.

If you have further questions, please let me know.

But don't use such a closing just because it is easy. Make your closing work for you.

The Complimentary Closing. Type the complimentary closing two spaces below the body. Use a standard expression like *Yours truly, Sincerely,* or *Sincerely yours.* (If the recipient is a friend as well as a business associate, you can use a less formal closing, such as *Best wishes* or *Best regards.*) Capitalize only the initial letter of the first word, and follow the expression with a comma. Type your full name four spaces below, aligned with the closing at the left. On the next line you may type in your business title, if it is appropriate to do so. Write your signature in the space between the complimentary closing and your typed name. If you are writing to someone with whom you are on a first-name basis, it is acceptable to sign only your given name; otherwise, sign your full name.

EXAMPLE Sincerely,

Thomas R. Castle

Thomas R. Castle
Treasurer

Sometimes the complimentary closing is followed by the name of the firm and then the signature, between the name of the firm and the typed name.

EXAMPLE Sincerely yours,
VIKING SUPPLY COMPANY, INC.

Laura A. Newland

Laura A. Newland
Controller

A Second Page. If a letter requires a second page, always carry at least two lines of the body text over to that page; do not use a continuation page to type only the letter's closing. The second page should be typed on plain (nonletterhead) paper of quality equivalent to that of the letterhead stationery. It should have a heading with the recipient's name, the page number, and the date. The heading may go in the upper left-hand corner or across the page, as shown in Figure 4.

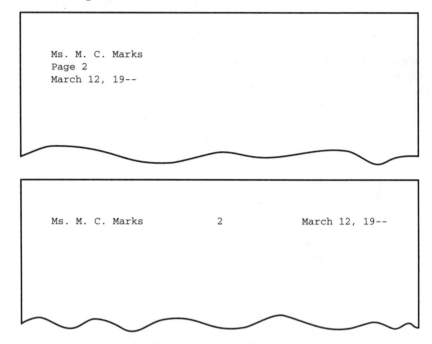

Figure 4 *Headings for the Second Page of a Letter*

Additional Information. Business letters sometimes require the typist's initials, an enclosure notation, or a notation that a copy of the letter is being sent to one or more people. Place any such information at the left margin, two spaces below the last line of the complimentary closing in a long letter, four spaces below in a short letter.

The *typist's initials* should follow the letter writer's initials, and the two sets of initials should be separated by either a colon or a slash. The writer's initials should be in capital letters, and the typist's initials should be in lower-case letters (when the writer is also the typist, no initials are needed).

    EXAMPLES CBG:pbg

                  APM/sjl

Enclosure notations indicate that the writer is sending material along with the letter (an invoice, an article, and so on). They may take several forms, as illustrated below; choose the form that seems most helpful to your readers.

    EXAMPLES Enclosure: Preliminary report invoice

                  Enclosures (2)

                  Enc. (Encs.)

Enclosure notations are included in long, formal letters or in any letters where the enclosed items would not be obvious to the reader. Remember, though, that an enclosure notation cannot stand alone. You must mention the enclosed material in the body of the letter.

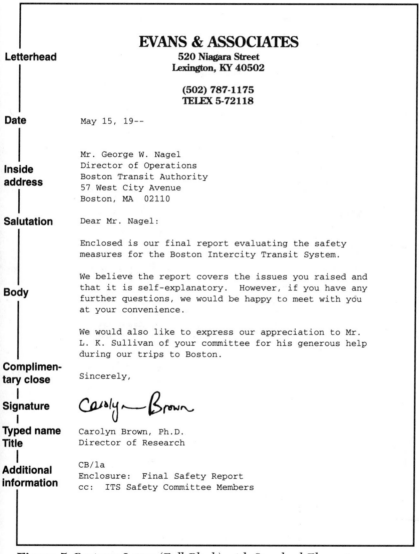

Figure 5 *Business Letter (Full Block) with Standard Elements*

Copy notations tell the reader that a copy of the letter is being sent to the named people.

EXAMPLE   cc: Ms. Marlene Brier
             Mr. David Williams
             Ms. Bonnie Ng
             Ms. Robin Horton

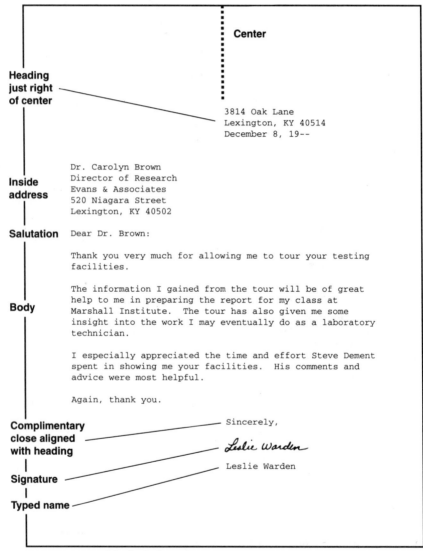

Figure 6 *Modified Block Style*

A business letter may, of course, contain all three items of additional information.

EXAMPLE Sincerely yours,

Jane T. Rogers

Jane T. Rogers

JTR/pst
Enclosure: Preliminary report invoice
cc: Ms. Marlene Brier
 Mr. David Williams
 Ms. Bonnie Ng
 Ms. Robin Horton

Figure 5 shows a typical business letter using most of the standard elements.

LETTER FORMATS

The two most common formats of business letters are the full block style shown in Figure 5 (see p. 149) and the modified block style shown in Figure 6 (see p. 150). The full block style, although easier to type because every line begins at the left margin, is suitable only with business letterhead stationery. In the modified block style, the return address, the date, and the complimentary closing all begin at the center of the page, and the other elements are aligned at the left margin. All other letter styles are variations of these two styles. Again, if your employer recommends or requires a particular style, follow it carefully.

electronic mail

Electronic mail (e-mail) refers to the transmission of messages from one person to another through a computer network. The messages are sent to and stored in a computer file called an electronic "mail box" until they are retrieved by the recipient. The recipient can display the message on the computer screen, print the message as a permanent record, forward the message to others, or send a reply to the original sender.

This method of communication offers a variety of advantages. The message—whether sent across the hall or across the continent—reaches its audience within minutes at a cost well below overnight mail service. Because the information is transmitted in machine-readable form, the text can be printed, revised and sent back, or incorporated directly into another computer file.

Although e-mail messages are like conventional job-related writing in most respects, they tend to be less formal, more conversational—somewhere between a telephone conversation and a memorandum—because of the immediacy of the transmission and the fact that it usually occurs directly between two people. Construct your messages accordingly. Avoid long, complicated sentences that are dense with unnecessary business jargon that can confuse the reader and convey the wrong message. Keep in mind, too, that although you want to keep sentences brief and words short, you should not use a telegraphic style that leaves important information unsaid or only partly said. Think carefully about your reader, the accuracy of your information, and the level of detail necessary to communicate your message clearly and concisely to that reader.

Avoid the temptation to "dash off" a first draft and send it as is. Unless carefully reviewed, the information sent could contain errors of fact and of grammar, be ambiguous, contain unintended implications, or inadvertently omit crucial details.

Consider privacy, too. Because e-mail messages are recorded in a computer for storage and retrieval, they could be read or printed by someone other than the intended recipient. This may happen not only during transmission, but also subsequent to it. Consider all your messages in the light of these possibilities.

inquiry letters and responses

An inquiry letter may be as simple as requesting a free brochure or as complex as asking a financial consultant to define the specific requirements for floating a multimillion-dollar bond issue.

WRITING AN INQUIRY LETTER

Your objective in writing the letter will probably be to obtain answers to specific questions. You will be more likely to receive a prompt, helpful reply if you make it easy for the reader to respond by following these guidelines:

1. Keep your questions concise but specific and clear.
2. Phrase your questions so that the reader will know immediately what type of information you are seeking, why you are seeking it, and how you will use it.
3. If possible, present your questions in a numbered list to make it easy for your reader to deal with them.
4. Keep the number of questions to a minimum.
5. Offer some inducement for the reader to respond, such as promising to share the results of what you are doing.
6. Promise to keep responses confidential.

At the end of the letter, thank the reader for taking the time to respond, and do not forget to include the address to which the material is to be sent. Your chances of getting a reply will improve if you enclose a stamped, self-addressed return envelope. Figure 1 is a typical inquiry letter.

P.O. Box 113
University of Dayton
Dayton, OH 45409
March 11, 19--

Ms. Jane Metcalf
Engineering Services
Miami Valley Power Company
P.O. Box 1444
Miamitown, OH 45733

Dear Ms. Metcalf:

I am an architectural student at the University of Dayton
and I need your help.

Could you please send me some information on heating
systems for a computer-controlled, energy-efficient,
middle-priced house that our systems design class at the
University of Dayton is designing. The house, which
contains 2,000 square feet of living space (17,600 cubic
feet), meets all the requirements stipulated in your
brochure "Insulating for Efficiency."

We need the following information:

1. The proper size heat pump to use in this climate for
   such a home;

2. The wattage of the supplemental electrical furnace
   that would be required for this climate; and

3. The estimated power consumption, and current rates, of
   these units for one year.

We will be happy to send you a copy of our preliminary
design report. Thank you very much.

Sincerely yours,

Kathryn J. Parsons

Kathryn J. Parsons

Figure 1 *Inquiry Letter*

RESPONSE TO AN INQUIRY LETTER

When you receive an inquiry letter, determine whether you are the right
person in your organization to answer it—that is, whether you are the one
who has both the information and authority to respond. Answer as promptly

as you can, and be sure to answer every question the writer has asked. How long and how detailed your response should be depends, of course, on the nature of the question and what you know about the person making the request. Even if the writer has asked a question to which the answer is obvious or a question that seems silly, answer it as completely as you can, and do so courteously. You may point out that the reader has omitted or misunderstood something, but be tactful.

■■■■■■■■■■■ MIAMI VALLEY POWER COMPANY ■■■■■■■■■■■
P.O. BOX 1444
MIAMITOWN, OH 45733
(513) 264-4800

March 15, 19--

Ms. Kathryn J. Parsons
P.O. Box 113
University of Dayton
Dayton, OH 45409

Dear Ms. Parsons:

Thank you for inquiring about the heating system we would recommend for use in homes designed according to the specifications outlined in our brochure "Insulating for Efficiency."

Since I cannot answer your specific questions, I have forwarded your letter to Mr. Michael Stott, Engineering Assistant in our development group. He should be able to answer the questions you have raised.

Sincerely,

Jane E. Metcalf

Jane E. Metcalf
Director of Public Information

JEM/mk
cc: Michael Stott

Figure 2 *Letter Indicating That the Inquiry Has Been Forwarded*

If you have received a letter that you feel you cannot answer, find out who can and forward the letter to that person. This person should state in the first paragraph of his or her letter that although the letter was addressed to you, it is being answered by someone else because he or she has the information needed to respond to the inquiry. Figure 2 (see p. 154) indicates to the inquirer that her letter has been forwarded, and Figure 3 shows a typical response to an inquiry.

MIAMI VALLEY POWER COMPANY
P.O. BOX 1444
MIAMITOWN, OH 45733
(513) 264-4800

March 24, 19--

Ms. Kathryn Parsons
P.O. Box 113
University of Dayton
Dayton, OH 45409

Dear Ms. Parsons:

Jane Metcalf has forwarded your letter of March 11 about the house that your systems design class is designing. I can estimate the insulation requirements of a typical home of 17,600 cubic feet, as follows:

1. We would generally recommend, for such a home, a heat pump capable of delivering 40,000 BTUs. Our model AL-42 (17 kilowatts) meets this requirement.

2. With the efficiency of the AL-42, you would not need a supplemental electrical furnace.

3. Depending on usage, the AL-42 unit averages between 1,000 and 1,500 kilowatt hours from December through March. To determine the current rate for such usage, check with the Dayton Power and Light Company.

I can give you an answer that would apply <u>specifically</u> to your house only with information about its particular design (such as number of stories, windows, and entrances). If you would send me more details, I would be happy to provide more precise figures--your project sounds interesting.

Sincerely,

Michael Stott

Michael Stott
Engineering Assistant

MS/mo

Figure 3 *Response to an Inquiry*

international correspondence

Many businesses now rely on overseas markets and suppliers, employ workers and managers from different countries, and maintain plants and offices abroad. Such companies need to communicate effectively with readers from diverse cultural and linguistic backgrounds.

STYLE AND USAGE IN INTERNATIONAL CORRESPONDENCE

Because English is not your reader's native language, it is especially important to write clear, complete sentences. (See **English as a second language** on the GRAMMAR tab.) Unusual syntax and rambling sentences will hinder a nonnative user of English from understanding your message.

When writing to nonnative readers, take special care to avoid American idioms, affectation, unusual figures of speech, and localisms—any of which could confuse your reader. Humor, particularly sarcasm, and euphemisms should also be avoided because they are easily misunderstood outside their cultural context. Elegant variation, especially the use of long variants or pretentious synonyms, will also impede the reader's understanding. Ask yourself whether the words you choose might be found in the English-language dictionary that your reader would likely have close at hand.

Proofread your letters carefully; a misspelled word will be particularly troublesome for someone reading in a second language (especially if that reader turns to a dictionary for help and cannot find the word because it is misspelled). Finally, read your writing aloud to identify overly long sentences and to eliminate any possible ambiguity.

Although it is important to choose your words carefully and to write clear, complete sentences, avoid using an overly simplified style. A reader who has studied English as a second language might be insulted by a condescending tone and childish language. Also avoid writing in short, choppy sentences and in a telegraphic style.

DATES, TIME, AND MEASUREMENT

Different countries use a variety of formats to represent dates, time, and other kinds of measurement. To represent dates, Europeans typically write the day before the month and year. In England, for example, 1/11/95 means 1 November 1995; in the United States, it means January 11, 1995. The numerical form for dates, therefore, should never be used in international correspondence. Writing out the name of the month makes the entire date immediately clear to any reader, whichever format you use. Time poses similar problems, particularly in this age of instantaneous communication and high-speed transportation, and you may need to specify time zones or to refer to international standards, such as Greenwich Mean Time, to ensure clarity.

Your use of other international standards, such as the metric system, will also help your reader. For up-to-date information about accepted conventions for numbers and symbols in chemical, electrical, data processing, radiation, pharmaceutical, and other fields, consult guides and manuals specific to the subject matter.

CULTURE, TRADITION, AND BUSINESS WRITING STYLE

In American business writing, traditional salutations like *Dear* and cordial closings like *Yours truly* have, through custom and long use, acquired meanings quite distinct from their dictionary definitions. Understanding the unspoken meanings of these forms and using them "naturally" is a significant mark of being a part of American business culture.

Such customary expressions and formal amenities vary from culture to culture; when you read foreign correspondence, be alert to these differences. Japanese business writers, for example, often use traditional openings that reflect on the season, compliment the reader's success, and offer hopes for the reader's continued prosperity. These traditional openings may strike some American readers as being overly elaborate. Where Americans value directness and employ a forthright tone in their correspondence, Japanese readers might find the writing blunt and tactless. Remember that our ideas about business writing have evolved in a particular educational, social, economic, and cultural context. Be sensitive to the expectations of readers who judge effective and appropriate communication from the vantage of a different cultural tradition.

memorandums

The memorandum is the standard form of communication among members of the same organization. Called *memos* for short, memorandums provide a record of decisions made and actions taken in an organization. The result of a carelessly prepared memo is a garbled message that could baffle readers, waste valuable time, produce costly errors, or irritate employees with an offensive tone.

Managers often use memos to inform employees about company goals, motivate them to achieve these goals, and keep their morale high in the process. To achieve these ends, managers must be clear and accurate in their memos. Consider the secondary messages the following notice conveys:

> EXAMPLE It has been decided that the office will be open the day after Thanksgiving.

The first part of the sentence ("It has been decided") not only sounds impersonal but also communicates an authoritarian management-versus-employee tone: *somebody* decides that *you* work. The passive voice also suggests that the decision maker does not want to say, "*I* have decided." One solution, of course, is to remove the first part of the sentence.

> EXAMPLE The office will be open the day after Thanksgiving.

But even this statement sounds impersonal. A better solution would be to suggest both that the decision is good for the company and that employees should be privy to (if not part of) the decision-making process.

> **EXAMPLE** Because we must meet our December 15 deadline to be eligible for the government contract, we must use the day after Thanksgiving as a normal work day.

WRITING MEMOS

Outline your memos, even if that means simply jotting down the points to be covered and then ranking them to fit a logical method of development. Adequate development is crucial to ensure clarity.

Don't assume your reader will know what you mean. State what you mean explicitly: readers aren't always careful, and some will provide their own interpretations if you are not as specific as possible.

> **CHANGE** Be more careful on the loading dock.
>
> **TO** To prevent accidents, follow these procedures:
>   1. Check . . .
>   2. Load only . . .
>   3. Replace . . .

Memos should normally deal with only one subject; if you need to cover two subjects, you may wish to write two memos, since multisubject memos are difficult to file.

MEMO OPENINGS

A memo should normally begin with a statement of its main idea.

> **EXAMPLE** Because of our inability to serve our present and future clients as efficiently as in the past, I recommend we hire an additional claims representative and a part-time receptionist.

The only exceptions to stating the main point first are (1) when the reader is likely to be highly skeptical and (2) when you are disagreeing with persons in positions of higher authority. In such cases, a more persuasive tactic is to state the problem first (rather than your solution) and then present the specific points that will support your final recommendation.

As with other writing, if your reader is not familiar with the subject or the background of a problem, provide an introductory background paragraph. A brief background is especially important in memos that serve as records that can provide crucial information months (or even years) later. Generally, longer memos or those dealing with complex subjects benefit most from developed introductions. However, even when you are writing a short memo and the recipient is familiar with the situation, you need to remind your reader of the context. Readers have so much crossing their desks that they need a quick orientation. (Words that provide context are shown below in italics.)

> EXAMPLES *As we decided after yesterday's meeting,* we need to set new guidelines for . . .
>
> *As Jane recommended, I reviewed the office reorganization plan.* I like most of the features; however, the location of the receptionist and word processor . . .

LISTS AND HEADINGS

It is often a good idea to use lists to emphasize your points in a memo. If you are trying to convince a skeptical reader, a list of your points—from most to least persuasive—will stand out rather than being lost in a lengthy paragraph.

Another useful device, particularly in long memos, is headings. Headings have a number of advantages:

1. They divide material into manageable segments.
2. They call attention to main topics.
3. They signal a shift in topic.
4. Readers interested only in one section of a memo can easily find it.

WRITING STYLE

The level of formality in memos depends entirely on your reader and objective. For example, is your reader a peer, a superior, or a subordinate? A memo to an associate who is of equal rank and a friend is likely to be informal and personal. However, a memo written as an internal proposal to several readers, or a memo to someone two or three levels higher in your organization, is likely to use a more formal style. Consider the following original and revised versions of a subordinate's statement to a superior:

> CHANGE I can't agree with your plan because I think it poses logistical problems. (informal, personal, and forceful)
>
> TO The logistics of moving the department may pose serious problems. (formal, impersonal, and cautious)

FORMAT AND PARTS

Memo format and customs vary greatly from organization to organization. Although there is no single, standard form, Figure 1 shows a typical memorandum format. When memos exceed one page, use a second page heading like the one shown in the **correspondence** entry in this tabbed section.

PROFESSIONAL PUBLISHING SERVICES
MEMORANDUM

DATE: April 14, 19--

TO: Hazel Smith, Publications Manager

FROM: Herbert Kaufman HK

SUBJECT: Schedule for Acme Electronics Brochure

Acme Electronics has asked us to prepare a comprehensive brochure
for their Milwaukee office by August 9, 19--.

We have worked with electronic firms in the past, so this job
should be relatively easy. My guess is that it will take nearly
two months. Ted Harris has requested time and cost estimates.
Fred Moore in accounting will prepare the cost estimates, and I
would like you to prepare a schedule for the estimated time.

Additional Personnel
In preparing the schedule, check the following:

    1. Production schedule for all staff writers.
    2. Available free-lance writers.
    3. Dependable graphic designers.

Ordinarily, we would not need to depend on outside personnel;
however, since our bid for the Wall Street Journal special project
is still under consideration, we could be pressed in June and
July. We have to keep in mind staff vacations that have already
been approved.

Time Estimates
Please give me time estimates by April 19. A successful job done
on time will give us a good chance to obtain the contract to do
Acme's publications for their annual stockholder's meeting this
fall.

I know your staff can do the job.

lcs
Copies: Ted Harris, Senior Vice-President
           Fred Moore, Accounting Manager

Figure 1 *Typical Memo Format*

Some companies also print short purpose statements on the side or bottom
of memos, with space for the writer to make a check mark.

     EXAMPLES ☐ For your information

                  ☐ For your action

                  ☐ For your reply

You can also use this quick-response system for memos sent to numerous readers whose responses you need to tabulate.

EXAMPLE I can meet at 1 p.m. ☐
2 p.m. ☐
3 p.m. ☐

Subject lines function much like the titles of reports, aiding in filing and later retrieval. Subject lines are also an important orientation when the reader first sees the memo. Therefore, it is important to make them specific.

CHANGE Subject: Tuition Reimbursement

TO Subject: Tuition Reimbursement for Time Management Seminar

Capitalize all major words in the title of a subject line (do not capitalize an article, conjunction, or preposition of fewer than four letters unless it is the first or last word).

The final step is signing or initialing a memo, which lets the reader know that you approve of its contents, especially if you did not type it. Where you sign or initial the memo depends on the practice of your organization. Some writers sign at the end and others initial next to their typed name.

order letters

Obviously, an order letter must be specific and complete if you are to receive the exact item you want. Above all, be accurate. Since a misspelled word or misplaced decimal point could cause a staggering error, proofread the letter carefully and double check all price calculations. If you order several items, it is best to list them.

Make sure that the order letter contains any of the following information that is appropriate:

1. The exact name and part (or product) number of the item.
2. A description of the item (size, style, color, and so on).
3. The quantity of each item.
4. The price of the item (both unit price and total price).
5. The shipping method (mail, air, express, or whatever).
6. The date of the order and the date by which you need the item if time is a factor.
7. The address of the place the material is to be shipped.
8. The method of payment (indicate that you will pay COD, include a purchase order number, or enclose a check or money order with your order letter).

Figure 1 shows a typical order letter.

HOLT TOOL COMPANY
1012 Clarke Street
Phoenix, AZ 85019

(602) 297-3100

                              September 5, 19--

Downtown Parts Company
109 South State Street
Chicago, IL 60650

Attention: Sales Department

Please send the following items listed in your current
parts catalog:

   2 Tempered steel cylinders, 2" diameter and 5"
      long, part number C5789S, @ $25.50 each $51.00

   4 Aluminum castings with corrosion-resistant
      coating, part number S312A, @ $8.18 each $32.72

  12 Special tempered sheet metal screen, 1₁/₄"
      long with hexagonal heads, @ $1.14 each $13.68

                                         TOTAL $97.40

The enclosed check for $104.22 covers the price, sales
tax, and parcel post charges.

Please send this material to me by October 1.

                         Sincerely,

                         James Siemer
                         James Siemer
                         Parts Manager

JS:tb
Enclosure: Check

Figure 1 *Order Letter*

refusal letters

When you receive a complaint letter or an inquiry letter to which you must give a negative reply, you may need to write a refusal letter.

In your letter you should lead up to the refusal. To state the bad news in your opening would certainly affect your reader negatively. The ideal refusal letter says *no* in such a way that you not only avoid antagonizing your reader but keep his or her goodwill. To achieve such an objective, you must convince your reader of the justness of your refusal *before refusing*. The following pattern is an effective way to deal with this problem:

1. A buffer opening
2. A review of the facts
3. The bad news, based on the facts
4. A positive and pleasant closing

The primary purpose of a buffer opening is to establish a pleasant and positive tone. You want to convince your reader that you are a reasonable person. If your refusal is in response to a complaint letter, do not begin by recalling the reader's disappointment ("We regret your dissatisfaction . . ."). Keep your buffer paragraph positive and pleasant. You can express appreciation for your reader's time and effort, if appropriate, to soften the disappointment and pave the way for future good relations.

EXAMPLE Thank you for your cooperation, your many hours of extra work answering our questions, and your patience with us as we struggled to make a very difficult decision. We believe our long involvement with your company certainly indicates our confidence in your products.

Next you should analyze the circumstances of the situation sympathetically. Place yourself in your reader's position and try to see things from his or her point of view. Establish clearly the reasons you cannot do what the reader wants—even though you have not yet said you cannot do it. A good explanation of the reasons should so thoroughly justify your refusal that the reader will accept your refusal as a logical conclusion.

EXAMPLE The Winton Check Sorter has all the features that your Abbott Check Sorter offers and, in fact, offers two additional features that your sorter does not. The more important of the two is a backup feature that retains totals in memory, even if the power fails, so that processing doesn't have to start again from scratch following a power failure. The second additional feature that the Winton Sorter offers is stacked pockets, which take less space than do the linear pockets on your sorter.

Don't belabor the bad news—state your refusal quickly, clearly, and as positively as possible.

EXAMPLE After much deliberation, we have decided to purchase Winton Check Sorters because of the extra features they offer.

Close your letter with a friendly remark, whether to assure the reader of your high opinion of his product or merely to wish him success.

EXAMPLE We have enjoyed our discussions with your company and feel we have learned a great deal about check processing. Although we did not select your sorter, we were very favorably impressed with your systems, your people, and your company. Perhaps we will work together in the future on another project.

The example shown in Figure 1 refuses a company credit for establishing an open account. Figure 2 refuses a claim.

Titus Packaging, Inc.

**2063 Eldorado Dr.
Billings, Montana 59102**

April 4, 19--

Ms. Edna Kohls
Graphic Arts Services, Inc.
936 Grand Avenue
Billings, Montana 59102

Dear Ms. Kohls:

**Buffer
opening**

We appreciate your interest in establishing an open account at Titus Packaging, Inc. In the two years since you began operations, your firm has earned an excellent reputation in the business community.

**Review of
the facts,
followed by
the bad news**

As you know, interest rates have been rising sharply this past year, while sales in general have declined. With the current negative economic climate, and considering the relatively recent establishment of your company, we believe that an open account would not be appropriate at this time.

**Positive and
pleasant
closing**

We will be happy to have you renew your request around the first of next year, when the economic climate is expected to improve and when your company will be even more firmly established. In the meantime, we will be happy to continue our present cash relationship, with a 2-percent discount for payment made in ten days.

Sincerely,

Conrad C. Atkins

Conrad C. Atkins
Manager, Credit Department

CCA/mo

Figure 1 *Refusal Letter*

General Television, Inc.
5521 West 23rd Street
New York, NY 10062

Customer Relations
(212) 574-3894

September 28, 19--

Mr. Fred J. Swesky
7811 Ranchero Drive
Tucson, AZ 85761

Dear Mr. Swesky:

Buffer opening

We have received your letter regarding the replacement of your KL-71 television set and have investigated the situation.

Review of the facts, followed by the bad news

You stated in your letter that you used the set on an uncovered patio. As our local service representative pointed out, this model is not designed to operate in extreme heat conditions. As the instruction manual accompanying your new set stated, such exposure can produce irreparable damage to this model. Since your set was used in such extreme heat conditions, therefore, we cannot honor the two-year replacement warranty.

Positive and pleasant closing

We trust you will understand our position and we hope to provide for your future television needs.

Sincerely yours,

Susan Siegel

Susan Siegel
Assistant Director

SS/ar

Figure 2 *Refusal Letter*

résumés

A résumé is an essential element in any job search because it is, in effect, a catalog of what you have to offer to prospective employers. Sent out with your application letter, it is the basis for their decision to invite you for a job interview. It tells them who you are, what you know, what you can do, what you have done, and what your job objectives are. It may be the basis for the questions you are asked in the interview, and it can help your prospective employer evaluate the interview.

Three steps will help you prepare your résumé:

1. Analyze yourself and your background.
2. Identify those to whom you will submit your résumé (your readers).
3. Organize and prepare the résumé.

ANALYZING YOUR BACKGROUND

The starting point in preparing a résumé is a thorough analysis of your experience, education and training, professional and personal skills, and personal traits.

List the major points for each category before actually beginning to organize and write your résumé. The following questions can serve as an inventory of what you should consider in each category.

Experience. Note all your employment—full-time, part-time, and free-lance work—and analyze each job on the basis of the following list of questions:

1. What was the job title?
2. What did you do (in reasonable detail)?
3. What experience did you gain that you can apply to another job?
4. Why were you hired for the job?
5. What special skills did you learn on that job?
6. Were you promoted or given a job with more responsibility?
7. Why did you leave it?
8. When did you start and when did you leave the job?
9. Would your former employer give you a reference?
10. What special traits were required of you on the job (initiative, leadership, ability to work with details, ability to work with people, imagination, ability to organize, and so on)?

Education. For the applicant with little work experience, such as a recent graduate, the education category is of primary importance. For the applicant with extensive work experience, education is still quite important, even though it is now secondary to work experience. List the following information about your education:

1. Colleges attended and the inclusive dates.
2. Degrees and the dates they were awarded.

3. Major and minor subjects.
4. Courses taken or skills acquired that might be important to the job you are applying for.
5. Internships, work-study programs, co-op positions.
6. Cumulative grade averages and academic honors.
7. Extracurricular activities.
8. Scholarships and awards.
9. Special training courses (academic or industrial).

ORGANIZING AND WRITING THE RÉSUMÉ

After listing all the items in the preceding two categories, analyze them in terms of the job you are seeking, evaluating the items, rejecting some of them, and finally selecting those that you will include in your résumé. Base your decision on the following questions:

1. What exact job are you seeking?
2. Who are the prospective employers?
3. What is most pertinent to that job and those employers?
4. What details should be included and in what order?
5. What information is most likely to get you an interview?

Résumés should be brief—preferably one or two pages, depending on your level of experience—and should include the following information:

1. Your name, address, and phone number.
2. Your immediate and long-range job objectives.
3. Your professional training.
4. Your professional experience, including the firms where you have worked, and your responsibilities.
5. Your specific skills.
6. Pertinent personal information.

FORMAT OF THE RÉSUMÉ

A number of different formats can be used. The most important thing is to make sure that your résumé is attractive, well organized, easy to read, and free of errors. A common format uses the following heads:

Employment Objective
Education
Employment Experience
Special Skills and Activities
References (optional)

Underline or capitalize the heads to make them stand out on the page. Whether you list education or experience first depends on which is stronger in your background. If you are a recent graduate, list education first; if you have substantial job experience, list your most recent experience first, your next most recent experience second, and so on.

The Heading. Center your name in all capital letters (and boldface if you're using a word processor) at the top of the page. Follow it with your address and telephone number, also usually centered.

Employment Objective. State both your immediate and long-range employment objectives. However, if an objective is not appropriate for a particular position (a temporary job, for example), you may exclude it.

Education. List the college or colleges you attended, the dates you attended each one, any degree or degrees received, your major field of study, and any academic honors you earned.

Employment Experience. List all your full-time jobs, from the most recent to the earliest that is appropriate. If you have had little full-time work experience, list your part-time and temporary jobs, too. Give the details of your employment, including the job title, dates of employment, and the name and address of your employer. Provide a concise description of your duties only for those jobs whose duties were similar to those of the job you are seeking; otherwise, give only a job title and a brief description. Specify any promotions or pay increases you received. Do not, however, list your present salary (salary depends on your experience and your potential value to an employer). If you have been with one company for a number of years, highlight your accomplishments during that time. List military service as a job, giving the dates you served, your duty specialty, and your rank at discharge. Discuss the duties only if they relate to the job you are applying for.

Some résumés arrange employment experience by function rather than by chronological time. Instead of listing your jobs first, starting with the most recent, you list the functions you've performed ("Management," "Project Development," "Training," "Sales," and the like). The functional arrangement is useful for persons who wish to stress their skills or who have been employed at one job and wish to demonstrate their diversity of experience at that single position. It is also used by those who have gaps in time on their résumé caused by unemployment or illness. Although the functional arrangement can be effective, employment directors know that it may be used to cover weaknesses, so you should use it carefully and be prepared to explain any gaps.

Special Skills and Activities. This category usually comes near the end. You may include such skills as knowledge of foreign languages, writing and editing abilities, specialized knowledge (such as experience with a computer language or a background in electronics), hobbies, student or community activities, professional or club memberships, and published works. Be selective: do not overload this category, do not duplicate information given in other categories, and do not include any items that do not support your employment objective.

Personal Data. Federal legislation limits the inquiries an employer can make before hiring an applicant—especially requests for such personal information as age, sex, marital status, race, and religion. Consequently, some job seekers exclude this category because they feel their personal data could have a negative impact on the employer. You may also eliminate this category simply because you need the space for more significant information about your qualifications. However, if you believe the personal data category will help you get a particular job, then include your date of birth and your marital status (it's better to give your date of birth than your age, so that

---

CAROL ANN WALKER
273 East Sixth Street
Bloomington, Indiana 47401
(913) 321-4567

EMPLOYMENT OBJECTIVE

Financial research assistant, leading to a management position in corporate finance.

EDUCATION

Indiana University (Bloomington)
Bachelor of Business Administration (Expected June 19--)
Major: Finance   Minor: Computer Science
Dean's List: 3.88 grade point average of possible 4.0
Senior Honor Society, 19--.

EMPLOYMENT EXPERIENCE

FIRST BANK (Bloomington, Indiana)
Research Assistant Intern, Summer and Fall Quarters, 19--.
    Assisted manager of corporate planning and developed computer model for long-range planning.

MARTIN FINANCIAL RESEARCH SERVICES (Bloomington, Indiana)
Editorial Assistant Intern, 19-- to 19--.
    Provided research assistance to staff and developed a design concept for in-house financial audits.

SPECIAL SKILLS AND ACTIVITIES

Associate Editor, Business School Alumni Newsletter.
    Wrote two articles on financial planning with computer models; surveyed business periodicals for potential articles; edited submissions.

President, Women's Transit Program.
    Coordinated activities to provide safe nighttime transportation to and from dormitories and campus buildings.

REFERENCES

Available upon request.

Figure 1 *Student Résumé*

your résumé won't become out of date after your next birthday). In any case, you should see yourself through the eyes of your prospective employers and provide whatever information would be most useful to them.

References. You can state on your résumé that "references will be furnished upon request" or include references as part of the résumé. Either

---

CAROL ANN WALKER
1436 W. Schantz Avenue
Dayton, Ohio 45401
(513) 339-2712

EMPLOYMENT OBJECTIVE

Senior Research Analyst in corporate offices of research-oriented manufacturing firm.

EMPLOYMENT EXPERIENCE

KERFHEIMER CORPORATION--November 19-- to Present
    Senior Financial Analyst
    Report to Senior Vice-President for Corporate Financial Planning.
    Develop manufacturing cost estimates for mining and construction equipment
    with Department of Defense procurement officers and engineers based on
    prototypes developed in corporation research laboratories.

    Financial Analyst
    Assisted in funding estimates for major Department of Defense contracts for
    troop carriers and digging and earth-moving machines.
    Researched funding options recommending those with most favorable rates and
    terms.
    Recommended by the senior financial analyst as his replacement upon his
    retirement.

FIRST BANK, INC., Bloomington, Indiana--September 19-- to August 19--
    Planning Analyst
    Developed computer models for short- and long-range planning.

EDUCATION

Master of Business Administration (In Progress)
Wharton School, University of Pennsylvania

Master of Science in Management in Business Administration, 19--
University of Wisconsin-Milwaukee
"Special Executive Curriculum" for employees identified as promising by their employers.

Bachelor of Business Administration (magna cum laude), 19--
Indiana University
    Major: Finance   Minor: Computer Science

SPECIAL SKILLS AND ACTIVITIES

Published "Developing Computer Models for Financial Planning." *Midwest Finance Journal* (Vol. 34, No. 2, 19--), pp. 126–136.

Association for Corporate Financial Planning, Senior Member.

REFERENCES

References and a portfolio of financial computer models are available upon request.

Figure 2 *Advanced Résumé: Organized by Job*

way, do not list anyone as a reference without first obtaining his or her permission to do so.

Style. As you write your résumé, use action verbs, and state your ideas concisely. You can avoid the pronoun *I,* since the résumé is only about you.

CHANGE   I was promoted to office manager in June 19--.

TO   Promoted to office manager in June 19--.

Be truthful in your résumé. If you give false data and are found out, the consequences could be serious. At the very least, you will have seriously damaged your credibility with your employer.

Make your résumé flawless before mailing it, by proofing it and verifying the accuracy of the information. Have someone else review it, too. And do not pinch pennies when you create the résumé. It, and the accompanying application letter, will be the sole means by which you are known to prospective employers until an interview. If you have access to a computer with word-processing software and a laser printer, create the résumé using them. (If you use a dot-matrix printer, make sure it is a high-quality printer.) The word processor also allows you to customize and update the résumé easily for future use. Otherwise, have the résumé professionally typeset and printed. Printing always produces a more professional-looking résumé than photocopying.

The sample résumés presented in Figures 1 and 2 (see pp. 169–170) are for the same person. Figure 1 is a student's first résumé, and Figure 2 is a résumé for the same person after she has been on the job a number of years. Examine as many résumés as possible, and select the format that best suits you and your goals.

sales letters

A sales letter promotes a product or a service. It might be a response to an inquiry letter or part of a direct-mail campaign. An effective sales letter (1) catches the attention of readers, (2) arouses their interest, (3) convinces them that your product or service will fulfill a need or desire, and then (4) confidently asks them to take the course of action you desire.

Before you can write an effective sales letter, you must determine who your readers will be. One good source of names is past and present customers. Those who have purchased a product or service from you in the past may well do so again. Another source is people who may be expected to be interested in certain products and services. Once you determine who is to receive your sales letter, learn as much as you can about the typical reader. The reader's sex, age, vocation, geographical location, financial status, and so on, will help determine your approach in your sales letter. You must be aware of your reader's needs and desires because they are what your product or service must satisfy.

With today's personal computers, a mail-merge feature enables you to address potential customers by name rather than as "Dear Homeowner," or whatever other general designation may be appropriate.

Be conscious of your legal liability when you write a sales letter. Make no claims that are not true, and be careful of overstatement. If you say that a product is safe, you are guaranteeing its absolute safety. Therefore, say that the product is safe *provided that normal safety precautions are taken.*

Naturally, you must have a thorough knowledge of the product or service you are offering if you are to convince your reader of its worth.

A sales letter consists of an opening, a body, and a closing.

OPENING

Begin your sales letter by identifying a need or a desire the reader may have—do not begin with a description of the product or service. The reader is much more likely to be interested in what you are selling if you show how it directly benefits him or her. The *you viewpoint* is essential here. A number of techniques can achieve this objective, as the following examples demonstrate:

Statement of problem	You have an inventory problem that is costing you money. Our staff of experts would like to help you solve that problem.
Unusual offer	How would you like to pay 50 cents for a complete restaurant meal? Or buy a $300 top coat for $80? Or save an incredible 37% on your monthly car payments? How would you like to see movies with your family absolutely free?
Surprising question	Would you be interested in a "magic" wand that would eliminate the drudgery of lawn care?
Appeal to normal desire	At this time each year, everyone's thoughts turn to vacation plans and home improvements. If you are considering a major recreational purchase or home improvement this year, you may want to find out about Superloans from Home National Bank.

BODY

The body of your sales letter should supply the details that will convince readers that your product or service will satisfy their needs or desires better than any other can. The body should point out and stress all the benefits your product can offer.

Analyze your product carefully to determine your strongest psychological sales points. (Psychological selling simply means stressing a product's benefits rather than its physical features.) Select the most important selling point about your product or service, and build your sales letter around it. Show how your product or service will make your reader's job easier, increase his or her status, make life more pleasant, and so on. In other words, the body of the letter should show how your product or service can satisfy the need or desire identified in your opening. Remember to describe the physical features of your product *in terms of their benefit to your reader.* Help your readers imagine themselves using your product or service—and enjoying the benefits of doing so.

> Superloan is a loan that is made against the equity that you have in your home. Remember that equity is money. You wouldn't keep your money stuffed under a mattress or buried in a tin can. Many people do not realize that equity money can be put to work just like any other asset. Because of the rapid increases in the value of real estate in this area, many people who purchased homes several years ago do not really know how much equity they have. In fact, you probably have more than you think. You may even have more than you need.
>
> Superloans can be used to buy the boat or car or airplane you've always wanted. They can also be used for those home improvements that cannot be financed under conventional FHA home improvement loans, such as a private swimming pool.
>
> Of course, a Superloan does not have to be used only for recreational items. You may want to use money that is now in equity to pay for college expenses for your children or grandchildren. You may want to open or expand your own business. Or you may need to install a more efficient heating system or put a new roof on your house.

You may need to provide evidence to convince your reader that your product or service is everything you claim it to be. There are many ways to do this. You can offer a money-back guarantee, a free trial use of your product, testimonials, case histories, and the like. Following are three examples:

Free trial use	As soon as I receive your okay, I will rush your copy to you. Read and use it for ten full days at no cost or obligation.
Testimonial	Senator William Worthington was so impressed by Peter Krump's *Breakthrough Rapid Reading* that he has written a glowing tribute to it. The senator writes that Krumf's method is "the least expensive and most efficient way" you can learn rapid reading.
Case history	Dozens of case histories are on file and available on request. To cite just one, Cynthia L. was fifty pounds overweight. She suffered constantly from severe arthritis, high blood pressure, and other ailments. Within three months of using negative energizer foods with her meals, she lost thirty pounds and her distressing symptoms began to disappear.

Try to minimize the negative effect price can have on your reader. There are a number of techniques that can help you do so. One is to mention the price along with a reminder of the benefits. Another technique is to state the price in terms of a unit rather than a set (50 cents per item instead of $6 per set). Another is to identify the daily, monthly, or even yearly cost based on the estimated life of the product (10 cents a night for a mattress sounds less expensive than $179). Suggest a series of payments rather than the total ($10 a month for the next year instead of $120). Or compare the cost with that of something the reader accepts readily ("for the cost of one beer a day, you can have streets that are free from potholes").

CLOSING

If effective, the body of your letter will make your reader want your product or service, or at least want more information about it. Your closing should ask the reader to do whatever is necessary to obtain the product or service. Some sales letters ask for the order; others ask only for a show of interest. You might request your reader to provide personal information on an enclosed card, to come to your showroom for a demonstration, or to authorize a home sales visit.

Your closing should offer incentives that will make your reader want to act. For example, you might send a complimentary item, stress an item's limited availability, offer a special discount for a limited period of time, or suggest a deferred payment plan. Make it as easy as possible for your reader to respond. Following are three examples:

Complimentary item By initiating and returning the enclosed postpaid card, you will receive at once the special handbook *Seven Steps to Better Managing* without cost—and you will begin to profit from your subscription to the new *Presidents' Letter.*

Time limit Just fill out and mail the enclosed invitation card. As soon as I receive it, I'll rush a copy of *How to Live Better and Spend 20% Less* for you to read and use for 10 full days at no cost or obligation. If at the end of 10 days you decide to keep *How to Live Better,* just send $10.95 plus postage and handling, and the book is yours. But act now—the cost will increase to $12.95 on November 30.

Appeal to normal desire So, if you have equity in your home and would like to talk with someone about the possibility of borrowing against that equity, please complete the postage-paid reply card included with this letter. Just drop it in the mail and a Home National Bank loan officer will call you to explain Superloan possibilities as well as to answer any questions you may have. Let us help to make your dreams come true.

Figure 1 illustrates how the parts of a sales letter work together.

**Home National Bank
902 Home Avenue
Portland, Oregon 97207**

October 8, 19--

Dear Mr. Jones:

    At this time each year, everyone's thoughts turn to vacation plans and home improvements. If you are considering a major recreational purchase or home improvement this year, you may want to find out about Superloans from Home National Bank.

    Superloan is a loan that is made against equity that you have in your home. Remember that equity is money. You wouldn't keep your money stuffed under a mattress or buried in a tin can. Many people do not realize that equity money can be put to work just like any other asset. Because of the rapid increases in the value of real estate in this area, many people who purchased homes several years ago do not really know how much equity they have. In fact, you probably have more than you think. You may even have more than you need.

    Superloans can be used to buy the boat or car or airplane you've always wanted. They can also be used for those home improvements that cannot be financed under conventional FHA home improvement loans, such as a private swimming pool.

    Of course, a Superloan does not have to be used only for recreational items. You may want to use money that is now in equity to pay for college expenses for your children or grandchildren. You may want to open or expand your own business. Or you may need to install a more efficient heating system or put a new roof on your house.

    So, if you have equity in your home and would like to talk with someone about the possibility of borrowing against that equity, please complete the postage-paid reply card included with this letter. Just drop it in the mail, and a Home National bank loan officer will call you to explain Superloan possibilities as well as to answer any questions you may have. Let us help make your dreams come true.

Sincerely,

John M. Peters

John M. Peters
President

JMP/ja
Enclosure

Figure 1 *Sales Letter*

transmittal letters

The transmittal letter, also known as a cover letter, identifies the item being sent, the person to whom it is being sent, and the reason for sending it. A transmittal letter provides a permanent record of the transmittal for both the writer and the reader.

WATERFORD PAPER PRODUCTS
P.O. BOX 413
WATERFORD, WI 53474

(414) 738-2191

January 16, 19--

Mr. Roger Hammersmith
Ecology Systems, Inc.
1015 Clarke Street
Chicago, IL 60615

Dear Mr. Hammersmith:

Enclosed is the report estimating our power consumption for the year as requested by John Brenan, Vice President, on September 4.

The report is a result of several meetings with the Manager of Plant Operations and her staff and an extensive survey of all our employees. The survey was delayed by the temporary layoff of key personnel in Building "A" from October 1 to December 5. We believe, however, that the report will provide the information you need to furnish us with a cost estimate for the installation of your Mark II Energy Saving System.

We would like to thank Diana Biel of ESI for her assistance in preparing the survey. If you need any more information, please let me know.

Sincerely,

James G. Evans
New Projects Office

JGE/fst
Enclosure

Figure 1 *Transmittal Letter*

Keep your remarks brief in a transmittal letter. Open with a paragraph explaining what is being sent and why. In an optional second paragraph, you might include a summary of any information you're sending. A letter accompanying a proposal, for example, might point out any sections in the proposal of particular interest to the reader. The letter could then go on to present evidence that the writer's organization is the best one to do the job. This paragraph could also mention the conditions under which the material was prepared, such as limitations of time or budget. The closing paragraph should contain acknowledgments, offer additional assistance, or express the hope that the material will fulfill its purpose.

Although writing is important, people on the job spend far more of their time speaking and listening. This section contains entries on these essential subjects, as well as on conducting meetings in organizations.

Since preparing an oral presentation is much like preparing to write, consider reviewing THE BUSINESS WRITING PROCESS tab, noting in particular the entries on **audience/readers, purpose/objective, methods of development,** and **organization.** The difference, of course, for oral presentations is in the delivery. Public speaking isn't natural for anyone, but everyone can learn to do it well with practice and with the techniques discussed in the **oral presentations** entry in this tabbed section.

Productive listening (an often overlooked skill) facilitates the exchange of ideas, opinions, and information. The **listening** entry discusses the barriers to effective listening, strategies for overcoming them, and techniques for becoming an effective listener.

Both the ability to speak and the ability to listen are crucial when you participate in meetings. Since meetings are so common in most organizations, you need to know how to conduct one, and you will find valuable the information in the entry on **conducting meetings.**

conducting meetings

Ideally, a meeting is a personal interchange among a group of people who have come prepared to make a contribution to a collective effort, an effort that will produce better results than any one of the participants in the meeting could have produced alone. If this definition does not apply to a situation, a meeting may not be necessary; an oral presentation or a written report might be a more effective method of communication.

As a form of oral communication, a meeting requires planning and preparation, just like writing and oral presentations. Although both the leader and the participants of a meeting are responsible for making the meeting an effective exercise of oral communication, the leader must plan the meeting and provide any necessary guidelines for the conduct of the meeting.

LEADERSHIP PHILOSOPHY

If you are a meeting leader, you could conduct yourself as a dictator, as a coach, or as a spectator. Ideally, you should conduct yourself as a coach most of the time, but you should be aware that there are times when you need to be a bit dictatorial (such as when a strong personality begins to take over) or when you need to be more of a spectator (such as when productive interaction among participants is taking place).

As a meeting leader, your focus needs to be on getting a group of people— all individuals—to come to an agreement in spite of their individual goals, preferences, and personalities. You must look at the big picture, and your goal should be to get the participants to focus on the collective goal rather than fragmenting into adversarial groups. As a meeting leader, you should see to it that individuals feel free to offer their thoughts, ideas, and facts in a receptive environment—thereby maximizing the contributions of each individual. You should encourage collective effort and make sure that one person does not dominate other participants.

MECHANICS OF A MEETING

The mechanics of a meeting include (1) planning, creating, and distributing an agenda for the meeting; (2) deciding on the meeting time and duration; (3) determining the best site for the meeting, as well as the best room setup; and (4) writing and distributing the minutes of the meeting.

Agenda.   The agenda is a road map of your meeting, and it is the primary mechanical factor in successful meetings. Never begin a meeting without an agenda, even if it is only a handwritten list of topics you want to cover. The agenda gives the chairperson a tool for steering the group. Since you cannot be aware of all the hidden agendas that people bring to meetings, tempers can flare, people can get off the issue, and things can start to bog down. With an agenda, the chairperson can simply look at it, look at the group, and calmly say, "All this is good, but let's get back to the agenda. These other issues may need to be addressed, but let's plan another time to address them. Now back to Item 4, . . ." This allows you to gently steer the group back to the appropriate topic. Without an agenda, the leader can only become a dictator or a spectator.

It is ideal if the agenda can be distributed a day or two before the meeting so that your group has time to prepare and gather the necessary materials. But if there is no time to distribute the agenda early, be sure to distribute it at the beginning of the meeting. For an elaborate meeting requiring that a participant do serious preparation (particularly of presentations), try to distribute the agenda a week or more in advance.

Planning the Agenda. Before attempting to write an agenda, you need to do some planning. To guide your planning, ask yourself the following questions.

- What is the specific purpose of this meeting? If you can't write a single sentence stating the precise purpose of the meeting, you are not ready to call a meeting.
- What topics need to be discussed to achieve the purpose of the meeting? The agenda should concentrate on just a few related major

points or issues. If a number of unrelated topics must be dealt with, consider holding several short meetings instead of one long one.
- What should the end result of the meeting be?
- What must happen to make the desired end result occur?
- Who must be there for the goal to be achieved?

Formatting the Agenda. In formatting the agenda, concentrate on just a few major items. Organize well, but not too tightly (if the agenda seems to be in control of the meeting, rather than just steering it, people may be hesitant to introduce new thoughts or ideas). Indicate who will attend. Indicate the place of the meeting. Be specific about times. Indicate the starting time, the amount of time allotted for each presentation, the time allotted for discussion, the time allotted for breaks, and the stopping time. Figure 1 (see p. 184) shows a sample agenda for a sales meeting.

Meeting Time and Duration.   The time of day of the meeting and the duration of the meeting can have a negative or positive effect on the meeting's success. Keep the following things in mind in planning your meeting.

The Four Worst Times to Have a Meeting. Following are the four worst times to have a meeting.

- *Monday morning*—People need Monday morning to get their work mode set for the week and to take care of anything urgent that has occurred over the weekend. It is a busy, harried time. People are distracted and unfocused from having been away for two days.
- *Friday afternoon*—People need Friday afternoons to wrap up the week and take care of anything that must be finished before the week ends. Again, people are challenged by distractions.
- *Immediately after lunch*—During the hour following lunch, most people fall victim to "post-prandial letdown," which is the body's natural need to regroup after lunch. Interestingly, the "down" feeling after lunch occurs as frequently in those who skip lunch as in those who eat lunch. It simply takes the body about a half hour to re-accelerate after being down for a break.
- *The end of the work day*—If you schedule a meeting during the last fifteen minutes of the day, you can be assured of a quick meeting, but it is likely that no one will know what you said.

The Duration of a Meeting. Psychologists tell us that group productivity tapers off considerably after an hour and a half, and after two hours it drops drastically. Therefore, any single session should be less than an hour, and a half hour is ideal. Several short meetings that are quick, sharp, and well planned are far more productive than fewer longer ones.

Breaks during a Meeting.   Breaks are critical in long meetings and the amount of the break time is equally critical. If a break is too long, participants can become detached, and it will take time to get the group back to the point where they were before the break. If a break is too short, it will not be refreshing enough.

Sales Meeting Agenda

Purpose: To introduce new products and plan both short-range and long-range sales strategy.

Date: January 27, 19--

Place: Conference Room 15-C

Time: 8:00 - 1:30

Attendees: Entire Sales Force

TOPIC	PRESENTER	TIME
New Products	Jim Lebatt	Presentation, 8:00 - 8:30 Discussion, 8:30 - 9:00
BREAK		9:00 - 9:15
Sales Strategy for New Products	Helen Kabal	Presentation, 9:15 - 9:45 Discussion, 9:45 - 10:15
BREAK		10:15 - 10:30
Future New Products	Walt McElvey	Presentation, 10:30 - 11:00 Discussion, 11:00 - 11:30
LUNCH		11:30 - 12:30
Long-Range Planning	Willa Brady	Presentation, 12:30 - 1:00 Discussion, 1:00 - 1:30

Figure 1 *Sample Agenda*

Meeting Site.   Give some thought to the best site for your meeting. There are certain advantages to having a meeting off site, or away from the office. However, it takes much more time, in addition to substantially increasing the cost. But meeting off site can have some good psychological benefits. Since it is neutral territory, it can encourage a more open discussion. Everyone loses the "home court" advantage. You are also assured that meeting participants will not be interrupted with messages and problems unrelated to the meeting topic.

Room Setup. How you have the room set up when the participants arrive will help you set the tone for the meeting. Whether or not the room is set up will, by itself, deliver a message. For example, having the room in disarray sends the message that things are not organized. In general you should have the chairs arranged in an orderly fashion; have note pads, pens or pencils, and a copy of the agenda (if not distributed prior to the meeting) at each seat; and have name tents assigning the seating (if that is appropriate in your organization).

Minutes of Meetings. All the time and planning you put into a meeting will be wasted if the results are all jumbled in the minds of the participants. Minutes are important for settling disputes about what happened or what was decided, and they can also be used as evidence in legal proceedings. Therefore, they must be accurate, complete, and clear.

Recruiting Someone to Take Minutes. In your premeeting personal call to participants, recruit someone to take the minutes. *Do not automatically choose a woman* for this job; your request could be considered sexist. Also avoid giving the responsibility to the quietest person in the room because that would only lead to that person's nonparticipation. Actually, this responsibility is excellent for someone who tends to talk a lot; the distraction of taking notes will help the talkative person concentrate on what's going on.

Help the person who is taking minutes by checking the accuracy of every decision made during the meeting. Do this by restating the decision, summarizing any action that needs to be taken, identifying who is responsible for the action, and specifying the deadline for the action. Be sure the minutes taker has that information down before you move on to the next topic.

Writing the Minutes. See the **minutes of meetings** entry on the BUSINESS WRITING FORMS AND ELEMENTS tab for detailed instructions on how to write minutes.

Distributing the Minutes. Issue your minutes as soon after the meeting as possible, certainly within three working days. The "action plan" represented by minutes provides participants with a good feeling of having accomplished forward motion.

listening

The primary difference between written and oral communication is that written documents are one-way communications (the reader cannot immediately respond), whereas oral communication is usually two-way communication (the listener can immediately respond). The listener who responds immediately must be able to listen effectively in order to respond appropriately.

Oral communication requires that a message be encoded effectively by the speaker and decoded accurately by the listener. Then the listener must formulate an effective response to the received message.

ENCODING THE MESSAGE

If you are the speaker, or the sender of the message, it is your responsibility to organize and present the message logically and succinctly. This is encoding the message.

Everything you have learned about organizing information effectively and composing clear and succinct sentences will help you encode oral messages effectively as well. What you have learned about knowing your reader will also help you determine the same things about your listener.

DECODING THE MESSAGE

If you are the listener, you must decode, or interpret, the message being sent by the speaker. Decoding is the listener's responsibility, just as encoding is the speaker's. Interpreting the message being sent by the speaker accurately and effectively requires conscious effort and a willingness on your part to become a *responder* rather than a *reactor.*

A responder is a listener who can slow the communication down, if necessary, to be certain that he or she is accurately receiving the exact message that is being sent by the speaker. To slow the communication down—increasing the amount of time that passes between the time the speaker talks and the listener answers—the listener should clarify his or her understanding, ask for more information, or paraphrase before offering his or her thoughts, opinions, input, or recommendations.

A reactor, on the other hand, simply says the first thing that comes to mind, based on limited information, and might easily take away from the conversation a confused version of the message that was intended.

FORMULATING A RESPONSE

Formulating a response is a very important facet of the oral communication process; but a problem that listeners often have is that they focus so much on formulating their response that they fail to take in all the information that is being given. Increase the amount of time you take to process your thoughts so you can produce a response instead of a reaction.

THE BENEFITS OF EFFECTIVE LISTENING

Effective listening has many benefits. It helps you avoid miscommunication, manage conflict, realize human benefits, achieve cooperation and synergy, and gather accurate information.

Avoiding Miscommunication. More often than not, we respond *not* to the message that was sent but to one or more of the following:

1. The manner in which the message was sent (you've heard people say, "It wasn't what he said, it's how he said it").
2. The way the speaker looks (frowning, closed appearance, purple hair, inappropriate dress for the situation).
3. A conscious or subconscious prejudice we may have about the subject or the speaker (someone we don't like or trust, a subject we feel strongly about, etc.).

Managing Conflict. Another benefit of effective listening is that it helps you effectively manage conflict. When you become emotional, your listening efficiency begins to drop—and the more emotional you become, the more your listening efficiency decreases. The amount of time spent thinking before speaking is reduced to practically nothing, and you begin letting emotion rather than intelligence rule your words. The only workable solution to this situation is to know how to detach from the emotions that are hampering listening efficiency so you can listen objectively and control the emotional barriers that are hampering effective listening. Asking questions and asking for clarification slows the development of conflict considerably. This and other good active listening techniques will help you avoid conflict, if possible, and give you a better chance of controlling it when it occurs.

Creating an Open Atmosphere. Good listening skills help create an open atmosphere, without which the continuing exchange of ideas and information could not occur. In an open atmosphere, people feel more at ease talking and sharing ideas, and they become more cooperative even if they don't share the same point of view. Listening with empathy for the speaker helps keep your own emotions from clouding the issue. Listening for clues that tell you what the speaker may be feeling (uncertainty, anger, excitement, etc.) can help you put the message into perspective more accurately so you can formulate a more accurate response and distance yourself from any emotions.

Reducing Tension and Stress. Effective listening reduces tension and stress by contributing to teamwork, trust, and a sense of belonging. When people really listen and try to understand the other person's point of view—without necessarily agreeing with it—even heated situations begin to calm down.

Stress is a serious side affect both of conflict and of not being able to voice your thoughts. By listening actively, stress levels can be reduced or eliminated because conflicts are less intense and everyone gets to speak.

A good listener begins a mutually beneficial chain reaction by demonstrating an interest in the speaker and what he or she has to say. Empathetic listening encourages better communication—which can result in more relevant questions and more valid information, less conflict, and a beneficial slowing down of everyone's communication process.

Achieving Cooperation and Synergy. Another benefit of effective listening is that good listening skills can help you achieve cooperation and synergy.

Cooperation means that no one gets his or her way entirely but that everyone's opinion is heard, understood, and taken into consideration. Without effective listening, this is unlikely to be true.

Synergy means that the "collective brain" of a group is more productive than any individual brain could be. The information from the collective brain is impossible to gather unless all the parts of the collective brain can be heard. Certainly, such an achievement could not occur without good listening skills.

Providing More Accurate Information.   When information you get from another person is accurate and complete, three things happen: (1) your own efficiency and productivity increases, (2) misunderstandings are eliminated, and (3) tensions are reduced. Poor listening habits result in less efficient work, with much time spent redoing things that could have been done right the first time. Many of us complain about our lack of time. Yet we rush through conversations only half listening, and end up bumbling through because we didn't listen effectively or check our understanding in the first place. Active, efficient listening is a great time saver.

STEPS TO MORE EFFECTIVE LISTENING

To listen more effectively on the job, you should (1) understand that different levels of listening efficiency are appropriate to different business situations, (2) decide to listen effectively, (3) increase your communication time, (4) define your purpose for listening, and (5) take specific actions to listen more efficiently.

Adapt Your Listening Efficiency to the Situation.   It is not necessary to listen at peak efficiency at all times. For example, when you are listening to a lecture, you are listening for specific information only. However, if you are on the job, working on a team project where the success of the project is dependent on everyone's contribution, your listening efficiency needs to be at its highest to enable you to not only gather information but also to pick up on other nuances the speakers may be communicating. It is helpful to identify for yourself the degree of listening intensity you need at the outset of any oral communication.

Decide to Listen Effectively.   Most of the battle with listening effectively can be won by simply making up your mind that you're going to do it. Effective listening requires conscious effort, something that does not come naturally. One way of thinking that can help you in the business world is to seek first to understand and then to be understood. If you let this rule of thumb be your guide, you may find it easier to take the steps or the time required to ensure that you are indeed exerting a conscious effort to listen effectively.

Increase Your Communication Time.   The first step is to tell yourself to stop reacting, instead of responding, and take the time to think and get additional input if necessary. It will take repetition and discipline, but if you don't take yourself firmly in hand now you'll never create the habit of slowing down your communication time so you can *respond* rather than *react.*

Seeking first to understand what the speaker is trying to tell you before you seek to make yourself understood is a most important factor in effective listening. By choosing to operate from this mindset, you will never speak too soon; you will never take incorrect action based on misunderstanding of a business situation; you will never suffer the consequences of your words or tone of voice being wrong; and you will never be out of control of your feelings, thoughts, and emotions. Once you've successfully prevented yourself from jumping on an emotional bandwagon, you can begin to listen objectively, without being thrown off course by emotion. When you've received more details about a business situation, it often becomes evident that the surface details really tell only a small part of the story.

To achieve the "seek first to understand and then to be understood" principle, you must do the following four things before you provide your answer, opinion, or response to the speaker's topic:

1. Acknowledge and validate the speaker
2. Check your understanding of the speaker's intended message
3. Demonstrate empathy
4. Encourage the speaker to talk

Acknowledge and Validate the Speaker. To make a speaker feel acknowledged and validated really doesn't take much effort. It can be done by:

- saying, "That's a good question."
- saying, "Yes, a lot of people feel that way."
- saying, "I can understand why you'd feel that way because . . ."
- showing interest through your words, vocal tone, gestures, and facial expressions.
- not raising your voice or seeming to react negatively, remaining calm and receptive.

Check Your Understanding of the Speaker's Intended Message. Like acknowledging and validating the speaker, verifying your understanding of the speaker's intended message is not difficult. It's a matter of saying:

- "It seems to me then that you're saying . . ."
- "Could you explain that further?"
- "What do you mean by . . . ?"
- "Let me see if I understand. . . ."

Demonstrate Empathy. Empathy is listening in a way that enables you to put yourself in the speaker's position, or to truly look at things from the speaker's perspective. It's a way of thinking that corresponds with the idea of not judging another until you've walked a mile in his or her moccasins.

The value of empathy is that it makes the speaker feel you are really try-ing to understand. It also helps keep your own emotions from clouding the issue. When people get this acknowledgment and feel they are being lis-tened to, they tend to respond with appreciation and cooperation. Empathy on the listener's part can begin a mutually beneficial chain reaction—empa-thetic listening encourages better communication.

Empathy is something you do mentally, first by picturing what the speaker is saying, and then by imagining how it must have felt or seemed for the speaker. The key is to let the speaker know you're putting yourself in his or her position. You could use phrases like:

- "That must have felt . . ."
- "You must have been . . ."

Let the Speaker Talk. One big problem for most people is that while they are listening to someone, they tend to want to talk. It's human nature. The same is true for the speaker; he or she wants and possibly needs to talk. When listeners get self-centered, they tend to forget this basic of human nature and focus on getting their turn to talk, completely disregarding the speaker's need. By encouraging the speaker, the listener is asking for more ideas or opinions, not necessarily words.

To encourage the speaker, you could say things like:

- "And then what happened?"
- "What more do you know?"
- "What are your feelings about all this?"

Define Your Purpose for Listening.   Much of the time, the biggest reason we don't listen effectively is that we haven't told ourselves *why* we are listening. Without some justification to ourselves, our minds may find something more interesting to think about while the speaker is talking.

Knowing why you are listening can go a long way toward managing the most common problems people have with listening: attention drifting while the speaker is talking, formulating your response while the speaker is still talking, and interrupting the speaker.

How to Define Your Purpose in a Planned Discussion. When you know you are going to be involved in a situation that will require you to listen actively, take the time to focus yourself for listening. Some possible ques-tions you may want to answer for yourself are:

- What kind of information do I hope to get from this conversation?
- What benefit will that information provide me?
- What kind of message do I want to send while I'm listening? (Do I want to portray understanding, determination, flexibility, competence, patience, etc.?)
- What kind of listening problems do I foresee during the interaction—boredom, mind wandering, anger, impatience, etc.? How can I keep these things from prohibiting me from listening effectively?

You may just want to give the questions some thought, or you may go as far as actually writing out your responses to them. By planning your communication, you can prevent problems that may arise as a result of reacting rather than responding—or "shooting from the hip." More often than not in business situations, we enter into interactions with people without giving any thought to possible problems or to what we hope to achieve.

Take Specific Actions.   Once you have made up your mind to listen actively and attentively throughout a business discussion, there are certain actions you can take that will help both you and the speaker. Make many of the following six actions part of your habitual and normal listening pattern:

1. Give the speaker your attention
2. Take notes
3. Use paraphrasing
4. Encourage the speaker
5. Ask probing questions
6. Use silence effectively

Give the Speaker Your Attention. Make the speaker aware that you are actively participating in the conversation. There are benefits in this behavior, both for the speaker and the listener. The *speaker* feels that you are showing an interest in the conversation, and you've begun creating a safe and open atmosphere for the speaker; this atmosphere is then usually reciprocated by the speaker, and you will have truly opened lines of communication. The *listener* helps himself or herself focus on the speaker, thereby sending good, positive signals to the speaker.

Following are some attention-giving behaviors.

- *Maintain eye contact* with the speaker *most* of the time. Eye contact is one of the strongest nonverbal signals. Think of eye contact as a mental handshake. Be careful that your eye contact doesn't turn into staring, however. Staring can be interpreted as a challenge or a threat.
- *Face the speaker* squarely and lean slightly toward him or her. This posture tells the speaker that you are truly focused.
- *Use positive nonverbal behavior* by nodding, smiling, opening your body posture, or looking pleased whenever it is appropriate. Take care, however, that this behavior doesn't make it appear to the speaker that you are simply faking listening.
- *Use empathetic listening* when it is appropriate. Sometimes people simply need to vent their feelings in a safe environment. To offer an empathetic ear, the listener should be leaning forward (if seated), make eye contact, and have a look of concern on his or her face. Possible comments could be something like, "It sounds as if you're really angry," or whatever the appropriate emotion may be. Or you can encourage the speaker to continue talking by asking "feeling" questions such as, "How does all this affect you now and in the long run?" or "How are you managing to cope?" Notice that you are not offering

advice or solutions but an atmosphere in which the speaker can feel safe expressing his or her emotions.

Take Notes. Taking notes while you are listening provides you with several benefits.

- *It helps you stay focused* on the speaker, especially during a presentation or lecture.
- *It helps you fill the time lag* between the speaker's rate of speaking and your rate of processing the information. Writing or expanding on what you hear will keep your mind from drifting off the subject.
- *It helps you remember* what you've heard, because you are reenforcing it by writing it.
- *It communicates* to the speaker that you are listening thoroughly and that you are interested in what he or she is saying.

Use Paraphrasing. To paraphrase means to restate in your own words what you believe the speaker said. Your paraphrasing should be concise and try to capture the essence of the speaker's message. Paraphrasing is a powerful and effective way to (1) let the speaker know that you are listening, (2) give the speaker an opportunity to clear up any misunderstanding you may have about what was said, (3) keep yourself focused, and (4) remember the discussion. Following are some ways to introduce paraphrases.

- "Let me see if I understand . . ."
- "So what you are saying is . . ."
- "Let me review what you've just said to see if I understand you correctly . . ."

Encourage the Speaker. "Encouragers" are those things you say that indicate to the speaker that you'd like to hear more. Encouragers are useful (1) to help you open a line of communication, (2) to help the speaker flesh out what he or she is trying to say, and (3) to show the speaker that you are interested in what he or she has to say. Common phrases you can use to encourage the speaker to continue are:

- "Then what happened?"
- "Tell me more."
- "How did it make you feel when . . . ?"
- "What do you think of all this?"

Many times your tone of voice will provide all the encouragement the speaker needs.

Ask Probing Questions. When your goal is to thoroughly understand the speaker, you must ask questions that will clarify your understanding. Unless your mind is set to seek first to understand, it probably won't occur to you to ask for more information.

Some cautions about questions: you can seem threatening or challenging to the speaker if your tone of voice reveals disapproval, mistrust, doubt, or disagreement. Also, avoid asking too many questions in rapid fire succession. Doing this puts the speaker on the defensive and may make him or her feel that you're getting too intense about whatever it is you're discussing. Questions, kindly and appropriately asked, will further your understanding greatly. Be aware, however, that they can do as much harm as good if you don't keep the speaker's feelings foremost in your mind.

Use Silence Effectively. Silence can be one of the most difficult things for human beings to handle. We tend to feel that we need to fill the vacuum with sound. We sometimes feel that to such a degree that we will fill the vacuum with any sound just to avoid the silence.

To listen effectively, the listener must be silent—even if the silence is sometimes uncomfortable. Some speakers need silence from the listener in order to gather their thoughts, and some need silence to show that the listener will wait for them to respond. If you are a quick responder, the speaker knows that if you ask a question and he or she waits long enough you will get impatient and fill the silence rather than wait it out.

oral presentations

DIRECTORY

Many of the steps required to prepare an effective oral presentation parallel the steps required to write a document. You must focus your presentation by determining its purpose and the audience to whom you will present it. You must find and gather the facts that will support your point of view and proposal, and you must then logically organize the information you have collected.

FOCUSING THE PRESENTATION

Focusing the presentation means (1) determining the specific purpose of the presentation and (2) determining your audience's needs. When your presentation is focused, the scope of coverage (the topics you need to include) fulfills your purpose in making the presentation and meets the needs of your audience.

Purpose.   The first step in focusing a presentation is to determine its purpose. Every presentation has a purpose—even if it is only to share information. One of the most frequent presentation problems is that the presenter does not have a specific enough purpose. Following is an example of a general purpose statement that, given a couple of attempts, gets tightened to a good, direction-giving purpose statement.

EXAMPLE I would like to discuss productivity with you today. (vague)

I would like to discuss how the productivity in Area B can be improved. (better)

The productivity in Area B can be improved with a few simple, inexpensive ideas that I want to share with you. (specific)

To determine the purpose of your presentation, use one or more of the following questions as a guide.

- What do I want the audience to *know* when I've finished this presentation?

  EXAMPLE When I've finished with this presentation, I want the audience to know that *Brand X copier is the best copier for us based on our finances, needs, and space.*

- What do I want the audience to *believe* when I've finished this presentation?

  EXAMPLE When I've finished with this presentation, I want the audience to believe that *I've thoroughly investigated all the applicable copiers, using identical criteria for each. To ensure that the audience believes that, I will show the system I used to evaluate each copier.*

- What do I want the audience to *do* when I've finished with this presentation?

  EXAMPLE When I've finished with this presentation, I want the audience to *approve the purchase of the Brand X copier. To get their approval, I need to assure them that the copier is within budget and that the money is being spent for a good, long-lasting product.*

You may need to answer all of these questions, or you may answer any one of them.

Once you've completed one or more of these statements, write a purpose statement for your presentation, based on the answers. This statement will most likely become a part of your presentation's introduction.

EXAMPLE The purpose of my presentation is to show the audience the copiers I compared and to make my recommendations *so that* the audience will approve funds to buy the copier I am recommending.

Audience Analysis.   The second step in focusing a presentation is to determine not only the type of information to give your audience, but also how to talk to your audience. To know both those things, you must analyze your audience by asking the following questions.

- What is my audience's level of knowledge and experience about my topic before hearing my presentation?

  EXAMPLE The experience or level of knowledge that my audience currently has about my topic is fairly basic. They know how to use a copier, and they know what they use it for. Beyond that, they have little knowledge. Therefore, I should begin with a basic description of how a copier works and how copiers differ so they will understand how I made my comparisons.

- What is the general educational level of my audience?

  EXAMPLE Since the general educational level of my audience is bachelor's degree and up, I don't need to worry about talking over their heads as far as general English vocabulary is concerned.

- What type of information will it take to move my audience to act on what I am presenting?

  EXAMPLE The type of information I should provide this audience in order to achieve my purpose is:

  - the basics of how a copier works;
  - the criteria used to compare copiers;
  - the benefits of Brand X over the other copiers in terms of quality, performance, how it fits our needs, and how it will be performing after 500,000 copies; and
  - how we can justify the extra expense up front—how that extra expense will save money in the long run.

Next, anticipate the questions that may come to the audience's mind during the presentation. Then incorporate the answers to those questions in your presentation.

    EXAMPLE Some questions the audience might have during the presentation are:

- Can Brand X handle the volume we do without breaking down during a project?
- Is a maintenance contract available?
- What is the response time for maintenance and supplies?
- Will the vendor provide us with a loaner should our copier need to go out for repairs?
- Does the vendor deliver supplies?
- How soon will our copier be installed should we approve the purchase?
- Will our people be trained, and if so what kind of schedule is proposed for training?

GATHERING INFORMATION

Now you need to find the facts that will support your point of view or proposal. While you are gathering information, keep in mind that you should give the audience only the facts it will need to enable you to accomplish your presentation goals. Too much information tends to overburden the audience, and too little information leaves your audience with a sketchy understanding of your topic. The trick is to know exactly what information you need to include to achieve your purpose and meet the needs of your audience.

Ask yourself the following question to help guide you in gathering information: "Based on what I know about the members of my audience, what do I need to include to meet their needs?"

EXAMPLE Based on what I know about the audience, I'll need to:

- explain how copiers work;
- provide an analysis of our needs in a copier;
- explain which copiers I chose to compare and why;
- go over the maintenance contract, comparing all brands (including cost per page for maintenance and supplies);
- show the long-term performance histories of all three copiers;
- show the quality of copies after 120,000 copies; and
- show the copier I recommend and why I am recommending it.

ORGANIZING THE PRESENTATION

Once you have your data collected, you need to organize it in a way that is logical and easy to understand. Organizing the presentation includes deciding (1) how to develop the topic and (2) how to structure the presentation.

Developing the Topic. Determine the best method for unfolding (or developing) your topic for your audience. Choosing a method of development means determining the best way to sequence your information to make it easiest to understand or most persuasive. An appropriate method of development will move the topic smoothly and logically from your opening to your closing.

Make certain that the method of development you select is appropriate to both your audience and your objective and that it is based on your audience's needs. For example, if you were trying to get approval to purchase a particular copier, you could *compare* the various brands available on the basis of features, price, maintenance and so forth. Or if you were trying to persuade your boss to reorganize your department, you might use *division and classification.* See the **methods of development** entry on THE BUSINESS WRITING PROCESS tab for a detailed discussion of methods of development.

Structuring the Presentation. A presentation has three distinct parts: an introduction, a body, and a closing. It is often best to write the body of your presentation first because you'll be able to write a better introduction after you decide what to include in the body.

Body. How to pull your presentation together is going to be evident now because you know what your purpose is, you know what your audience needs, you know how to talk to your audience, and you have collected the appropriate data and decided on the best way to develop your topic.

Now it is only a matter of listing your major points, in the most appropriate order, and incorporating the data you have collected under the appropriate major points. To structure your presentation, create an outline. Begin by dividing your topic into its major points or divisions. You should know your topic well enough that you can readily identify its major divisions. Write them down in a sequence that reflects your method of development. Then consider them carefully to make sure they divide the topic logically.

Continuing with the copier example, you could start with the following major divisions:

Introduction
How a Copier Works
Construction of Compared Copiers
Quality of Copies by Compared Copiers
Maintenance Contracts of Compared Copiers
Cost of Compared Copiers
Proposal
Closing

The next step is to outline your presentation. This permits you to recognize at a glance the relative importance of divisions within your topic. The copier example could be broken down as follows:

I. Introduction
II. How a Copier Works
  A. Overhead with Drawing
III. Construction of Compared Copiers
  A. Brand X
  B. Brand Y
  C. Brand Z
IV. Quality of Copies by Compared Copiers
  A. Brand X
  B. Brand Y
  C. Brand Z
V. Maintenance Contracts of Compared Copiers
  A. Brand X
  B. Brand Y
  C. Brand Z
VI. Cost of Compared Copiers
  A. Brand X
  B. Brand Y
  C. Brand Z
VII. Proposal
  A. A Comparison Chart of All Three Copiers

Introduction. The introduction may include an opening—a catchy beginning that is designed to focus the audience's attention. In the copier presentation, you could use any of the following types of openings.

- *An attention-getting statement,* such as, "The Brand X copier exceeds the ability of Brands Y and Z in several areas by a wide margin."
- *A rhetorical question,* such as, "Are all copiers alike?"

- *A dramatic or entertaining story,* such as, "When I first began re-searching these three brands of copiers, I thought there really couldn't be much difference. Boy, was I wrong!"
- *A personal experience,* such as, "I first saw the Brand X copier at our branch office in Memphis. After using it a few times, I feel sure this copier is just what we need."
- *An appropriate quotation,* such as, "The bitterness of poor quality lingers long after the sweetness of low price is forgotten."
- *A historical event,* such as, "When the first copy machine came out, there weren't many options. There have been a lot of changes since then, some better than others."
- *A reference to a current news story.*
- *A joke or humorous story* that ties directly to your topic. Just be sure your humor is related and is not off-color.

Following your opening, if you have one, create a formal introduction that sets the stage for your audience. The following questions will help you create your introduction:

- *What is the purpose of your presentation?* Not every presentation needs to announce its purpose in the introduction, but many do. If there is a good strategic reason to wait until the closing to announce your purpose, by all means do so.
- *What general information will your audience need* in order to understand the more detailed information in the body of your presentation?
- *What is your method of development?* It is often useful to tell your audience how you are going to tell them what it is you have to say.

> EXAMPLE The purpose of my presentation is to show the copiers I compared and to recommend the one I believe will best meet our needs. To do that, I'm going to show you:
>
> - how a copier works;
> - the criteria I used to compare copiers;
> - the brands of copiers I compared, and why;
> - which copier I propose we buy.

Closing. The closing should be designed to achieve the goals of your presentation. If your purpose is to motivate the audience to take action, ask them to do what you want them to do; if your purpose is to get your audience to think about something, summarize what you want them to think about. The mistake presenters make most frequently with closings is that they fail to close at all—they simply quit talking, shuffle papers around, and then ask, "Are there any questions?"

Since your closing is what your audience is most likely to remember, it's the time to be strong and persuasive. Let's return to our copier example and take a look at one possible closing.

> EXAMPLE Based on all the data, I have concluded that Brand X is the copier for us. The fact that it is $600 higher in price than the other brands

I looked at is unimportant compared to the value that we would be getting. If you could allocate the money to buy this copier by the fifteenth of this month, we can not only be up and running by the first of next month, but we'll be well equipped to prepare for next quarter's customer presentations.

This closing brings the presentation full cycle and asks the audience to fulfill the purpose of the presentation—exactly what a closing should do.

Transition. Planned transitions should appear between the body and the closing. Transitions let the audience know you're moving from one topic to the next, and provides you with assurance that you know where you're going and how to get there.

Most delivery problems in a presentation happen at points of transition. When you are on a point that you know, it is easy to speak. The problems usually occur when you have to move from one point to the next. Most of a presenter's fidgeting and audible pauses ("uh," "okay?" and "you know") happen when the presenter can't figure out how to get off one point and on to the next. Transition neatly solves that problem.

EXAMPLE Before getting into the specifics of each of the copiers I compared, I'd like to show how copiers in general work. That knowledge will provide you with the background you'll need to compare the different brands of copiers.

It is also a good idea to pause for a moment after you have delivered a transitional line between topics to let the audience shift gears with you. Remember, they don't know your plan.

Visual Aids. Well planned visual aids can not only add interest and emphasis to your presentation, but they can also clarify and simplify your message because they communicate clearly, quickly, and vividly. Use visual aids, however, *only* if they clarify or emphasize a point. Don't try to use visual aids to flesh out a skimpy or weak presentation, and don't use them to deflect the attention of your audience away from you. And don't use visual aids, especially overheads, simply because "everyone else does." Visual aids that don't aid communication just get in the way of communication.

It is a good idea to start planning your visual aids when you begin to gather information. For example, the bulleted list of the kinds of information needed for the sample presentation described under "Gathering Information" in this entry could have been altered as follows to include the kind of visuals that would most likely be needed.

EXAMPLE Based on what I know about the audience, I'll need to:

- explain how copiers work—*good place for a drawing that shows the process as simply as possible*
- provide an analysis of our needs in a copier—*perhaps a bulleted list on an overhead transparency*
- explain which copiers I chose to compare and why—*perhaps a chart that lists the necessary criteria*

- go over the maintenance contracts, comparing all brands (including cost per page for maintenance and supplies)—*overhead transparency*
- show the long-term performance histories of all three copiers
- show the quality of copies after 120,000 copies
- state the copier I recommend and why I am recommending it—*perhaps on an overhead that lists the advantages of Brand X over the others*

Keep your visual aids simple and uncluttered. Keep the amount of information on each visual aid to a minimum (usually one idea per visual). When the visual contains text, space the lines of type so the audience can read them easily, and make the letters large enough to be read easily.

Slide projectors and overhead projectors are easy to use. As you prepare your presentation, decide which visuals you will use and where each one will go. If you have a large number of them, use slides rather than overheads to avoid the distraction of constantly changing overheads. Have visuals made up far enough in advance so you can rehearse with them.

PREPARING TO DELIVER A PRESENTATION

When you have taken all the steps outlined so far, you are ready to think about delivery techniques. It is *only* after you have the presentation carefully created that you can begin practicing your delivery.

Practice. Begin by familiarizing yourself with the sequence of the material in your outline. Then you are ready to practice your presentation. Remember the following points about practicing.

Practice on your feet and out loud. The reason for practicing out loud rather than just mentally rehearsing is that you can process the information in your mind many times faster than you can possibly speak it. Mental rehearsing will not tell you how long your presentation will take or if there are any problems, such as awkward transitions.

Videotape your practice session if possible. Seeing yourself will show you not only what you are doing wrong but also what you are doing right. If you can't videotape yourself, at least use an audiotape recorder to evaluate your vocal presentation.

Force yourself to exaggerate gesturing, physical movement, and vocal inflection in your practice sessions. Continue practicing those things until you don't feel awkward with any of them.

Practice with your visual aids. The more you actually handle your visuals and practice using them, the more smoothly you'll use them during the presentation. And even then things may still go wrong, but being prepared and practiced will give you the confidence and poise to go on.

Try to get a practice session in the room where you'll be giving the presentation. This will let you learn the idiosyncrasies of the room: acoustics, lighting, how the chairs will most likely be arranged, where electrical outlets and switches are located, and so forth.

Delivery Techniques. Delivery is both audible and visual. Your audience is affected by all of you, not just your words or message. Therefore, you need to breathe life into your presentation. To make an impact on your audience members and keep them mentally with you, you must be animated. Words will have more punch when they are delivered with physical and vocal animation. The audience must believe in your enthusiasm for your topic if you want them to share your point of view.

When using visuals, give your audience time to absorb the information before you comment on it. Don't talk while you are changing visuals or doing something physical. Pause while you do it.

During the practice sessions, point to the visual aid—with both gestures and words. Be sure you are talking to your audience, however, rather than to the visual aid, and be sure you do not block the visual aid with your body.

If possible, don't distribute handouts early in the presentation. Hold them until you are ready for your audience to look at them.

There are a number of techniques you should use to give your presentation the animation it needs to make you look enthusiastic: eye contact, movement, gestures, and pace.

Eye Contact. Eye contact is the best way to establish rapport with your audience. The smaller the audience, the more important it is that you make eye contact with as many people as possible. In a large audience, find people in different parts of the audience who are responding to you, and talk directly to those people, one at a time. Look at one person and talk to that person for several seconds. Then go to the next person and do the same thing, and so on.

Movement. To get maximum interest from your audience, use physical movement to add animation to your presentation. Movement can mean that you simply take a step or two to one side or the other after you have been talking a minute or so. The strategic points at which movement is most likely to be effective is between points, before transitionary words or phrases, after pauses, or after a point of emphasis. Be careful, however, to stay in one place for a minute or so—do not pace.

Another way to get movement into your presentation is to walk to the screen and point with a pointer. Touch the screen with the pointer, to hold it in place, and then turn back to the audience before beginning to speak (touch, turn, and talk). Or you can leave the screen and go to the overhead projector, pointing by placing the pointer on the overhead (the pointer will cast a shadow pointing to the appropriate item on the overhead).

Gestures. Gestures not only help provide animation to your presentation, but they can help you communicate your message. Most people gesture naturally when they talk; however, nervousness can inhibit you from gesturing when you make a presentation. If you discipline yourself to always keep one hand free and above your waist during your presentation, you will almost certainly use that hand to gesture. Leave your other hand by your side or in your pocket, but be sure your pocket is empty of keys, change, and other temptations to fidget. Be careful not to put both hands above your waist and then lock them together; there is nothing wrong with bringing them together for effect, but don't lock them up and keep them together, because that inhibits gesturing. If you make yourself gesture during practice, you will automatically gesture at the appropriate time and in the appropriate way when you make your presentation.

Voice. The effective use of your voice is another way to get animation into your presentation—and a very important one. Since much of your believability is projected through your vocal tone, your ability to use your voice effectively is of enormous importance. Hypnotists use a monotone speech pattern to hypnotize people, and as a speaker you can have the same effect on your audience if you speak in a monotone. Vocal variety also allows you to emphasize and de-emphasize different points.

Your vocal delivery should sound conversational rather than contrived and formal. By using simple, everyday words, you will draw your audience into your subject more quickly and easily. When your delivery is conversational, each member of the audience feels as though he or she is the only one you are speaking to. Using the personal pronoun *you*, speaking as though you are talking to only one person, can make this easier to do.

Projection. Most speakers think they are projecting more loudly than they are. Just remember that if anyone in the audience cannot hear you, your presentation has been ineffective for that person—and that if the audience has to strain to hear you, they will usually give up.

Inflection. Vocal inflection is the rise and fall of your voice at different times, such as the way your voice naturally rises at the end of a question. It is like using a musical scale in your speaking. Vocal inflection helps you communicate your meaning more effectively.

Pace. Pace is the speed at which you deliver your presentation. If the pace is too fast, your words will run together, making it difficult for your audience to follow you. If your pace is too slow, the audience will get impatient and their minds are likely to wander to another topic.

MANAGING NERVOUSNESS

It is natural to be apprehensive, and that feeling will probably never go away. Stage fright shouldn't worry you. Perhaps the lack of it should, in fact, because nerves can be a helpful stimulant. But nervousness and fear are not the same thing. Fear is the result of a lack of confidence, and nervousness is the energy you feel when you are as well prepared as possible. If you are prepared, you can expect to be nervous; however, if you know what you are going to say and how you are going to say it, you will probably relax as you start to speak. You can use the power of positive imaging (imagining yourself making the presentation perfectly) to overcome your nervousness. You can also use the "as if" technique: act "as if" you are completely in control, or act "as if" you can't wait to get started with the presentation. You can also give yourself a pep talk to control nervousness: "My subject is important. I am ready. My listeners are here to listen to what I have to say."

OVERVIEW

Graphics often express ideas or convey information in ways that words alone cannot. They communicate by showing how things look (photographs, drawings, and maps), by visualizing numbers and quantities (graphs and tables), by depicting relationships (in charts and diagrams), and by making abstract concepts and relationships concrete (schematics and organizational charts). They also condense information and emphasize key concepts by setting them off from their surrounding text. Information made concrete and concise in graphic form focuses reader attention and promotes understanding.

Take your graphics requirements into account when you plan and organize information for your document. Then treat graphics as an integral part of your document outline, noting approximately where each should appear throughout the outline. At each such place, either make a rough pencil sketch of the visual, if you can, or write "illustration of . . ." and enclose each suggestion in a box. Like other information in an outline, these boxes and sketches can be moved, amended, or deleted, as required. Planning your graphics requirements from the beginning stages of your outline ensures their harmonious integration throughout all versions of the draft to the finished document.

All of the graphic elements that comprise the "look" of information on a page are also crucial to the success of a document. These include the size and style of type for text and headings, the number and width of text columns, the graphics elements, the headers and footers, the lists, and other reader cues that make up the page layout. Collectively, these design elements should:

- highlight the structure, hierarchy, and order of information,
- help readers find the information they need,
- achieve visual simplicity, and
- convey the image of your organization.

Desktop publishing and even word processing software allow writers knowledgeable about document design to combine page-layout techniques with the visual presentation of information to transform the individual page into an organizing unit within itself.

Even the best writing, however, may fail to reach its audience if the primary delivery vehicle—the visual design of the page and text—remains inadequate to the audience's needs and the document's purpose. Accordingly, plan the general design of a document at the outset when you assess purpose, audience, and the scope of information to include in your document.

Tips for Using Illustrations

Each type of illustration has unique strengths and weaknesses. The guidelines presented here apply to most visual materials you might use to supplement or clarify the information in your text. These tips will help you create and present your visual materials to good effect.

1. Make reference to the illustration in the text. The amount of discussion each illustration requires varies with its importance. The complexity of the illustration will also affect the discussion, as will the background your readers bring to the information (nonexperts require lengthier explanations than experts).
2. Keep the illustration brief and include only information necessary to the discussion in the text.
3. Present only one type of information in each illustration.
4. Keep terminology consistent. Don't refer to something as a "proportion" in the text and as a "percentage" in the illustration.
5. When appropriate, specify the units of measurement used or include a scale of relative distances.
6. Position the lettering of any explanatory text or labels horizontally for ease of reading, if possible.
7. Give each illustration a concise title that clearly describes its contents.
8. Assign a figure number to each illustration in your document (the same is true of tables). The figure or table number precedes the title: (Figure 1. Widget Production for Fiscal 19--.) Graphics (graphs, maps, etc.) are labeled "figures," and tables are labeled "tables."
9. Refer to illustrations in text by their figure or table number.
10. Ensure that illustrations always follow their first mention in the text as closely as possible.
11. Allow adequate white space on the page, around and within illustrations.

12. To use an illustration from a copyrighted source, obtain written permission to do so from the copyright owner. Acknowledge the source in a source or credit line below the caption for a figure and below any footnotes under a table.

computer graphics

Computer graphics are among the fastest developing areas of applications software for personal computers. Both new software and novel combinations of existing software are continually being developed. Accordingly, rather than attempting a definitive classification of this field, this entry provides a concise, basic introduction to the most common types of graphics software and their capabilities. The discussion focuses on graphics produced primarily for use in documents rather than for use in oral or multimedia presentations.

Graphics software for personal computers can be divided into two broad categories: *bitmapped graphics* and *vector graphics*.

BITMAPPED GRAPHICS

Bitmapped graphics are composed of an array of evenly spaced "pixel elements." Pixels are similar to the dots that make up the images on a television screen. Because bitmapped graphics are composed of a finite number of pixel elements, they tend to produce images with a distinctive jagged-edge appearance (see Figure 1). Bitmapped graphics tend to require large amounts of computer memory to manipulate and store.

Bitmapped graphics can be obtained in several ways: by *scanning* an existing image, by using *bitmapped clip art,* or by using a *bitmap editor.*

Scanned images are created by using a computer device called a scanner to convert an existing paper copy graphic (graph, diagram, photograph, etc.) into a bitmapped image on a computer screen through a process called digitizing. Once digitized in bitmap form, the scanned graphic can be modified on screen by using a bitmap editor and then printed for use in a document. If you scan a copyrighted image for use in your document, of course, you must obtain prior written permission to do so.

A *bitmap editor* is a computer software application that permits the editing and manipulation of bitmapped graphics. In their simplest form, bitmap editors allow you to modify an image by adding and removing pixels (or dots) from it. More sophisticated bitmap editors allow you to rotate, reduce, and enlarge images. Bitmap editors also allow you to create freehand images from scratch, much as an artist wields pencil, brush, charcoal, and other tools to create images on paper and canvas.

Bitmapped clip art is computer artwork created by professional graphic artists and sold on diskette or CD-ROM. Clip art graphics are frequently grouped and sold by topics, such as vehicles, animals, symbols, children, insignia, and many others. Figure 2 shows a grouping of typical clip art images.

Figure 1 *Image Created from a Bitmapped Program*

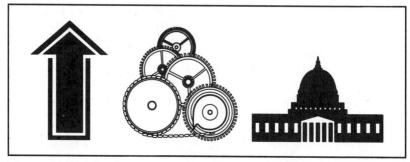

Figure 2 *Sample Clip Art Images*

Since clip art images are not copyrighted, you need not obtain prior approval to use these images after you purchase the software.

VECTOR GRAPHICS

Vector graphics are composed of predefined shapes, called graphic primitives (boxes, triangles, arcs, circles, lines, and so forth), instead of pixels (Figure 3). Vector graphics are far easier to manipulate than pixel graphics and they produce images that are of higher resolution (better visual quality) than bitmap images. Note the crispness of the image in Figure 4 compared with the bitmapped image in Figure 1.

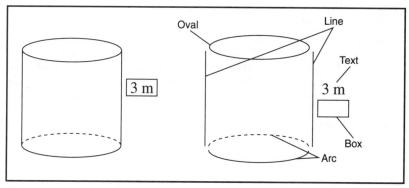

Figure 3 *Graphics Primitives*

Figure 4 *Image Created from a Vector Graphic Program*

Vector graphics can be obtained either by *vector drawing programs* or by *vector clip art*.

Vector drawing programs are a class of computer software applications that allows you to create complex graphic images. These images are manipulated by using the coordinates, or vectors, of the beginning and end points of the primitives that form them. By modifying the primitives, you can quickly modify the image. In general, vector graphics are ideal for creating graphs, charts, and diagrams.

Vector clip art is like that described for bitmapped clip art, except for the technology by which the images are created.

USES OF COMPUTER GRAPHICS

Business graphics programs, also called *charting* programs, produce preformatted charts, graphs, and tables based on numerical data taken either from a computer spreadsheet program, as in Figure 5, or from text and data entered from the computer keyboard. Figure 6 shows a range of typical bar and pie charts created by business graphics software. After creating your graphics, you can integrate them into your document by following "Tips for Using Illustrations" on p. 206.

Other computer graphics programs are available for creating maps, statistical analyses, animation, and computer-aided design (CAD) images

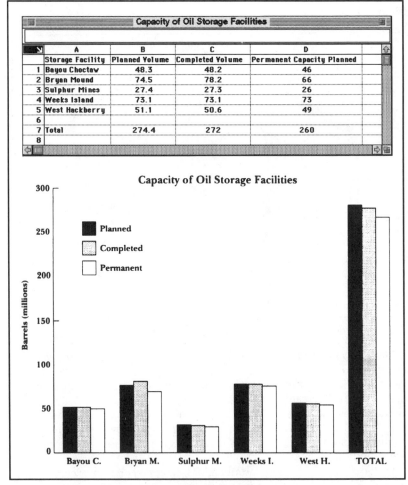

Figure 5 *Spreadsheet Table to Graph Image*

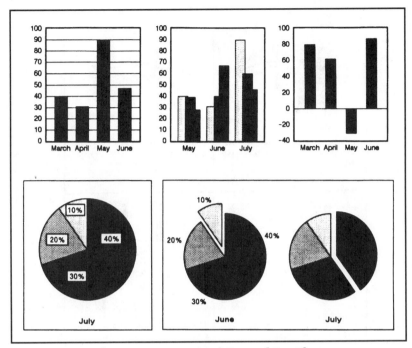

Figure 6 *Typical Computer-Generated Bar and Pie Charts*

used in engineering and manufacturing. They offer specialized applications for the graphics, engineering, architectural, or scientific professional that are beyond the scope of this text.

drawings

A drawing can focus on details or relationships that a photograph cannot capture. A drawing can emphasize the significant part of a mechanism, or its function, and omit what is not significant. However, if the actual appearance of an object is necessary to your report or document, include a photograph.

There are various types of drawings, each with unique advantages. The type of drawing used for an illustration should be determined by the specific purpose it is intended to serve. If your reader needs an impression of an object's general appearance or an overview of a series of steps or directions, a conventional drawing of the type illustrated by Figure 1 will suffice. To show the internal parts of a piece of equipment in such a way that their relationship to the overall equipment is clear, use a cutaway drawing, as in Figure 2. To show the proper sequence in which parts fit together or to show the details of each individual part, use an exploded-view drawing such as Figure 3.

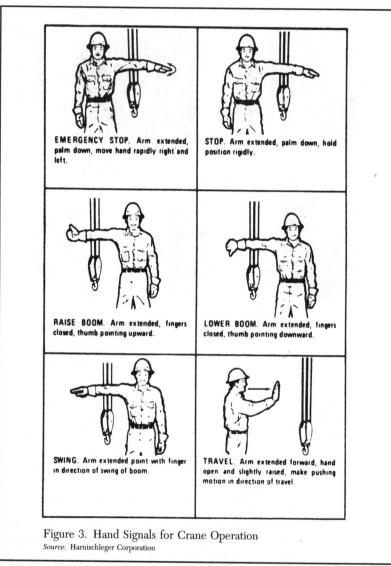

Figure 3. Hand Signals for Crane Operation
Source: Harnischleger Corporation

Figure 1 *Drawing That Illustrates Instructions*

TIPS FOR CREATING AND USING DRAWINGS

Many organizations have their own format specifications for creating drawings. In the absence of such specifications, follow the "Tips for Using Illustrations" on page 206. In addition, follow these guidelines specific to drawings:

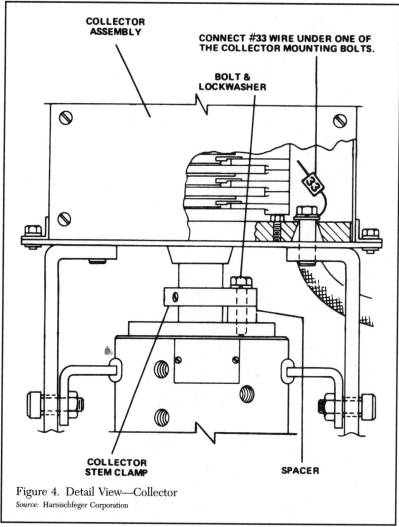

Figure 4. Detail View—Collector
Source: Harnischfeger Corporation

Figure 2 *Cutaway Drawing*

1. Show equipment and other objects from the point of view of the person who will use them.
2. When illustrating a subsystem, show its relationship to the larger system of which it is a part.
3. Draw the different parts of an object in proportion to one another, unless you indicate that certain parts are enlarged.

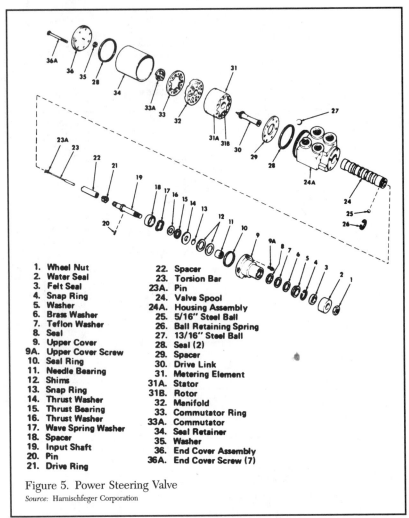

Figure 5. Power Steering Valve
Source: Harnischfeger Corporation

1. Wheel Nut
2. Water Seal
3. Felt Seal
4. Snap Ring
5. Washer
6. Brass Washer
7. Teflon Washer
8. Seal
9. Upper Cover
9A. Upper Cover Screw
10. Seal Ring
11. Needle Bearing
12. Shims
13. Snap Ring
14. Thrust Washer
15. Thrust Bearing
16. Thrust Washer
17. Wave Spring Washer
18. Spacer
19. Input Shaft
20. Pin
21. Drive Ring

22. Spacer
23. Torsion Bar
23A. Pin
24. Valve Spool
24A. Housing Assembly
25. 5/16" Steel Ball
26. Ball Retaining Spring
27. 13/16" Steel Ball
28. Seal (2)
29. Spacer
30. Drive Link
31. Metering Element
31A. Stator
31B. Rotor
32. Manifold
33. Commutator Ring
33A. Commutator
34. Seal Retainer
35. Washer
36. End Cover Assembly
36A. End Cover Screw (7)

Figure 3 *Exploded View Drawing*

4. When a sequence of drawings is used to illustrate a process, arrange them from left to right or from top to bottom.
5. Label parts in the drawing so that text references to them are clear and consistent.
6. Depending on the complexity of what is shown, place labels on the parts themselves, or give the parts letter or number symbols, with an accompanying key (see Figure 3).

flowcharts

A flowchart is a diagram of a process that involves stages, with the sequence of stages shown from beginning to end. The flowchart presents an overview of the process that allows the reader to grasp the essential steps of the process quickly and easily. The process being illustrated could range from the steps involved in assembling a bicycle to the stages by which bauxite ore is refined into aluminum ingots for fabrication.

Flowcharts can take several forms to represent the steps in a process. They can consist of labeled blocks (Figure 1), pictorial representations (Figure 2), or standardized symbols (Figure 3). The items in any flowchart are always connected according to the sequence in which the steps occur. The normal direction of flow in a chart is left to right or top to bottom. When the flow is otherwise, be sure to indicate it with arrows.

Flowcharts that document computer programs and other information-processing procedures use standardized symbols. The standards are set forth in *Information Processing—Documentation Symbols and Conventions for Data, Program and System Flowcharts, Program Network Charts, and System Resources Charts,* published by the International Organization for Standardization, publication ISO 5807-1985 (E).

TIPS FOR CREATING AND USING FLOWCHARTS

When creating a flowchart, follow the general guidelines for creating and integrating illustrations with text on page 206, in addition to the following guidelines specific to flowcharts:

1. Label each step in the process, or identify it with a conventional symbol. Steps can also be represented pictorially or by labeled blocks.
2. With flowcharts made up of labeled blocks and standardized symbols, use arrows to show the direction of flow only if the flow is opposite to the normal direction. With pictorial representation, use arrows to show the direction of all flow.
3. Include a key if the flowchart contains symbols your readers may not understand.

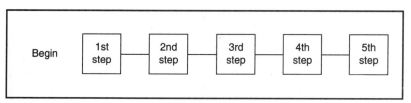

Figure 1 *Example of a Block Flowchart*

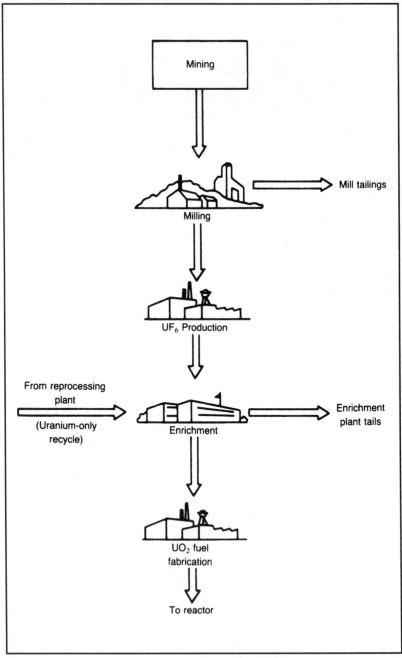

Figure 2 *Pictorial Flowchart of Light-Water Reactor Uranium Fuel Cycle*

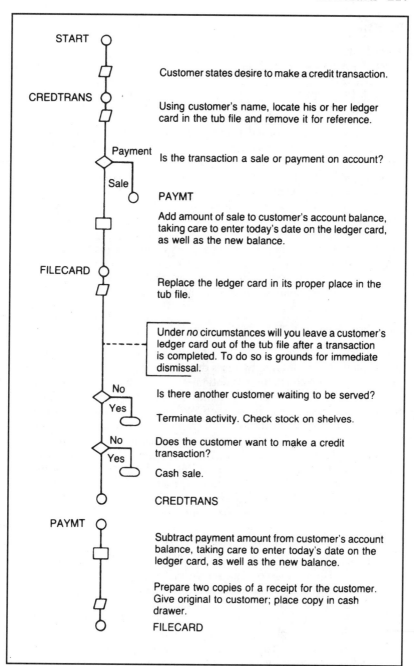

START

Customer states desire to make a credit transaction.

CREDTRANS

Using customer's name, locate his or her ledger card in the tub file and remove it for reference.

Payment

Is the transaction a sale or payment on account?

Sale

PAYMT

Add amount of sale to customer's account balance, taking care to enter today's date on the ledger card, as well as the new balance.

FILECARD

Replace the ledger card in its proper place in the tub file.

Under *no* circumstances will you leave a customer's ledger card out of the tub file after a transaction is completed. To do so is grounds for immediate dismissal.

No

Is there another customer waiting to be served?

Yes

Terminate activity. Check stock on shelves.

No

Does the customer want to make a credit transaction?

Yes

Cash sale.

CREDTRANS

PAYMT

Subtract payment amount from customer's account balance, taking care to enter today's date on the ledger card, as well as the new balance.

Prepare two copies of a receipt for the customer. Give original to customer; place copy in cash drawer.

FILECARD

Figure 3 *Flowchart of a Credit Transaction*

graphs

A graph presents numerical data in visual form. This method has several advantages over presenting data in tables or within the text. Trends, movements, distributions, and cycles are more readily apparent in graphs than they are in tables. By providing a means for ready comparisons, a graph often shows a significance in the data not otherwise immediately apparent. Be aware, however, that although graphs present statistics in a more interesting and comprehensible form than tables do, they are less accurate. For this reason, they are often accompanied by tables giving exact data. The main types of graphs are line graphs, bar graphs, pie graphs, and picture graphs. When creating graphs, follow the general guidelines for creating illustrations and integrating them with text that is found on page 206, in addition to the guidelines throughout this entry.

LINE GRAPHS

A line graph shows the relationship between two sets of numbers by means of points plotted in relation to two axes drawn at right angles. The points, once plotted, are connected to form a continuous line. In this way, what was merely a set of dots having abstract mathematical significance becomes graphic, and the relationship between the two sets of figures can easily be seen.

The line graph's vertical axis usually represents amounts, and its horizontal axis usually represents increments of time, as shown in Figure 1.

Line graphs with more than one line are common because they allow for comparisons between two sets of statistics for the same period of time. In creating such graphs, be certain to identify each line with a label or a legend, as shown in Figure 2 (see p. 220). The difference between the two lines can be emphasized by shading the space between them.

Tips for Creating and Using Line Graphs

1. Indicate the zero point of the graph (the point where the two axes meet). If the range of data shown makes it inconvenient to begin at zero, insert a break in the scale, as in Figure 3 (see p. 220).
2. Graduate the vertical axis in equal portions from the least amount at the bottom to the greatest amount at the top. Ordinarily, the caption for this scale is placed at the upper left.
3. Graduate the horizontal axis in equal units from left to right. If a caption is necessary, center it directly beneath the scale.

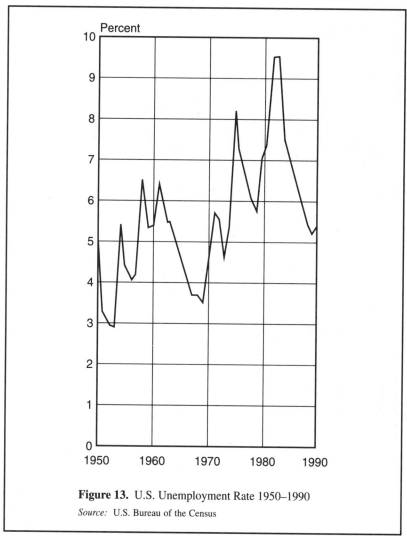

Figure 13. U.S. Unemployment Rate 1950–1990

Source: U.S. Bureau of the Census

Figure 1 *Single-Line Graph*

4. Graduate the vertical and horizontal scales so that they give an accurate visual impression of the data, since the angle at which the curved line rises and falls is determined by the scales of the two axes. The curve can be kept free of distortion if the scales maintain a constant ratio with each other. See Figures 4 and 5 on page 221.

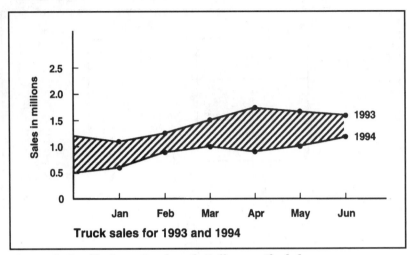

Figure 2 *Double-Line Graph with Difference Shaded*

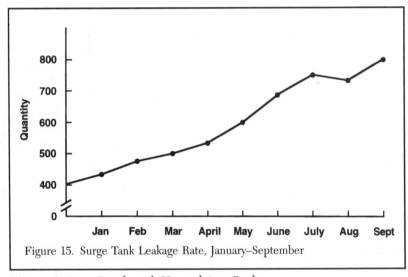

Figure 3 *Line Graph with Vertical Axis Broken*

5. Hold grid lines to a minimum so that curved lines stand out. Since precise values are usually shown in a table of data accompanying a graph, detailed grid lines are unnecessary. Note the increasing clarity of the three graphs in Figures 6, 7, and 8 on pages 221 and 222.
6. When necessary, include a key that lists and explains symbols, as in Figure 7. At times a label will do just as well, as in Figure 8.

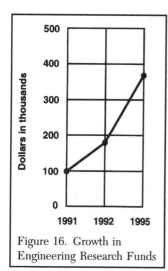

Figure 16. Growth in
Engineering Research Funds

Figure 4 *Distorted
Expression of Data*

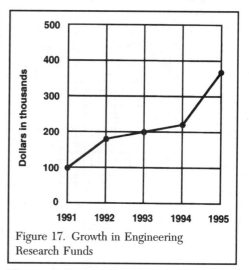

Figure 17. Growth in Engineering
Research Funds

Figure 5 *Distortion-Free
Expression of Data*

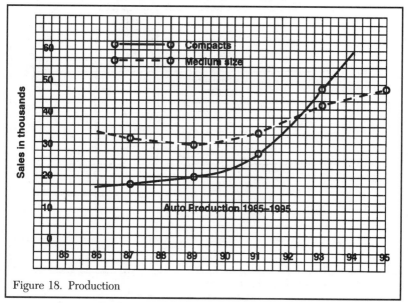

Figure 18. Production

Figure 6 *Line Graph That Is Difficult to Read*

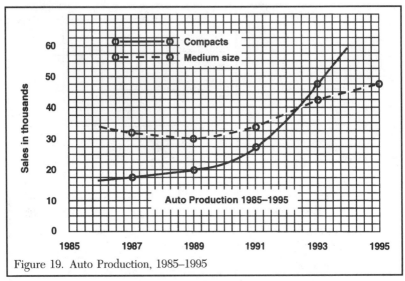

Figure 19. Auto Production, 1985–1995

Figure 7 *A More Legible Version of Figure 6*

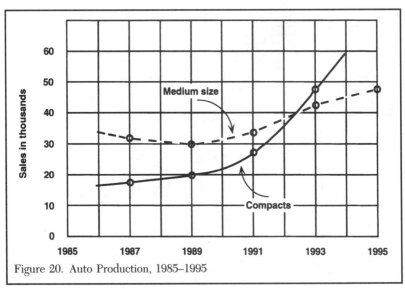

Figure 20. Auto Production, 1985–1995

Figure 8 *A Clear Version of Figure 6*

BAR GRAPHS

Bar graphs consist of horizontal or vertical bars of equal width, but scaled in length to represent some quantity. They are commonly used to show (1) quantities of the same item at different times, (2) quantities of different items for the same time period, or (3) quantities of the different parts of an item that make up the whole.

Figure 9 is an example of a bar graph showing varying quantities of the same item (population) at the same time (1980). Here each bar, which represents a different quantity of the same item, includes specific population data.

Supercity*	1980 Population
New York City/Northeastern New Jersey/ Southern Connecticut	17,606,680
Los Angeles/Long Beach/San Bernardino/Riverside	10,184,611
Chicago/Northwest Indiana/Aurora/Elgin/Joliet	7,212,778
Philadelphia/Wilmington/Trenton	4,779,796
San Francisco/San Jose	4,434,650
Detroit	3,809,327
Boston/Brockton/Lowell/Lawrence/Haverhill	3,225,386
Miami/Fort Lauderdale/Hollywood/West Palm Beach	3,103,729
Washington, D.C.	2,763,105
Houston/Texas City/Lamarque	2,521,856
Cleveland/Akron/Lorain/Elyria	2,493,475
Dallas/Fort Worth	2,451,390
St. Louis	1,848,590
Pittsburgh	1,810,038
Seattle/Everett/Tacoma	1,793,612
Minneapolis/St. Paul	1,787,564
Baltimore	1,755,477
San Diego	1,704,352
Atlanta	1,613,357
Phoenix	1,409,279
Tampa/St. Petersburg	1,354,249
Denver	1,352,070
Cincinnati/Hamilton	1,228,438
Milwaukee	1,207,008
Newport News/Hampton/Norfolk/Portsmouth	1,099,360
Kansas City	1,097,793
New Orleans	1,078,299
Portland	1,026,144
Buffalo	1,002,285

*Cities in bold type lost population in the 1980's.

Figure 14. Urban areas of 1 million or more population, with land area and population density. Source: *Scientific American*.

Figure 9 *Bar Graph of Varying Quantities of the Same Item at the Same Time*

Some bar graphs show the quantities of different items for the same period of time. See Figure 10. (A bar graph with vertical bars is also called a column graph.)

Bar graphs can also show the different portions of an item that make up the whole. Here the bar is equivalent to 100 percent. It is then divided according to the appropriate proportions of the item sampled. This type of graph can be constructed vertically or horizontally and can indicate more than one whole when comparisons are necessary. See Figures 11 and 12.

If the bar is not labeled, each portion must be marked clearly by shading or crosshatching. Include a key that identifies the subdivisions.

PIE GRAPHS

A pie graph presents data as wedge-shaped sections of a circle. The circle must equal 100 percent, or the whole, of some quantity (a tax dollar, a bus fare, the hours of a working day), with the wedges representing the various

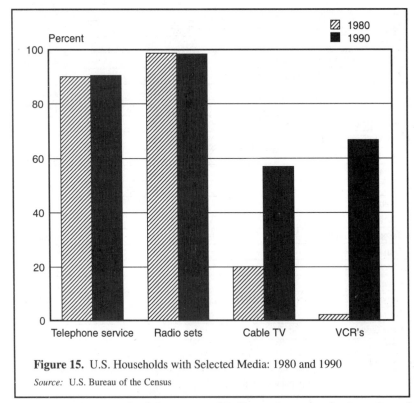

Figure 15. U.S. Households with Selected Media: 1980 and 1990

Source: U.S. Bureau of the Census

Figure 10 *Bar Graph of Quantities of Different Items for the Same Period (Shown for Two Separate Years)*

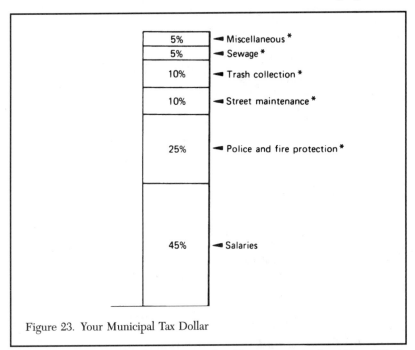

Figure 23. Your Municipal Tax Dollar

Figure 11 *Bar Graph of Quantities of Different Parts Making Up a Whole*

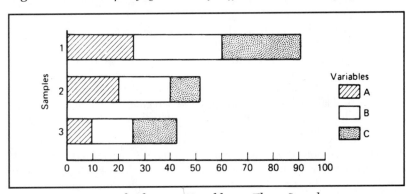

Figure 12 *Bar Graph Showing Variables in Three Samples*

ways the whole is divided. In Figure 13, for example, the circle stands for a city tax dollar, and it is divided into units equivalent to the percentage of the tax dollar spent on various city services.

Pie graphs provide a quicker way of presenting the same information that can be shown in a table; in fact, a table with a more detailed breakdown of the same information often accompanies a pie graph.

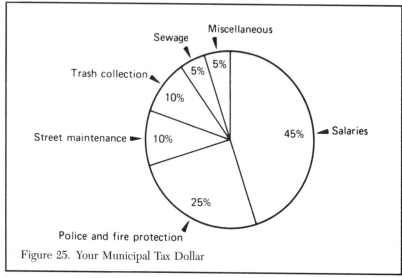

Figure 25. Your Municipal Tax Dollar

Figure 13 *Pie Graph*

Tips for Creating and Using Pie Graphs

1. The complete 360° circle is equivalent to 100 percent; therefore, each percentage point is equivalent to 3.6°.
2. When possible, begin at the 12 o'clock position and sequence the wedges clockwise, from largest to smallest. (Adhering to this guidance is not always possible because some computer-drawn pie charts appear counter clockwise.)
3. If you shade the wedges, do so clockwise and from light to dark.
4. Keep all labels horizontal, and give the percentage value of each wedge.
5. Finally, check to see that all wedges, as well as the percentage values given for them, add up to 100 percent.

Although pie graphs have strong visual impact, they also have drawbacks. If more than five or six items are presented, the graph looks cluttered. Also, since they usually present percentages of something, they must often be accompanied by a table listing precise statistics. Further, unless percentages are shown on the sections, the reader cannot compare the values of the sections as accurately as with a bar graph. (The terms that identify each segment of the graph are referred to as *callouts*.)

PICTURE GRAPHS

Picture graphs are modified bar graphs that use picture symbols of the item presented. Each symbol corresponds to a specified quantity of the item. See

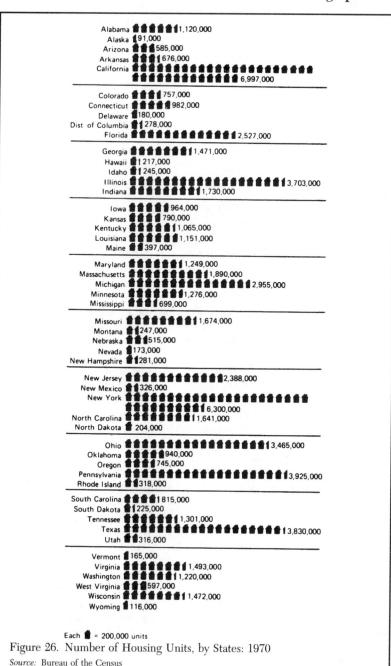

Each 🏠 = 200,000 units

Figure 26. Number of Housing Units, by States: 1970

Source: Bureau of the Census

Figure 14 *Picture Graph*

Figure 14 (p. 227). Note that precise figures are included, since the graph can present only approximate figures.

Tips for Preparing Picture Graphs

1. Make the symbol self-explanatory.
2. Have each symbol represent a single unit.
3. Show larger quantities by increasing the number of symbols rather than by creating a larger symbol (it is difficult to judge relative sizes accurately).

heads

Heads (also called headings) are titles or subtitles within the body of a long piece of writing that divide the material into manageable segments, call attention to the main topics, and signal changes of topic. A formal report or proposal may need several levels of heads to indicate major divisions, sub-divisions, and even smaller units of those. Some business material may need as many as five levels of heads, but it is rarely necessary (and usually confusing) to use more than three levels of heads.

Heads typically represent the major topics of a good topic outline. In a short document, you can use the major divisions of your topic outline as heads, but in a longer document you may need to use both the major and minor divisions.

If your document requires only one level of head, use any form (all capital letters, initial capital letters only, etc.). Capitalizing the first letter of all the main words (as in a title) and then underlining them is common.

Although the second-, third-, and fourth-level heads are indented in an outline or table of contents, they are flush left as headings in the body of the report. Every head is typed on a separate line, with an extra line of space above and below the head.

There is no one correct format for heads. Sometimes a company settles on a standard format, which everyone within the company follows. Or a customer for whom a report or proposal is being prepared may specify a particular format. In the absence of such guidelines, the system used in Figure 1 should serve you well. Note the following format characteristics: (1) The first-level head is in all capital letters, typed flush to the left margin, on a line by itself, and separated by a line space from the material it introduces. (2) The second-level head is in capital and lowercase letters, also typed flush to the left margin on a line by itself and also separated by a line space from the material it introduces. (3) The third-level head is in capital and lowercase letters, but it is "run in" right on the same line with the first sentence of the material it introduces (therefore, it is followed by a period to set it apart from what follows, and it is underlined or italicized so that it will stand out clearly on the page).

Title

Interim Report of the Committee to Investigate New Factory Locations

The committee initially considered thirty possible locations for the proposed new factory. Of these, twenty were eliminated almost immediately for one reason or another (unfavorable tax structure, remoteness from rail service, inadequate labor supply, etc.). Of the remaining ten locations, the committee selected for intensive study the three that seemed most promising: Chicago, Minneapolis, and Salt Lake City. These three cities we have now visited, snd our observations on each of them follow.

First-level head

CHICAGO

Of the three cities, Chicago presently seems to the committee to offer the greatest advantages, although we wish to examine these more carefully before making a final recommendation.

Second-level head

Location

Though not at the geographical center of the United States, Chicago is centrally located in an area that contains more than three-quarters of the U.S. population. It is within easy reach of our corporate headquarters in New York. And it is close to several of our most important suppliers of components and raw materials—those, for example, in Columbus, Detroit, and St. Louis.

Second-level head

Transportation

Third-level head

Rail Transportation. Chicago is served by the following major railroads. . . .

Sea Transportation. Except during the winter months when the Great Lakes are frozen, Chicago is an international seaport. . . .

Third-level heads

Air Transportation. Chicago has two major airports (O'Hare and Midway) and is contemplating building a third. Both domestic and international air cargo service are available. . . .

Transportation by Truck. Virtually all of the major U.S. carriers have terminals in Chicago. . . .

Figure 1 *The Use of Heads*

TIPS FOR USING HEADS

The following are some important points to keep in mind about heads:

1. They should signal a shift to a new topic (or, if they are lower level heads, a new "subtopic" within the larger topic).
2. Within the unit they subdivide, all heads at one level should be consistent in their relationship to the topic of the unit.
3. The fact that one unit at a particular level is subdivided by lower-level heads does not mean that every unit at that particular level must also include lower-level heads.
4. All heads at any one level should be parallel with one another in structure (see the **parallel structure** entry on the STYLE AND CLARITY tab). For instance, most heads are nouns or noun phrases.
5. Too many heads, or too many levels of heads, can be as bad as too few.
6. If your document needs a table of contents, create it from your heads and subheads. Be sure that the wording in your table of contents is the same as the wording in your text.
7. The head does not substitute for the discussion; the text should read as if the head were not there.

(See also the **layout and design** entry, following.)

layout and design

DIRECTORY

Good visual design is crucial to the success of a document. A well-designed document should make even complex information look accessible and give readers a favorable impression of the writer and the organization. To accomplish those goals, a design should

- be visually simple and uncluttered
- highlight structure, hierarchy, and order
- help readers find information they need
- help reinforce an organization's image

Good design achieves visual simplicity by establishing compatible or harmonious relationships, such as using the same family of type in a document or the same highlighting device for similar items. Effective design reveals hierarchy by signaling the difference between topics and subtopics, between primary and secondary information, and between general points and examples. Writers can achieve effective layout and design through their selection of type for the text, their choice of devices that highlight information, and their arrangement of text and visual components on a page. Visual cues make information easy to find the first and subsequent times it is sought. They also make information accessible to different readers by allowing them to locate the information they need. Finally, the design of a document should project the appropriate image of an organization.

USING TYPOGRAPHY

Typography refers to the style and arrangement of type on a printed page. The letters comprising a typeface have a number of distinctive characteristics, some of which are shown in Figure 1.

A complete set of all the words, numbers, and symbols available in one typeface (or style) is called a *font*.

Selecting a Typeface. For most on-the-job writing, select a typeface primarily for its legibility, which is the speed with which readers can recognize each letter and word. Avoid typefaces that may distract readers with contrasts in thickness or with odd features, as is often the case with script or cursive typefaces. In addition, avoid typefaces that fade when printed or copied. Choose popular typefaces with which readers are familiar, such as the following typefaces:

- Baskerville
- Bodoni
- Caslon
- Century
- Futura
- Garamond
- Gill Sans
- Helvetica
- Times Roman
- Universe

Do not use more than two families of typeface in a document, even though you may have access to many more. To create a dramatic contrast between headlines and text, as in a newsletter, use a typeface that is distinctively different from the text. You may also use a noticeably different typeface *inside* a graphic element. In any case, experiment before making final decisions,

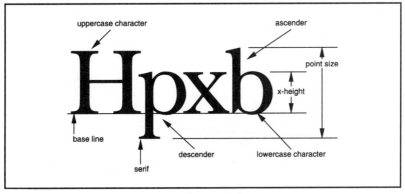

Figure 1 *Primary Components of Letter Characters*

and keep in mind that not all fonts have the same assortment of symbols and other characters.

One distinction of typefaces is between *serif* and *sans serif* type. Serifs, shown in Figure 1, are the small projections at the end of each stroke in a letter. Serif type styles have these lines; sans (French for "without") serif styles do not. Although sans serif type has a modern look, serif type is easier to read, especially in the smaller sizes. Sans serif, however, does work well for headings. If you do choose sans serif typefaces for text, pick one with large "counters," the fully or partially enclosed white spaces in letters like *c* and *b*.

Do not use a type that is too small for text because it will cause eye strain and make the text look crammed and uninviting. Six-point type is the smallest that can be read without a magnifying glass (see Figure 2). Type that is too large may use more space than necessary, can make reading difficult and inefficient, and can make readers perceive words in parts rather than wholes.

Ideal point sizes for text range from 8 to 12 points (see Figure 2); 10-point type is most commonly used. Look at samples of text in various type sizes and typefaces—and trust your reaction to them.

The distance from which a document will be read should help determine type size. For example, a set of instructions on a table at which the reader stands requires a larger typeface. Consider the age of your readers too. Visually impaired readers and some older adults may need large type sizes.

Line Length. Designers sometimes use this general rule for determining optimal line length in typeset copy: Double the point size of the typeface for line length in picas. (There are six picas to an inch.) Thus, if the type size is 12 points, the line length should be 24 picas (or 4 inches). Other designers suggest that a maximum of 10 to 12 words on a line is acceptable for many typefaces, depending on the amount of white space on the page, as well as other elements discussed later in this entry.

Leading. The word leading refers to the space between lines. Leading should be proportional to line length and point size—about 20 percent of the point size. The table in Figure 3 shows standard type sizes with recommended proportional line lengths and leading. Ranges are given (in parentheses) because some typefaces can affect the leading you should use. You may also use extra leading between paragraphs, as well as indention for paragraphs, to achieve maximum readability.

6 pt.	Type size can determine legibility.
8 pt.	Type size can determine legibility.
10 pt.	Type size can determine legibility.
12 pt.	Type size can determine legibility.
14 pt.	Type size can determine legibility.

Figure 2 *Samples of 6- to 14-Point Type*

Type Size (in points)	Line Length (in picas)	(in inches)	Leading (in points)
6	12	2	1 (0–1)
8	16	2 ⅔	1 ½ (0–2)
9	18	3	2 (0–3)
10	20	3 ⅓	2 (0–3)
11	22	3 ⅔	2 (1–3)
12	24	4	3 (2–4)

Figure 3 *Optimal Type Sizes, Line Lengths, and Leading*

Justified and Ragged Right Margins. Ragged right margins are generally *easier* to read than justified right margins because the uneven contour of the right margin provides the eyes with more landmarks to identify. Ragged right may also be preferable if justification or proportional spacing of your word processing software inserts irregular-sized spaces between words, producing unwanted white space or unevenness in blocks of text.

Because ragged right margins look informal, justified text is appropriate for publications aimed at a broad readership that expects a more formal, polished appearance. Further, justification is often useful with multiple-column formats because the spaces between the columns (called *alleys*) need the definition that justification provides. Do not justify short lines, however, because doing so will leave huge gaps between words.

USING HIGHLIGHTING DEVICES

Writers use a number of means to emphasize important words, passages, and sections within documents:

- typographical devices
- headings and captions
- headers and footers
- rules and boxes
- icons and pictograms
- color and screening

When used thoughtfully, such highlighting devices give a document a visible sense of logic and organization. For example, they can set off steps or illustrations from surrounding explanations. Keep in mind also that typographical devices and special graphic effects should be used in moderation. In fact, too many design devices clutter a page and interfere with comprehension.

Consistency is important. When you choose a highlighting technique to designate a particular feature, always use the same technique for that feature throughout your document.

Typographical Emphasis. One method of typographical emphasis is the use of uppercase or capital letters. BUT ALL UPPERCASE LETTERS ARE DIFFICULT TO READ AT LONG STRETCHES BECAUSE THEIR UNIFORMITY OF SIZE AND SHAPE DEPRIVES READERS OF IMPORTANT VISUAL CLUES AND THUS SLOWS READING. Letters in lowercase have ascenders and descenders (see Figure 1) that make the letters distinctive and easy to identify; therefore, a mixture of uppercase and lowercase is most readable. Use all uppercase letters only in short spans—three or four words, as in headings.

As with all uppercase letters, use italics sparingly. *Continuous italic type reduces legibility and thus slows readers.* Of course, italics may be useful when you wish to slow readers, as in cautions and warnings. Boldface may be the best cuing device because it is visually different, yet it retains the customary shape of the letters and numbers.

Headings and Captions. Headings (or heads) reveal the organization of the document and indicate hierarchy within it. Headings should therefore help readers decide which sections they need to read. Using too few headings forces readers to work to find their way; conversely, using too many headings can confuse readers and make a document look like an outline. Captions are key words that highlight or describe illustrations or blocks of text. Captions often appear in the left or right margins of textbooks to summarize passages.

Headings may appear in many typeface variations (boldface being most common) and often use sans serif styles. The most common positions for headings and subheadings are centered, flush left, indented, or by themselves in a wide left margin. Major section or chapter headings normally appear at the top of a new page. Never leave a heading on the final line of a page. Instead, carry it to the start of the next page. Insert one additional line of space or extra leading above a heading to emphasize that it marks a logical division.

Rules, Icons, and Color. Rules are vertical or horizontal lines used to divide one area of the page from another. Rules can also be combined to box off elements on the page. Do not overuse rules; too many rules and boxed elements can create a cluttered look.

An *icon* is a pictorial representation of an idea; it can be used to identify specific actions, objects, or sections of a document. The most widely used icons include the symbols used to designate men's and women's restrooms, wheelchair accessibility, and parking for the physically challenged. To be effective, icons must be simple and intuitively recognizable—or at least easy to define. Icons can be placed in headers, in footers, next to headings, or in the open left column of a page.

Color and *screening* can distinguish one part of a document from another or unify a series of documents. (Screening refers to shaded areas on a page.) Color and screening can set off sections within a document, highlight examples, or emphasize warnings.

Designing the Page

Page design is the process of combining the various design elements on a page. The flexibility of your design will be based on the capabilities of your word-processing or typesetting equipment, how the document will be reproduced, and the budget available. (Color printing, for example, is far more expensive than black-and-white printing.)

Thumbnail Sketch. Before you put actual text and visuals on a page, you may wish to create a *thumbnail sketch,* with blocks indicating the placement of elements. You can go further by laying out a rough assembly of all the thumbnail pages showing size, shape, form, and general style of a publication. This mock-up, called a *dummy,* allows you to see how a publication will look. As you work with elements on the page, experiment with different designs. Often what seems a useful concept in principle turns out not to work in practice.

Defining Columns. As you design pages, consider the size and number of columns. Figure 4 shows eight ways of placing text on a page. Pattern A provides maximum text; patterns B and C provide more white space; patterns D and E combine maximum text and readability; and patterns F, G, and H provide ample illustrative space. For typewritten material, such as reports, the maximum block (pattern A) is acceptable if double-spaced. For fairly solid prose set in type, the traditional two-column structure (pattern D) enhances legibility by keeping text columns narrow enough so that readers need not scan back and forth across the width of the entire page for every line.

Avoid both widows and orphans. A word at the end of a column is called a *widow.* This term is also used for carried-over letters of hyphenated words. If a widow is carried over to the top of the next column or page, it is called an *orphan.*

Using White Space. White space visually frames information and breaks it into manageable chunks. Even white space between paragraphs helps readers see the information in that paragraph as a unit. Use extra white space between sections to signal to the reader that one section is ending and another is beginning—a visual cue indicating the organization of a document. You need not have access to sophisticated equipment to make good use of white space. You can easily indent and skip lines for paragraphs, lists, and other blocks of material.

Using Lists. Lists provide an effective way to highlight words, phrases, and short sentences. Lists are particularly useful for certain types of information:

- steps in sequence
- materials or parts needed
- items to remember
- criteria for evaluation
- concluding points
- recommendations

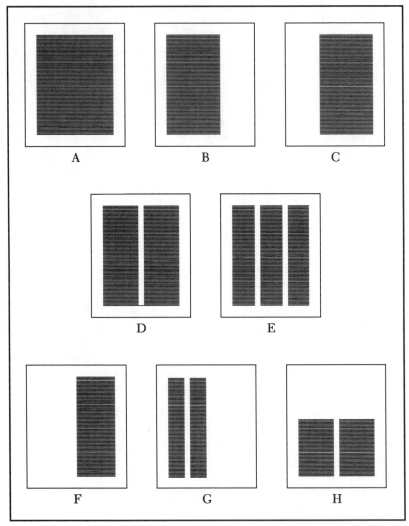

Figure 4 *Eight Ways of Using Columns (Courtesy of* Designing with Type *by James Craig; copyright © 1971 by Watson-Guptill Publications)*

Follow the advice given in the entry on **lists** in this tabbed section, such as avoiding both too many lists and too many items in lists.

Using Illustrations. Readers notice illustrations before they notice text, and they notice large illustrations before they notice small ones. Thus, the size of an illustration is the reader's gauge of its importance. Consider the proportion of the illustration to the text. Proportion often means employing the three-fifths rule: page layout is more dramatic and appealing when the major element (photo, drawing, and so on) occupies three-fifths rather than half of the available space.

Although illustrations can be gathered in one place (as at the end of a report), placing them within the text makes them more effective by putting them closer to their accompanying explanations, as well as providing visual relief. (See "Tips for Using Illustrations" on p. 206.)

lists

Lists can save readers time by allowing them to see specific items at a glance. Lists also help readers by breaking up complex statements that include figures and by allowing key ideas to stand out.

> EXAMPLE Before we agree to hold the convention at the Brent Hotel, we should make sure the hotel facilities meet the following criteria:
>
> 1. At least eight meeting rooms that can accommodate 25 people each.
> 2. Ballroom and dining facilities for 250 people.
> 3. Duplicating facilities that are adequate for the conference committee.
> 4. Overhead projectors, flip charts, and screens that are sufficient for eight simultaneous sessions.
> 5. Ground-floor exhibit area that can provide room for thirty 8 × 15-foot booths.
>
> To confirm that the Brent Hotel is our best choice, perhaps we should take a look at its rooms and facilities during our stay in Kansas City.

Notice that all the items in this example are parallel in structure. In addition, all the items are balanced—that is, all points are relatively equal in importance and are of the same general length.

To ensure that the reader understands how a list fits with the surrounding sentences, always provide adequate transitions before and after any list. If you do not wish to indicate rank or sequence, which numbered lists suggest, you can use bullets, as shown in the list of tips that follows. In typography a bullet is a small "o" that is filled in with ink.

TIPS FOR USING LISTS

- List only comparable items.
- Use parallel structure throughout.
- Use only words, phrases, or short sentences.
- Provide adequate transitions before and after lists.
- Use bullets when rank or sequence is not important.
- Do not overuse lists.

maps

Maps can be used to show specific geographic features (roads, mountains, rivers, and the like) or to show information according to geographic distribution (population, housing, manufacturing centers, and so forth). Bear these points in mind in creating and using maps:

1. Label the map clearly.
2. Assign the map a figure number if you are using enough illustrations to justify use of figure numbers. (See Figure 1.)
3. Make sure all boundaries within the map are clearly identified. Eliminate unnecessary boundaries.

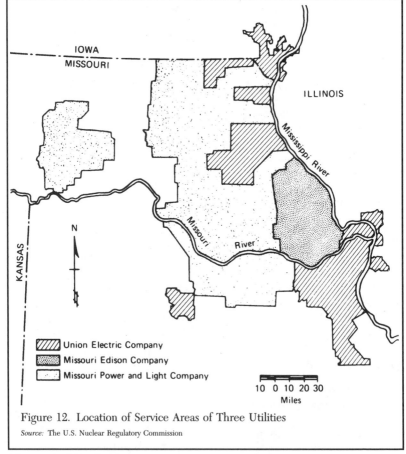

Figure 12. Location of Service Areas of Three Utilities

Source: The U.S. Nuclear Regulatory Commission

Figure 1 *Sample Map*

4. Eliminate unnecessary information from your map (if population is important, do not include mountains, roads, rivers, and the like).
5. Include a scale of miles or feet to give your reader an indication of the map's proportions.
6. Indicate which direction is north.
7. Show the features you want emphasized by using shading, dots, cross-hatching, or appropriate symbols when color reproduction cannot be used.
8. If you use only one color, remember that only three shades of a single color will show up satisfactorily.
9. Include a key or legend telling what the different colors, shadings, or symbols represent.
10. Place maps as close as possible to the portion of the text that refers to them.

organizational charts

An organizational chart shows how the various components of an organization are related to one another. It is useful when you want to give your readers an overview of an organization or to show them the lines of authority within it.

The title of each organizational component (office, section, division) is placed in a separate box. These boxes are then linked to a central authority. (See Figure 1.) If your readers need the information, include the name of the person occupying the position identified in each box. (See Figure 2.)

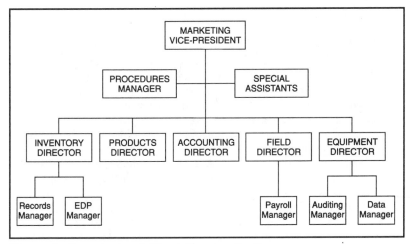

Figure 1 *Organizational Chart Showing Positions*

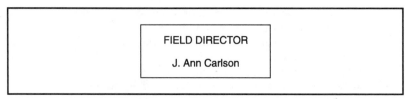

Figure 2 *Organizational Box with Name of Person and Position*

As with all illustrations, place the organizational chart as close as possible to the text that refers to it.

photographs

Photographs are the best way to show the surface appearance of an object or to record an event or the development of a phenomenon over a period of time. Not all representations, however, call for photographs. They cannot depict the internal workings of a mechanism or below-the-surface details of objects or structures. Such details are better represented in drawings.

HIGHLIGHTING PHOTOGRAPHIC SUBJECTS

Stand close enough to the object that it fills your picture frame. To get precise and clear photographs, choose camera angles carefully. Select the important details and the camera angles that will record them. To show relative size, place a familiar object—such as a ruler or a person—near the object being photographed.

USING COLOR

The preparation and printing of color photographs are complex technical tasks performed by graphics and printing experts. If you are planning to use color photographs in your publication, discuss the type and quality of photographs required with these experts. Generally, they prefer color transparencies (slides) and color negatives (negatives of color prints) for reproduction.

The advantages of using color illustrations are obvious: color is a good way of communicating crucial information. In medical, chemical, geological, and botanical publications, to name but a few, readers often need to know exactly what an object or phenomenon looks like. In these circumstances, color reproduction is the only legitimate option available.

Be aware, however, that color reproduction is significantly more expensive than black and white. Color can also be tricky to reproduce accurately without losing contrast and vividness. For this reason, the original must be sharply focused and rich in contrast.

Tips for Using Photographs

Like all illustrative materials, photographs must be handled carefully. When preparing photographs for printing, observe the following guidelines:

1. Mount photographs on white bond paper with spray adhesive (available at art supply stores) and allow ample margins.
2. If the photograph is the same size as the paper, type the caption, figure and page numbers, and any other important information on labels and fasten them to the photograph with spray adhesive. The labels that identify key features in the photograph are referred to as *callouts*. (Photographs are given figure numbers in sequence with other illustrations in a publication; see Figure 1.)
3. Position the figure number and caption so that the reader can view them and the photograph from the same orientation.
4. Do not draw crop marks (lines showing where the photo should be trimmed for reproduction) directly across a photograph. Draw them at the very edge of the photograph.
5. Do not write on a photograph, front or back. Tape a tissue-paper overlay over the face of the photograph, and then write very lightly on the overlay with a soft-lead pencil. Never write on the overlay with a ball-point pen.
6. Do not use paper clips or staples directly on photographs.

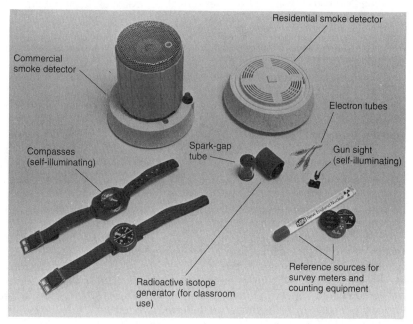

Commercial smoke detector

Residential smoke detector

Electron tubes

Compasses (self-illuminating)

Spark-gap tube

Gun sight (self-illuminating)

Radioactive isotope generator (for classroom use)

Reference sources for survey meters and counting equipment

Figure 1   Example of a Photograph

7. Do not fold or crease photographs.
8. If only a color photograph or slide is available for black-and-white reproduction, have a photographer produce a black-and-white glossy copy or slide for printing. Otherwise, the printed image will not have an accurate tone.

tables

A table is useful for showing large numbers of specific, related facts or statistics in a small space. A table can present data more concisely than text can, and it is more accurate than graphic presentations are because it provides numerous facts that a graph cannot convey. A table facilitates comparisons among data because of the arrangement of the data into rows and columns. Overall trends about the information, however, are more easily seen in charts and graphs. But do not rely on a table (or any illustration) as the only method of conveying significant information.

GUIDELINES FOR CREATING AND USING TABLES

Tables typically include the following elements, as shown in Figure 1.

Table Number. If you are using several tables, assign each a number, and then center the number and title above the table. The numbers are usually Arabic, and they should be assigned sequentially to the tables throughout the text. Tables should be referred to in the text by table number rather than by direction ("Table 4" rather than "the above table"). If there are more than five tables in your report or paper, include a "List of Tables" and list the tables by title and page number on a separate page following the table of contents. The first text reference to a table should precede the table. If a document contains several chapters or sections, tables can be numbered by chapter or section (Table 1-1, 1-2, . . . 3-1, 3-2).

Table Title. The title, which is placed just above the table, should describe concisely what the table represents.

Boxhead. The boxhead carries the column headings (or titles). These should be kept concise but descriptive. Units of measurement, where necessary, should be specified either as part of the heading or enclosed in parentheses beneath the heading. Avoid vertical lettering if possible.

Stub. The left-hand vertical column of a table is the stub. It lists the items about which information is given in the body of the table.

Body. The body comprises the data below the boxhead and to the right of the stub. Within the body, columns should be arranged so that the terms to be compared appear in adjacent rows and columns. Leaders (a row of spaced periods) are sometimes used between figures to aid the eye in following data from column to column. Where no information exists for a specific item, leave an empty space to acknowledge the gap.

Labels (annotations): Table number, Boxhead, Stub, Rule, Footnote, Source line, Table title, Column headings, Body

Geographical Regions	Reservoirs	Manmade Ponds	Natural Lakes & Ponds	Rivers & Streams	Farm Ponds
New England	130	40	570	410	410
Middle Atlantic	710	290	780	1200	630
East North Central	1200	760	3100	1600	1300
West North Central	810	550	1200	970	980
South Atlantic	1100	760	640	1500	1600
East South Central	890	630	190	670	1200
West South Central	1700	610	430	880	1300
Mountain	820	50	280	600	230
Pacific	950	200	820	1400	470
Totals	8300	3900	8000	9200	7800

Table 1. Recreational Fresh Water Angling by Water-Body Type and Geographical Region*

*In thousands of anglers. Anglers who fished in more than one water body or region are represented in more than one category.

SOURCE: U.S. Department of the Interior

Figure 1 *Table of Data*

Rules. These are the lines that separate the table into its various parts. Horizontal lines are placed below the title, below the body of the table, and between the column headings and the body of the table. They should not be closed at the sides. The columns within the table may be separated by vertical lines if they aid clarity.

Footnotes. Footnotes are used for explanations of individual items in the table. Symbols (such as ° and #) or lowercase letters (rather than numbers) are ordinarily used to key table footnotes, because numbers might be mistaken for the data in a numerical table.

Source Line. When appropriate a source line, which identifies where the information was obtained, appears below any footnotes.

Continued Lines. When a table must be divided so that it can be continued on another page, repeat the boxhead and give the table number at the head of each new page with a "continued" label ("Table 3, continued").

INFORMAL TABLES

To list relatively few items that would be easier for the reader to grasp in tabular form, use an informal table.

EXAMPLE The sound intensity levels (decibels) for the three frequency bands (in Hertz) were determined to be:

Frequency Band (Hz)	Decibels
600–1200	68
1200–2400	62
2400–4800	53

Although informal tables do not need titles or table numbers to identify them, they do require column headings that accurately describe the information listed.

OVERVIEW

Usage describes the choices we make among the various words and constructions available in our language. The line between standard or nonstandard English, or between formal and informal English, is determined by these choices. (See also the STYLE AND CLARITY tab.) Your guideline in any situation requiring such choices should be appropriateness: Is the word or expression you use appropriate to your audience and subject? When it is, you are practicing good usage.

The entries in this section have been designed to help you sort out the appropriate from the inappropriate: Just look up a word or term in question alphabetically or in the Index. A good dictionary is also an invaluable aid in your selection of the right word.

a/an

See the **articles** entry on the GRAMMAR tab.

a lot/alot

A *lot* is often incorrectly written as one word *(alot)*. If you use it, write the phrase as two words: *a lot*. It is very informal, however, and should not normally be used in business writing.

> CHANGE The peer review group had *a lot* of objections.
>
> TO The peer review group had many objections.

above

Avoid using *above* to refer to a preceding passage unless the reference is very clear. The same is true of *aforesaid, aforementioned, the former,* and *the latter,* which not only risk vagueness but also make your writing difficult to follow. To refer to something previously mentioned, repeat the noun or pronoun or construct your paragraph so that your reference is obvious.

> CHANGE Please fill out and submit the *above* by March 1.
>
> TO Please fill out and submit your time card by March 1.

accept/except

Accept is a verb meaning "consent to," "agree to take," or "admit willingly."

EXAMPLE I *accept* the responsibility that goes with the appointment.

Except is normally a preposition meaning "other than" or "excluding."

EXAMPLE We agreed on everything *except* the schedule.

adapt/adept/adopt

Adapt is a verb meaning "adjust to a new situation." *Adept* is an adjective meaning "highly skilled." *Adopt* is a verb meaning "take or use as one's own."

EXAMPLE The company will *adopt* a policy of finding executives who are *adept* administrators and who can *adapt* to new situations.

affect/effect

Affect is a verb that means "influence."

EXAMPLE The public utility commission's decisions *affect* all state utilities.

Effect can function either as a verb that means "bring about" or "cause," or as a noun that means "result." It is best, however, to avoid using *effect* as a verb; a less formal word, such as *made,* usually contributes to smoother reading.

CHANGE The new manager *effected* several changes that had a good *effect* on morale.

TO The new manager *made* several changes that had a good *effect* on morale.

all right/alright

All right means "all correct," as in "The answers were *all right.*" In formal writing it should not be used to mean "good" or "acceptable." It is always written as two words, with no hyphen; *alright* is incorrect.

CHANGE The decision that the committee reached was *all right.*

TO The decision that the committee reached was acceptable.

allude/elude/refer

Allude means to make an indirect reference to something not specifically mentioned.

EXAMPLE The report simply *alluded* to the problem, rather than stating it clearly.

Elude means to escape notice or detection.

EXAMPLES The discrepancy in the account *eluded* the auditor.
The leak *eluded* the inspectors.

Refer is used to indicate a direct reference to something.

EXAMPLE He *referred* to the chart three times during his speech.

already/all ready

Already is an adverb expressing time.

EXAMPLE We had *already* shipped the transistors when the stop order arrived.

All ready is a two-word phrase meaning "completely prepared."

EXAMPLE He was *all ready* to start work on the project when it was suddenly canceled.

also

Also is an adverb that means "additionally."

EXAMPLE Two 500,000-gallon tanks have recently been constructed on site. Several 10,000-gallon tanks are *also* available, if needed.

Also should not be used as a connective in the sense of "and."

CHANGE He brought the reports, letters, *also* the section supervisor's recommendations.

TO He brought the reports, letters, *and* the section supervisor's recommendations.

Avoid opening sentences with *also*. It is a weak transitional word that suggests an afterthought rather than planned writing.

CHANGE *Also* he brought statistical data to support his proposal.

TO He *also* brought statistical data to support his proposal.

amount/number

Amount is used with things thought of in bulk (mass nouns).

EXAMPLE The *amount* of electricity available for industrial use is limited.

Number is used with things that can be counted as individual items (count nouns).

> EXAMPLE   The *number* of employees who are qualified for early retirement has increased in recent years.

and/or

And/or means that either both circumstances are possible or only one of two circumstances is possible; however, it is clumsy and awkward because it makes the reader stop to puzzle over your distinction.

> CHANGE   Use A *and/or* B.
>
> TO   Use A *or* B *or* both.

as/since/because

All three of these words are commonly used to mean "because." All can be used as subordinating conjunctions to indicate to the reader that what follows is subordinate to the main clause.

> EXAMPLES   *Because* he did not have a college degree, he was turned down for the job.
>
> *Since* he did not have a college degree, he was turned down for the job.
>
> *As* he did not have a college degree, he was turned down for the job.

Because is the strongest subordinator of these three words, and *as* is the weakest. *As* is so weak, in fact, that it should never be used to introduce a clause. *Since* should also be used with caution because it is considerably weaker in establishing the cause-and-effect relationship than *because*.

as much as/more than

These two phrases are sometimes incorrectly run together, especially when intervening phrases delay the completion of the phrase.

> CHANGE   The engineers had *as much,* if not *more,* influence in planning the program *than* the accountants.
>
> TO   The engineers had *as much* influence in planning the program *as* the accountants, if not *more.*

as such

The phrase *as such* is seldom useful and should be omitted.

> CHANGE This program is poor. *As such,* it should be eliminated.
>
> TO This program is poor and should be eliminated.

as well as

Do not use *as well as* together with *both.* The two expressions have similar meanings; use one or the other.

> CHANGE Both General Motors, *as well as* Ford, are developing electric cars.
>
> TO *Both* General Motors *and* Ford are developing electric cars.

augment/supplement

Augment means to increase or magnify in size, degree, or effect.

> EXAMPLE Many employees *augment* their incomes by working overtime.

Supplement means to add something to make up for a deficiency.

> EXAMPLE The physician told him to *supplement* his diet with vitamins.

average/mean/median

The *average,* or arithmetical *mean,* is determined by dividing a sum of two or more quantities by the number of items totaled. For example, if one report is 10 pages, another is 30 pages, and a third is 20 pages, their *average* (or *mean*) length is 20 pages. It is incorrect, therefore, to say that "each averages 20 pages" because each report is a specific length.

> CHANGE Each report *averages* 20 pages.
>
> TO The three reports *average* 20 pages.

A *median* is the middle number in a sequence of numbers.

> EXAMPLE The *median* of the series, 1, 3, 4, 7, 8 is 4.

bad/badly

Bad is the adjective form that follows such linking verbs as *feel* and *look.*

> EXAMPLE We don't want our department to look *bad* at the meeting.

Badly is an adverb.

> **EXAMPLE** The test model performed *badly* during the trial run.

To say "I feel *badly*" would mean, literally, that your sense of touch was impaired. (See also the **good/well** entry in this tabbed section.)

balance/remainder

One meaning of *balance* is "a state of equilibrium"; another meaning is "the amount remaining in a bank account after balancing deposits and withdrawals." *Remainder*, in all applications, is "what is left over." *Remainder* is the more accurate word, therefore, to mean "that which is left over."

> **EXAMPLES** The accounting department must attempt to maintain a *balance* between looking after the company's best financial interests and being sensitive to the company's research and development work.
>
> The *balance* in the corporate account after the payroll has been met is a matter for concern.
>
> Round the fraction off to its nearest whole number and drop the *remainder*.

between/among

Between is normally used to relate two items or persons.

> **EXAMPLE** The roll pin is located *between* the grommet and the knob.

Among is used to relate more than two.

> **EXAMPLE** The subcontracting was distributed *among* the three firms.

bi/semi

When used with periods of time, *bi* means "two" or "every two." *Bimonthly* means "once in two months"; *biweekly* means "once in two weeks."

When used with periods of time, *semi* means "half of" or "occurring twice within a period of time." *Semimonthly* means "twice a month"; *semiweekly* means "twice a week."

Both *bi* and *semi* are normally joined with the following element without space or hyphen.

both ... and

Statements using the *both ... and* construction should always be balanced grammatically and logically.

EXAMPLE A successful photograph must be *both* clearly focused *and* adequately lighted.

Notice that *both* and *and* are followed logically by ideas of equal weight and grammatically by identical constructions.

CHANGE For success in management, it is necessary both *to develop* writing skills and *mastering* speaking.

TO For success in management, it is necessary both *to develop* writing skills and *to master* speaking.

can/may

In writing, *can* refers to capability, and *may* refers to possibility or permission.

EXAMPLES I *can* have the project finished by January 1. (capability)

I *may* be in Boston on Thursday. (possibility)

May I proceed with the project? (permission)

center on/center around

Substitute *on* or *in* for *around* in this phrase.

CHANGE The experiments *center around* the new discovery.

TO The experiments *center on* the new discovery.

Usually the idea intended by *center around* is best expressed by *revolve around.*

EXAMPLE The subcommittee hearings on computer security *revolved around* access codes.

chair/chairperson

The terms *chair, chairperson, chairman,* and *chairwoman* all are used to refer to a presiding officer. The titles *chair* and *chairperson,* however, avoid any sexual bias that might be implied by the other titles.

EXAMPLE Mary Roberts preceded John Stevens as *chair* (or *chairperson*) of the executive committee.

comprise/compose

Comprise means "include," "contain," or "consist of." The whole *comprises* the parts.

EXAMPLE The mechanism *comprises* 13 moving parts.

Compose means "create" or "make up the whole." The parts *compose* the whole.

CHANGE The 13 moving parts *compose* the mechanism.

TO The mechanism is *composed* of 13 moving parts.

connotation/denotation

The *denotation* of a word is its dictionary definition. The *connotations* of a word are its emotional associations. For example, *cheap* and *frugal* both refer to a reluctance to spend money, but they have different connotations, as the following sentences show.

EXAMPLES Her company was *cheap*. (negative connotation)

Her company was *frugal*. (positive connotation)

Clear writing requires words with both the most accurate denotation and the most appropriate connotations.

criteria/criterion

Criterion means "an established standard for judging or testing." *Criteria* and *criterions* are both acceptable plural forms of *criterion,* but *criteria* is generally preferred.

EXAMPLES In evaluating this job, we must use three *criteria.*

The most important *criterion* is quality of workmanship.

data/datum

In much business writing, *data* is considered a collective singular. In formal scientific and scholarly writing, however, *data* is generally used as a plural, with *datum* as the singular form. Base your decision on whether your reader should consider the data as a single collection or as a group of individual facts. Whatever you decide, be sure that your pronouns and verbs agree in number with the selected usage.

EXAMPLES The *data are* voluminous. *They indicate* a link between smoking and lung cancer. (formal)

The *data is* now ready for evaluation. *It is* in the mail. (less formal)

different from/different than

In formal writing, the preposition *from* is used with *different.*

EXAMPLE The personal computer is *different from* the mainframe computer.

Different than is acceptable when it is followed by a clause.

> EXAMPLE The job cost was *different than* we had estimated it.

each

When *each* is used as a subject, it takes a singular verb or pronoun.

> EXAMPLE *Each* of the reports is to be submitted ten weeks after it is assigned.

When *each* occurs after a plural subject with which it is in apposition, it takes a plural verb or pronoun.

> EXAMPLE The reports *each have* white embossed titles on *their* covers.

e.g./i.e.

The abbreviation *e.g.* stands for the Latin *exempli gratia,* meaning "for example"; *i.e.* stands for the Latin *id est,* meaning "that is." Since perfectly good English expressions exist for the same uses (*for example* and *that is*), there is no need to use a Latin expression or abbreviation except in notes and illustrations where you need to save space.

> CHANGE Some terms of the contract (*e.g.,* duration and job classification) were settled in the first two bargaining sessions.
>
> TO Some terms of the contract (*for example,* duration and job classification) were settled in the first two bargaining sessions.
>
> CHANGE We were a fairly heterogeneous group; *i.e.,* there were managers, foremen, and vice-presidents at the meeting.
>
> TO We were a fairly heterogeneous group; *that is,* there were managers, foremen, and vice-presidents at the meeting.

If you must use *i.e.* or *e.g.,* punctuate them as follows. If *i.e.* or *e.g.* connects two independent clauses, a semicolon should precede it and a comma should follow it. If *i.e.* or *e.g.* connects a noun and appositive, a comma should precede and follow it.

> EXAMPLES We were a fairly heterogeneous group, *i.e.,* managers, foremen, and vice-presidents.
>
> We were a fairly heterogeneous group; *i.e.,* we were managers, foremen, and vice-presidents.

etc.

Etc. is an abbreviation for the Latin *et cetera,* meaning "and others" or "and so forth"; therefore, *etc.* should not be used with *and.*

CHANGE He brought pencils, pads, erasers, a calculator, *and etc.*

TO He brought pencils, pads, erasers, a calculator, *etc.*

Do not use *etc.* at the end of a list or series introduced by the phrases *such as* or *for example* because these phrases already indicate that there are other things of the same category that are not named.

CHANGE He brought camping items, *such as* backpacks, sleeping bags, tents, *etc.*, even though he didn't need them.

TO He brought camping items, *such as* backpacks, sleeping bags, and tents, even though he didn't need them.

explicit/implicit

An explicit statement is one expressed directly, with precision and clarity. An implicit meaning may be found within a statement, even though it is not directly expressed.

EXAMPLES His directions to the new plant were *explicit,* and we found it with no trouble.

Although he did not mention the nation's financial condition, the danger of an economic recession was *implicit* in the president's speech.

fact

Expressions containing the word *fact* ("due to the *fact* that," "except for the *fact* that," "as a matter of *fact,*" or "because of the *fact* that") are often wordy substitutes for more accurate terms.

CHANGE *Due to the fact that* the sales force has a high turnover rate, sales have declined.

TO *Because* the sales force has a high turnover rate, sales have declined.

The word *fact* is, of course, valid when facts are what is meant.

EXAMPLE Our research has brought out numerous *facts* to support your proposal.

Do not use the word *fact* to refer to matters of judgment or opinion.

CHANGE *It is a fact that* sales are poor in the Midwest because of insufficient market research.

TO In my opinion, sales are poor in the Midwest because of insufficient market research.

female

Female is usually restricted to scientific, legal, or medical contexts (a *female* patient or suspect). Keep in mind that this term sounds cold and impersonal. The terms *girl, woman,* and *lady* are acceptable substitutes in other contexts; however, be aware that these substitute words have connotations involving age, dignity, and social position. (See also the **male** entry in this tabbed section.)

few/a few

In certain contexts, *few* carries more negative overtones than the phrase *a few* does.

> **EXAMPLES** There are *a few* good things about your report. (positive)
>
> There are *few* good things about your report. (negative)

fewer/less

Fewer refers to items that can be counted (count nouns).

> **EXAMPLE** *Fewer* employees took the offer than we expected.

Less refers to mass quantities or amounts (mass nouns).

> **EXAMPLE** The crop yield decreased this year because we had *less* rain than necessary for an optimum yield.

first/firstly

Firstly is an unnecessary attempt to add the *-ly* form to an adverb. *First* is an adverb in its own right, and sounds much less stiff than *firstly.* The same is true of other numbers as well.

> **CHANGE** *Firstly,* we should ask for an estimate.
>
> **TO** *First,* we should ask for an estimate.

flammable/inflammable/nonflammable

Both *flammable* and *inflammable* mean "capable of being set on fire." Since the *-in* prefix usually causes the word following to take its opposite meaning (*incapable, incompetent*), *flammable* is preferable to *inflammable* because it avoids possible misunderstanding.

> **EXAMPLE** The cargo of gasoline is *flammable.*

Nonflammable is the opposite, meaning "not capable of being set on fire."

> EXAMPLE The asbestos suit was *nonflammable.*

former/latter

Former and *latter* should be used to refer to only two items in a sentence or paragraph.

> EXAMPLE The president and his aide emerged from the conference, the *former* looking nervous and the *latter* looking glum.

Because these terms often make the reader look back to previous material to identify the reference, they impede reading and are best avoided.

good/well

Good is an adjective and *well* is an adverb.

> EXAMPLES John presented a *good* plan.
>
> The plan was presented *well.*

However, *well* can also be used as an adjective to describe someone's health.

> EXAMPLE She is not a *well* woman.

he/she

Because the use of a masculine pronoun to refer to both sexes is offensive to many people, it is better to rewrite the sentence in the plural or avoid use of a pronoun altogether rather than to offend.

> EXAMPLES *Employees* should take advantage of their insurance benefits.
>
> *Whoever* is appointed will find the task difficult.

You could also use the phrases *he or she* and *his or her.*

> EXAMPLE Whoever is appointed will find *his or her* task difficult.

Unfortunately, *he or she* and *his or her* are clumsy when used repeatedly and the *s/he* construction is awkward; the best advice is to reword the sentence to use a plural pronoun. Be sure also, however, to change the noun to which the pronoun refers to its plural form.

> CHANGE The administrator cannot do *his or her* job until *he or she* understands the concept.
>
> TO *Administrators* cannot do *their* jobs until *they* understand the concept.

imply/infer

If you *imply* something, you hint or suggest it. If you *infer* something, you reach a conclusion on the basis of evidence.

EXAMPLES His memo *implied* that the project would be delayed.

The general manager *inferred* from the memo that the project would be delayed.

in/into

In means "inside of"; *into* implies movement from the outside to the inside.

EXAMPLE The equipment was *in* the test chamber, so she sent her assistant *into* the chamber to get it.

in order to

The phrase *in order to* is sometimes essential to the meaning of a sentence.

EXAMPLE If the vertical scale of a graph line would not normally show the zero point, use a horizontal break in the graph *in order to* include the zero point.

In order to can also help control the pace of a sentence, even when it is not essential to the meaning of the sentence.

EXAMPLE The committee must know the estimated costs *in order to* evaluate the feasibility of the project.

Most often, however, the phrase *in order to* is just a meaningless filler phrase that is dropped into a sentence without thought.

CHANGE *In order to* start the engine, open the choke and throttle and then press the starter.

TO *To* start the engine, open the choke and throttle and then press the starter.

Search for these thoughtless uses of *in order to* in your writing and eliminate them.

insure/ensure/assure

Insure, ensure, and *assure* all mean "make secure or certain." *Assure* refers to persons, and it alone has the connotation of setting a person's mind at rest. *Ensure* and *insure* also mean "make secure from harm." Only *insure* is widely used in the sense of guaranteeing the value of life or property.

EXAMPLES I *assure* you that the equipment will be available.

We need all the data to *ensure* the success of the project.

We should *insure* the contents of the building.

interface

An *interface* is the surface providing a common boundary between two bodies or areas. The bodies or areas may be physical (the *interface* of a piston and a cylinder) or conceptual (the *interface* of mathematics and statistics). Do not use *interface* as a substitute for the verbs *cooperate, interact,* or even *work.*

CHANGE The Water Resources Department will *interface* with the Department of Marine Biology on the proposed project.

TO The Water Resources Department will *work* with the Department of Marine Biology on the proposed project.

irregardless/regardless

Irregardless is nonstandard English because it expresses a double negative. The prefix *ir-* is designed to render the word following it negative, and the word *regardless* is already negative, meaning, "unmindful." Always use *regardless* or *irrespective.*

CHANGE *Irregardless* of the difficulties, we must increase the strength of the outer casing.

TO *Regardless* of the difficulties, we must increase the strength of the outer casing.

its/it's

Its is a possessive pronoun, whereas *it's* is a contraction of *it is.*

EXAMPLE *It's* important that the factory meet *its* quota.

Although pronouns normally form the possessive by the addition of an apostrophe and an *s,* the contraction of *it is* (*it's*) has already used that device; therefore, the possessive form of the pronoun *it* is formed by adding only the *s.*

kind of/sort of

Kind of and *sort of* should be used in writing only to refer to a class or type of things.

EXAMPLE They used a special *kind of* metal in the process.

Do not use *kind of* or *sort of* to mean "rather," "somewhat," or "somehow."

CHANGE It was *kind of* a bad year for the firm.

TO It was a bad year for the firm.

lay/lie

Lay is a transitive verb (a verb that requires a direct object to complete its meaning) that means "place" or "put." Its present tense form is *lay*.

EXAMPLE We are *laying* the foundation of the building one section at a time.

The past tense form of *lay* is *laid*.

EXAMPLE We *laid* the first section of the foundation on the 27th of June.

The perfect tense form of *lay* is also *laid*.

EXAMPLE Since June we have *laid* all but two sections of the foundation.

Lay is frequently confused with *lie*, which is an intransitive verb (a verb that does not require an object to complete its meaning) that means "recline" or "remain." Its present tense form is *lie*.

EXAMPLE Injured employees should *lie* down and remain still until the doctor arrives.

The past tense form of *lie* is *lay*. (This form causes the confusion between *lie* and *lay*.)

EXAMPLE The injured employee *lay* still for approximately five minutes.

The perfect tense form of *lie* is *lain*.

EXAMPLE The injured employee had *lain* still for approximately five minutes when the doctor arrived.

leave/let

As a verb, *leave* should never be used in the sense of "allow" or "permit."

CHANGE *Leave* me do it my way.

TO *Let* me do it my way.

As a noun, however, *leave* can mean "permission granted."

EXAMPLE Employees are granted a *leave* of absence if they have a chronic illness.

like/as

To avoid confusion between *like* and *as,* remember that *like* is a preposition and *as* is a conjunction. Use *like* with a noun or pronoun that is not followed by a verb.

> EXAMPLE   The new supervisor behaves *like* a novice.

Use *as* before clauses (which contain verbs).

> EXAMPLES   He acted *as though* he owned the company.
>
> He responded *as* we expected he would.

Like may be used in elliptical constructions that omit the verb.

> EXAMPLE   She took to architecture *like* a bird to nest building.

like/such as

Like and *such as* are so close in meaning that they can often be used interchangeably. The slight difference between them is that *such as* leads the reader to imagine an indefinite group of objects.

> EXAMPLE   He referred to mankind's great inventions, *such as* the wheel, the steam engine, the gasoline engine, and the computer.

Like, on the other hand, suggests a closer resemblance among the things compared.

> EXAMPLE   He referred to the satisfactions of sense, *like* sight, sound, odor, and touch.

male

The term *male* is usually restricted to scientific, legal, or medical contexts (a male patient or suspect). Keep in mind that this term sounds cold and impersonal. The terms *boy, man,* and *gentleman* are acceptable substitutes in other contexts; however, be aware that these substitute words also have connotations involving age, dignity, and social position. (See also the **female** entry in this tabbed section.)

media/medium

Media is the plural of *medium* and should always be used with a plural verb.

> EXAMPLES   The *media* are a powerful influence in presidential elections.
>
> The most influential *medium* is television.

Ms./Miss/Mrs.

Ms. is a convenient form of addressing a woman, regardless of her marital status, and it is now almost universally accepted. *Miss* is used to refer to an unmarried woman, and *Mrs.* is used to refer to a married woman. Some women indicate a preference for *Miss* or *Mrs.*, and such a preference should be honored. An academic or professional title *(Doctor, Professor, Captain)* should take preference over *Ms., Miss,* or *Mrs.*

nature

Nature, when used to mean "kind" or "sort," can often be vague. Avoid the word in your writing. Say exactly what you mean.

> CHANGE   The *nature* of the engine caused the problem.

> TO   The compression ratio of the engine caused the problem.

OK/okay

The expression *okay* (also spelled *OK* or *O.K.*) is common in informal writing but should be avoided in more formal correspondence and reports.

> CHANGE   The solution is *okay* with me.

> TO   The solution is acceptable to me.

on/onto/upon

On is normally a preposition meaning "supported by," "attached to," or "located at."

> EXAMPLE   Install the telephone *on* the wall.

Onto implies movement to a position on or movement up and on.

> EXAMPLE   The union members surged *onto* the platform after their leader's defiant speech.

Similarly, *on* stresses a position of rest and *upon* emphasizes movement.

> EXAMPLES   A book lay *on* the table.

> She put a book *upon* the table.

only

In writing, the word *only* should be placed immediately before the word or phrase it modifies.

CHANGE We *only* lack financial backing.

TO We lack *only* financial backing.

oral/verbal

Oral refers to what is spoken.

EXAMPLE He offered an *oral* commitment to the policy.

Although it is sometimes used synonymously with *oral, verbal* literally means "in words" and can refer to what is spoken *or written*. To avoid possible confusion, do not use *verbal* if you can use *written* or *oral*.

CHANGE He offered a *verbal* agreement to complete the work.

TO He offered a *written* agreement to complete the work.

OR He offered an *oral* agreement to complete the work.

per

When *per* is used to mean "by means of," "through," or "on account of," it is appropriate.

EXAMPLES *per* annum, *per* capita, *per* diem, *per* head

When used to mean "according to" (*per* your request, *per* your order), the expression is jargon and should be avoided. Equally incorrect is the phrase *as per*.

CHANGE *As per* our discussion, I will send revised instructions.

TO As we agreed, I will send revised instructions.

per cent/percent/percentage

Percent, which is replacing the two-word *per cent*, is used instead of the symbol (%) except in tables, where space is at a premium.

EXAMPLE Only 25 *percent* of the members attended the meeting.

Percentage, which is never used with numbers, indicates a general size.

EXAMPLE Only a small *percentage* of the managers attended the meeting.

phenomenon/phenomena

A *phenomenon* is an observable thing, fact, or occurrence. Its plural form is *phenomena*.

EXAMPLES The natural *phenomenon* of earth tremors is a problem we must anticipate in designing the California installation.

The *phenomena* associated with atomic fission were only recently understood.

reason is because

The redundant phrase *reason is because* is a colloquial expression that should be avoided in writing. In *the reason is because,* the word *because* (which in this phrase only repeats the notion of cause) should be replaced by *that.* You could also just delete *the reason is* and use only *because.*

CHANGE Sales have increased more than 20 percent. The *reason is because* our sales force has been more aggressive this year.

TO Sales have increased more than 20 percent this year *because* our sales force has been more aggressive.

OR Sales have increased more than 20 percent this year. The *reason is that* our sales force has been more aggressive this year.

same

When used as a pronoun, *same* is awkward and outdated.

CHANGE Your order has been received, and we will respond to *same* next week.

TO Your order has been received, and we will respond to *it* next week.

shall/will

Although traditionally *shall* was used to express the future tense with *I* and *we, will* is now generally accepted with all persons. *Shall* is commonly used today only in questions requesting an opinion or a preference rather than a prediction (compare "Shall we go?" to "Will we go?") and in statements expressing determination ("I shall return").

that

Do not delete *that* from a sentence if it is necessary for the reader's understanding.

CHANGE Some managers fail to recognize sufficiently the human beings who operate the equipment constitute an important safety system.

TO Some managers fail to recognize sufficiently *that* the human beings who operate the equipment constitute an important safety system.

Avoid the unnecessary repetition of *that*.

> CHANGE   You will note *that*, as you assume greater responsibility and as your years of service with the company increase, *that* your benefits will increase accordingly.

> TO   You will note *that* your benefits will increase as you assume greater responsibility and your years of service with the company increase.

that/which/who

Who refers to persons, whereas *that* and *which* refer to animals and things.

> EXAMPLES   John Brown, *who* is retiring tomorrow, has worked for the company for twenty years.

> Companies *that* fund basic research must not expect immediate results.

> The jet stream, *which* is approximately eight miles above the earth, blows at an average of 64 miles per hour.

That is often overused. However, do not eliminate it if to do so would cause ambiguity or problems with pace.

> CHANGE   On the file specifications input to the compiler for any chained file, the user must ensure the number of sectors per main file section is a multiple of the number of sectors per bucket.

> TO   On the file specifications input to the compiler for any chained file, the user must ensure *that* the number of sectors per main file section is a multiple of the number of sectors per bucket.

Which, rather than *that,* should be used with nonrestrictive clauses (clauses that do not change the meaning of the basic sentence).

> EXAMPLES   After John left the restaurant, *which* is one of the best in New York, he came directly to my office. (nonrestrictive)

> Companies *that* diversify usually succeed. (restrictive)

there/their/they're

There is an expletive or an adverb.

> EXAMPLES   *There* were more than 1,500 people at the conference. (expletive)

> More than 1,500 people were *there.* (adverb)

Their is the possessive form of *they.*

> EXAMPLE   Our employees are expected to keep *their* desks neat.

They're is a contraction of *they are.*

EXAMPLE If *they're* right, we should change the design.

to/too/two

To, too, and *two* are confused only because they sound alike. *To* is used as a preposition or to mark an infinitive.

EXAMPLES Send the report *to* the district manager. (preposition)

I wish *to* go. (mark of the infinitive)

Too is an adverb meaning "excessively" or "also."

EXAMPLES The price was *too* high. ("excessively")

I, *too,* thought it was high. ("also")

Two is a number.

EXAMPLE Only *two* buildings have been built this fiscal year.

try and

The phrase *try and* is colloquial for *try to.* Unless you are writing a casual personal letter, use *try to.*

CHANGE Please *try and* finish the report on time.

TO Please *try to* finish the report on time.

up

Adding the word *up* to verbs often creates a redundant phrase.

CHANGE Next open *up* the exhaust valve.

TO Next open the exhaust valve.

utilize

Utilize should not be used as a long variant of *use,* which is the general word for "employ for some purpose." When you are tempted to use this term, substitute *use.* It will almost always prove a clearer and less pretentious word.

CHANGE You can *utilize* the word processor to write your correspondence.

TO You can *use* the word processor to write your correspondence.

via

Via is Latin for "by way of."

EXAMPLE The equipment is being shipped to Los Angeles *via* Chicago.

The term should be used only in routing instructions.

CHANGE His project was funded *via* the recent legislation.

TO His project was funded *as the result of* the recent legislation.

where/that

Do not substitute *where* for *that* to anticipate an idea or fact to follow.

CHANGE I read in the *Wall Street Journal where* computer chips will be used in the new process.

TO I read in the *Wall Street Journal that* computer chips will be used in the new process.

whether or not

When *whether or not* is used to indicate a choice between alternatives, omit *or not;* it is redundant, since *whether* communicates the notion of a choice.

CHANGE The project director asked *whether or not* the request for proposals had been issued.

TO The project director asked *whether* the request for proposals had been issued.

while

Do not use *while* to mean *although* or *whereas.*

CHANGE *While* Ryan Patterson wants the job of sales manager, he has not yet asked for it.

TO *Although* Ryan Patterson wants the job of sales manager, he has not yet asked for it.

Restrict *while* to its meaning of "during the time that."

EXAMPLE I'll have to catch up on my reading *while* I am on vacation.

who/whom

See the **who/whom** entry on the GRAMMAR tab.

whose/of which

Whose should normally be used with persons and *of which* with inanimate objects.

EXAMPLES The man *whose* car had been towed away was angry.

The mantle clock, the parts *of which* work perfectly, is over one hundred years old.

If these uses cause a sentence to sound awkward, however, *whose* may be used with inanimate objects.

EXAMPLE There are added fields, for example, *whose* totals should never be zero.

who's/whose

Who's is a contraction of *who is.*

EXAMPLE *Who's* scheduled to attend the productivity seminar next month?

Whose is the possessive for *who* or *of which.*

EXAMPLE *Whose* department will be affected by the budget cuts?

Who's and *whose* are not interchangeable.

your/you're

Your is a personal pronoun denoting possession; *you're* is a contraction of *you are.*

EXAMPLE If *you're* going to the seashore, be sure to wear *your* sweater.

The entries in this section are intended to help you develop a style that is clear and effective—and that follows the conventions of standard English. For a number of related entries, see THE BUSINESS WRITING PROCESS, USAGE, and GRAMMAR tabs.

A dictionary definition of style is "the way something is said, as distinguished from its substance." Writers' styles are reflected by the way they use words, sentences, images, figures of speech, and so on. A writer's style is also determined by the way his or her language functions in particular situations. For example, a letter to a friend would be informal, relaxed, even chatty in tone; a job application letter, on the other hand, would be more formal, restrained, and deliberate.

No clear-cut line delineates what is formal and what is informal, and some writing may call for a combination of the two. Nevertheless, certain material is clearly formal, such as scholarly and scientific articles in professional journals, lectures read at meetings of professional societies, and legal documents. Examples of informal writing include private letters, nonfiction books of general interest, mass-circulation magazines, and even some business memorandums.

Whether you should use a formal style in a particular instance depends on your audience and objective. When you attempt to force a formal style when it should not be used, you are likely to fall into affectation and awkwardness. When you consciously attempt to create any "style," you are likely to defeat your purpose. Just keeping your reader and your purpose clearly in mind as you prepare and write any document will help you achieve an appropriate writing style for the document.

In general, business writing style should be simple, clear, direct, and interesting. A judicious use of the active voice, parallel structure, and appropriate emphasis and subordination will help you produce a readable and interesting business writing style.

absolute words

Absolute words (such as *round, unique, exact,* and *perfect*) are not logically subject to comparison *(rounder, roundest);* nevertheless, these words are sometimes used comparatively.

> CHANGE Phase-locked loop circuits make the FM tuner performance *more exact* by decreasing tuner distortion.
>
> TO Phase-locked loop circuits make the FM tuner performance *more accurate* by decreasing tuner distortion.

Absolute words should be used comparatively only with the greatest caution in business writing, where accuracy and precision are crucial.

abstract words/concrete words

The difference between abstract and concrete words is the difference between *durability* (abstract) and *stone* (concrete).

Abstract words refer to general ideas, qualities, conditions, acts, or relationships—to something that is intangible, something that cannot be discerned by the five senses.

> EXAMPLES work, courage, crime, kindness, idealism, love, hate, fantasy, sportsmanship

Abstract words must frequently be qualified by other words.

> CHANGE What the members of the Research and Development Department need is *freedom.*
>
> TO What the members of the Research and Development Department need is *freedom to explore the problem further.*

Concrete words refer to specific persons, places, objects, and acts that can be perceived by the senses.

> EXAMPLES wrench, book, house, scissors, gold, water
>
> *Skiing* (concrete) is a strenuous *sport* (abstract).

Concrete words are easier to understand, for they create images in the mind of your reader. Still, you cannot express ideas without using some abstract words. Actually, the two kinds of words are usually used best together, in support of each other. For example, the abstract idea of *transportation* is made clearer with the use of specific concrete words, such as *subways, jets,* or *automobiles.*

> EXAMPLE *Transportation* was limited to the *subway* and *automobiles.*

affectation

Affectation is the use of language that is more business, formal, or showy than is necessary to communicate information to the reader. A writer who is unnecessarily ornate or pretentious is usually attempting to impress the reader by showing off a repertoire of fancy words and phrases. Using unnecessarily formal words (such as *herewith*) and outdated phrases (such as *please find enclosed*) is another cause of affectation.

EXAMPLES   *pursuant to* (instead of *about* or *regarding*)

            in view of the foregoing (instead of *therefore*)

            in view of the fact that (instead of *because*)

            it is interesting to note that (omit)

            it may be said that (omit)

Affected writing, which forces the reader to work harder to understand the writer's meaning, typically contains abstract, highly technical, pseudotechnical, pseudolegal, or foreign words and is often liberally sprinkled with vogue words. Jargon can become affectation if it is misused, and euphemisms can contribute to affected writing if their purpose is to hide the facts of a situation rather than treat them with dignity or restraint. Attempts to make the trivial seem important can also cause affectation.

The easiest kind of affectation to be lured into is the use of long variants: words created by adding prefixes and suffixes to simpler words (*utilize* for use, *analyzation* for analysis, *telephonic communication* for telephone call). The practice of elegant variation—attempting to avoid repeating the same word in the same paragraph by substituting pretentious synonyms—is also a form of affectation. Another contributor to affectation is gobbledygook, which is wordy, roundabout writing that has many pseudolegal and pseudoscientific terms sprinkled throughout.

Affectation is a widespread problem in business writing because many people apparently feel that affectation lends a degree of formality, and hence authority, to their writing. Nothing could be further from the truth.

awkwardness

To avoid awkwardness, make your writing as direct and concise as possible. The following three guidelines will help you smooth out most awkward passages: (1) keep your sentences uncomplicated, (2) use the active voice unless you have a reason to use the passive voice, and (3) tighten up your writing by eliminating excess words and phrases.

business writing style

At one time business writing style was as formal as the starched collars every businessperson wore. The following example was typical.

My Dear Sir:

Yours of the 12th received and in reply beg to state that herewith are forwarded the reports under consideration. Please be advised of general concurrence in desire to expedite matters. . . .

This style is extremely formal and impersonal by today's standards. Business writing today is generally much more personal and conversational, as the following revision of the previous example illustrates.

> Dear Mr. Watson:
>
> I have received your letter of the 12th, and I am enclosing the reports for you to study. Certainly, we agree with you that time is important to the project. . . .

Even though business writing style is less formal today, it must adhere to the conventions of standard English by using conventional spelling and standard grammatical forms.

Business writing may legitimately vary all the way from the chatty style you might use with a close business associate to the very formal style found in contracts. In memorandums and letters, however, a position between the two extremes is generally appropriate. Writing that is too formal can be irritating to the reader, and an obvious attempt to be casual and informal may strike the reader as insincere. In business writing, as in all writing, knowing your reader is critical.

> CHANGE Dear Jane,
> I'm crazy about your proposal! . . . .
>
> TO Dear Jane:
> Your proposal arrived today, and it seems fine. . . .

Your use of personal pronouns is important in letters and memos. Do not use *one* (or *the writer*) to refer to yourself; it is perfectly natural and appropriate to refer to yourself as *I* and to the reader as *you.* In a report, however, you may not be writing to a single reader and may not necessarily want to refer to collective readers as *you.* Be careful also when you use the pronoun *we* in a business letter on company stationary, since it commits your company to what you have written. When a statement is your opinion, use *I;* when it is company policy, use *we.*

The best writers strive to write in a style that is so clear that their message cannot be misunderstood. Clarity should be the ultimate goal of your business writing style. A clear style is achieved primarily through the proper and conscientious use of the different steps of the writing process as presented ON THE BUSINESS WRITING PROCESS tab.

One way to achieve a clear style, especially during revision, is to eliminate the overuse of the passive voice, which is prevalent in most poor business writing. The passive voice not only saps the life of your writing, but it can sometimes be ambiguous, uninformative, or overly impersonal.

> CHANGE It was discovered that salary totals were incorrect. (Who discovered it?)
>
> TO The Accounting Department discovered that salary totals were incorrect.

You can also achieve clarity with conciseness. Proceed cautiously here, however, because business writing should not be telegraphic, with an endless series of short, choppy sentences. (See also **telegraphic style** in this tabbed section.)

Furthermore, don't be so concise that you become blunt. If you respond to a written request that you cannot understand with, "Your request was un-

---

PLR Air Conditioning Center 27 West Elm Street • Plaines City, IA 50705

March 6, 19--

Ms. Harriet L. Bussman, President
Bussman Engineering, Inc.
2731 Janus Street
Plaines City, IA 50505

Dear Ms. Bussman:

Thank you very much for allowing us to present our recommendation for a PLR Air Conditioning System. We would like also to express our appreciation to Mr. Lindsay and Mrs. Smoot for the time and courtesy they extended to us as we collected the data necessary for this proposal.

After thoroughly analyzing your company's management and engineering requirements, we believe that this proposed PLR system will provide the maximum return on your investment dollar. In addition, the PLR system protects you against obsolescence in the near future--if your business continues to experience the normal growth you have experienced the last few years--because the equipment PLR proposes to install is a modular design to which you may add additional units as the need arises. The system we have designed for you provides flexibility, allowing for any special conditions your company may wish to incorporate.

We believe that you will find this system practical, efficient, and economical for your company, both now and in the future. It is our sincere hope that the information in the enclosed proposal will make your decision to install a PLR Air Conditioning System much easier.

Sincerely yours,

James P. Callahan

James P. Callahan
Sales Manager

JPC/mo
Enclosure

Figure 1 *Business Writing Style*

clear" or "I don't understand your question," you will probably offend your reader. Instead of attacking the writer's ability to phrase a request, consider that what you are really doing is asking for more information. Say so: "I will need more information before I can answer your request. Specifically, can you give me the title and the date of the report you are looking for?" The second version is a little longer than the first, but it is both more polite and more helpful.

Finally, clarity is achieved through the wise use of punctuation. A misplaced comma, or other mark of punctuation, can often cause misunderstanding and confusion.

In Figure 1 (see p. 277), notice that the tone is dignified, yet neither too formal nor too informal. Extensive use of the active voice keeps the pace of the letter moving well, and use of personal pronouns and a positive point of view keeps the writing interesting.

clichés

Clichés are expressions that have been used for so long that they are no longer fresh, but they come easily to mind because they have been used continually over a long period of time. In addition to being stale, clichés are usually wordy and often vague. Each of the following clichés is followed by better, more direct words, or expressions:

> **EXAMPLES**   *quick as a flash* (quickly, in five minutes)
>
> *straight from the shoulder* (frank)
>
> *last but not least* (last, finally)
>
> *as plain as day* (clear, obvious)
>
> *abreast of the times* (up to date, current)
>
> *the modern business world* (business today)

Clichés are often used in an attempt to make writing elegant or impressive (see also the entry on **affectation** in this tabbed section). Because they are wordy and vague, however, they slow communication and can even irritate your reader. So, although clichés come to mind easily while you are writing the draft, they normally should be eliminated during the revision phase of the writing process.

coherence

Writing is coherent when the relationships among ideas are made clear to the reader. Coherent writing moves logically and consistently from point to point. Each idea should relate clearly to the others, with one idea flowing smoothly to the next. Many elements contribute to smooth and coherent writing; however, the major components are (1) a logical sequence of ideas and (2) clear transitions between ideas.

A logical sequence of presentation is the most important single requirement in achieving coherence, and the key to achieving the most logical
sequence of presentation is the use of a good outline. The outline forces you
to establish a beginning (introduction), a middle (body), and an end (conclusion), and this alone contributes greatly to coherence. The outline also enables
you to lay out the most direct route to your objective without digressing into
interesting but only loosely related side issues, a habit that inevitably defeats
coherence. Drawing up an outline permits you to experiment with different
sequences and choose the best one.

Thoughtful transition is also essential to coherence, for without it your
writing cannot achieve the smooth flow from sentence to sentence and from
paragraph to paragraph that is required for coherence. Notice the difference
between the following two paragraphs; the first has no transition and the
second has transition added.

CHANGE The moon has always been an object of interest to human beings.
Until the 1960s, getting there was only a dream. Some thought that
we were not meant to go to the moon. In 1969 Neil Armstrong
stepped onto the lunar surface. Moon landings became routine to
the general public.

TO The moon has always been an object of interest to human beings,
but until the 1960s, getting there was only a dream. *In fact,* some
thought that we were not meant to go to the moon. *However,* in
1969 Neil Armstrong stepped onto the lunar surface. *After that*
moon landings became routine to the general public.

The transitional words and phrases of the second paragraph fit the ideas
snugly together, making that paragraph read more smoothly than the first.
Attention to transition in longer works is essential if your reader is to move
smoothly from point to point in your writing.

Providing your readers with sentence variety also contributes to making
your writing coherent. Provide variety in (1) sentence construction (don't
begin every sentence with an article and a noun); (2) in sentence types (use
complex sentences in addition to simple sentences and compound sentences); and (3) in sentence length (if you write only long sentences, you'll
put your readers to sleep; if you write only short sentences, you'll have a
jackhammer effect on them).

Check your draft carefully for coherence during revision; if your writing
is not coherent, you are not really communicating with your reader.

compound words

A compound word is made from two or more words that are either hyphenated or written as one word. (If you are not certain whether a compound
word should be hyphenated, check a dictionary.)

EXAMPLES   nevertheless, mother-in-law, courthouse, run-of-the-mill, low-level, high-energy

Be careful to distinguish between compound words and words that frequently appear together but do not constitute compound words, such as *high school* and *post office*. Also be careful to distinguish between compound words and word pairs that mean different things, such as *greenhouse* and *green house*.

Plurals of compound words are usually formed by adding an *s* to the last letter.

EXAMPLES   bedrooms, masterminds, overcoats, cupfuls

When the first word of the compound is more important to its meaning than the last, however, the first word takes the *s* (when in doubt, check your dictionary).

EXAMPLES   editors-in-chief, fathers-in-law

Possessives are formed by adding *'s* to the end of the compound word.

EXAMPLES   the *vice-president's* speech, his *brother-in-law's* car, the *pipeline's* diameter, the *antibody's* action

conciseness/wordiness

Effective writers make all words, sentences, and paragraphs count by eliminating unnecessary words and phrases. Wordiness results from needless repetition of the same idea in different words.

CHANGE   Modern students *of today* are more technologically sophisticated than their parents. (The phrase *of today* repeats the thought already expressed by the adjective *modern*.)

TO   Modern students are more technologically sophisticated than their parents.

Careful writers remove every word, phrase, clause, or sentence they can remove without sacrificing clarity. In doing so, they are striving to be as concise as clarity permits—but note that conciseness is not a synonym for brevity. In fact, when brevity is overdone it can become telegraphic style (see also the entry on **telegraphic style** in this tabbed section). Brevity may or may not be desirable in a given passage depending on the writer's objective, but conciseness is always desirable. The writer must distinguish between language that is used for effect and mere wordiness that stems from lack of care or judgment.

A concise sentence is not guaranteed to be effective, but a wordy sentence always loses some of its readability and coherence because of the extra load it must carry. Wordiness is to be expected in a first draft, but it should never survive revision.

CAUSES OF WORDINESS

Modifiers that repeat an idea already implicit or present in the word being modified contribute to wordiness by being redundant.

EXAMPLES *active* consideration   balance *of equilibrium*

final outcome   *present* status

personal opinion   descended *down*

completely finished   circle *around*

basic essentials   worthy *of merit*

advance planning   the reason *is because*

Coordinating synonyms that merely repeat one another contribute to wordiness.

EXAMPLES any and all   each and every

finally and for good   basic and fundamental

first and foremost

Excess qualification also contributes to wordiness, as the following examples demonstrate:

EXAMPLES *utterly rejected*—rejected

perfectly clear—clear

completely compatible—compatible

completely accurate—accurate

radically new—new

The use of expletives, relative pronouns, and relative adjectives, although they have legitimate purposes, often results in wordiness.

CHANGE *There are* (expletive) many supervisors in the area *who* (relative pronoun) are planning to attend the workshop *which* (relative adjective) is scheduled for Friday.

TO Many supervisors in the area plan to attend the workshop scheduled for Friday.

Circumlocution (a long, indirect way of expressing things) is a leading cause of wordiness.

CHANGE The payment to which a subcontractor is entitled should be made promptly so that in the event of a subsequent contractual dispute we, as general contractors, may not be held in default of our contract by virtue of nonpayment.

TO Pay subcontractors promptly. Then if a contractual dispute should occur, we cannot be held in default of our contract because of nonpayment.

Conciseness can be overdone. If you respond to a written request that you cannot understand with "Your request was unclear" or "I don't understand," you will probably offend your reader. Instead of attacking the writer's ability to phrase a request, consider that what you are really doing is asking for more information. Say so.

> EXAMPLE   I will need more information before I can answer your request. Specifically, can you give me the title and the date of the report you are looking for?

This version is a little longer than the others, but it is both more polite and more helpful. Although conciseness and clarity usually reinforce each other, there are times when clarity legitimately demands more words.

HOW TO ACHIEVE CONCISENESS

Conciseness can be achieved by effective use of subordination. This is, in fact, the best means of tightening wordy writing.

> CHANGE   The chemist's report was carefully illustrated, *and it covered five pages.*
>
> TO   The chemist's *five-page* report was carefully illustrated.

Conciseness can be achieved by using simple words and phrases.

> CHANGE   It is the policy of the company to provide the proper equipment to enable each employee to conduct the telephonic communication necessary to discharge his responsibilities; such should not be utilized for personal communications.
>
> TO   Your telephone is provided for company business; do not use it for personal calls.

Conciseness can be achieved by eliminating undesirable repetition.

> CHANGE   Postinstallation testing, which is offered to all our customers at no further cost to them whatsoever, is available with each Line Scan System One purchased from this company.
>
> TO   Free postinstallation testing is offered with each Line Scan System One.

Conciseness can sometimes be achieved by changing a sentence from the passive to the active voice or from the indicative to the imperative mood. The following example does both:

> CHANGE   Card codes are normally used when it is known that the cards are to be processed by a computer, and control punches are normally used when it is known that the cards are designed to be processed at a tab installation.
>
> TO   Use card codes when you process the cards on a computer, and use control punches when you process them at a tab installation.

Eliminate wordy introductory phrases or pretentious words and phrases of any kind.

EXAMPLES	In view of the foregoing	As you may recall
	It appears that	As you know
	In the case of	Needless to say
	It may be said that	In view of the fact that

CHANGE in order to, so as to, so as to be able to, with a view to

TO *to*

CHANGE due to the fact that, for the reason that, owing to the fact that, the reason for

TO *because*

CHANGE by means of, by using, utilizing, through the use of

TO *by* or *with*

CHANGE at this time, at this point in time, at present, at the present

TO *now*

CHANGE at that time, at that point, at that point in time, as of that date, during that period

TO *then*

Overuse of intensifiers (such as *very, more, most, best, quite*) contributes to wordiness; conciseness can be achieved by eliminating them. The same is true of excessive use of adjectives and adverbs.

euphemisms

A euphemism is a word that is an inoffensive substitute for one that could be distasteful, offensive, or too blunt.

EXAMPLES *remains* for *corpse*

passed away for *died*

marketing representative for *salesman*

previously owned (or *preowned*) for *used*

Used judiciously, a euphemism might help you avoid embarrassing or offending someone. Overused, however, euphemisms can hide the facts of a situation (such as *incident* for *accident*) or be a form of affectation. (See also the entry on **word choice** in this tabbed section.)

expletives

An expletive is a word that fills the position of another word, phrase, or clause. *It* and *there* are the usual expletives.

>   **EXAMPLE** *It* is certain that he will go.

In this example, the expletive *it* occupies the position of subject in place of the real subject, *that he will go.* Although expletives are sometimes necessary to avoid awkwardness, they are commonly overused and most sentences can be better stated without them.

>   **CHANGE** *There are* several reasons that I did it.
>   **TO** I did it for several reasons.

>   **CHANGE** *There were* many orders lost for unexplained reasons.
>   **TO** Many orders were lost for unexplained reasons.

figures of speech

A figure of speech is an imaginative comparison, either stated or implied, between two things that are basically unlike but have at least one thing in common. If a device is cone shaped with an opening at the top, for example, you might say that it looks like a volcano.

Business people may find themselves using figures of speech to clarify the unfamiliar by relating a new and difficult concept to one with which the reader is familiar. In this respect, figures of speech help establish a common ground of understanding between the specialist and the nonspecialist. Business people may also use figures of speech to help translate the abstract into the concrete; in the process of doing so, figures of speech also make writing more colorful and graphic.

Although figures of speech are not used extensively in business writing, a particularly apt figure of speech may be just the right tool when you must explain or describe a complex concept. A figure of speech must be appropriate, however, to achieve the desired effect.

>   **CHANGE** Without the fuel of tax incentives, our economic engine would operate less efficiently. (It would not operate at all without fuel.)
>   **TO** Without the fuel of tax incentives, our economic engine would sputter and die. (This is not only apt, but it also states a rather dry fact in a colorful manner—always a desirable objective.)

A figure of speech must also be consistent to be effective.

>   **CHANGE** We must get our research program *back on the track,* and we are counting on you to *carry the ball.* (inconsistent)
>   **TO** We must get our research program back on the track, and we are counting on you to do it. (inconsistency removed)

A figure of speech should not, however, attract more attention to itself than to the point the writer is making.

> **EXAMPLE** The whine of the engine sounded like ten thousand cats having their tails pulled by ten thousand mischievous children.

Trite figures of speech, which are called *clichés,* defeat the purpose of a figure of speech—to be fresh, original, and vivid. A surprise that comes "like a bolt out of the blue" is not much of a surprise. It is better to use no figure of speech than to use a trite one.

TYPES OF FIGURES OF SPEECH

Analogy is a comparison between two objects or concepts that shows ways in which they are similar. It is very useful in business writing, especially when you are writing to an educated but nontechnical audience. In effect, analogies say "A is to B as C is to D." The resemblance between these concepts is partial but close enough to provide a striking way of illuminating the relationship the writer wishes to establish.

> **EXAMPLE** Pollution (A) is to the environment (B) as cancer (C) is to the body (D).

Antithesis is a statement in which two contrasting ideas are set off against each other in a balanced syntactical structure.

> **EXAMPLES** Art is long, but life is short.

Hyperbole is gross exaggeration used to achieve an effect or emphasis.

> **EXAMPLE** He *murdered* me on the tennis court.

Litotes are understatements, for emphasis or effect, achieved by denying the opposite of the point you are making.

> **EXAMPLES** Seventy dollars is not a small price for a book.

Metaphor is a figure of speech that points out similarities between two things by treating them as though they were the same thing. Metaphor states that the thing being described *is* the thing to which it is being compared.

> **EXAMPLE** He is the sales department's *utility infielder.*

Metonymy is a figure of speech that uses one aspect of a thing to represent it, such as *the red, white, and blue* for the American flag, *the blue* for the sky, and *wheels* for an automobile. This device is common in everyday speech because it gives our expressions a colorful twist.

> **EXAMPLE** *The hard hat* area of the labor force was especially hurt by the current economic recession.

Simile is a direct comparison of two essentially unlike things, linking them with the word *like* or *as.*

EXAMPLE   His feelings about his business rival are so bitter that in recent conversations with his staff he has returned to the subject compulsively, *like a man scratching an itch.*

Personification is a figure of speech that attributes human characteristics to nonhuman things or abstract ideas. One characteristically speaks of the *birth* of a planet and the *stubbornness* of an engine that will not start.

EXAMPLE   Early tribes of human beings attributed scientific discoveries to gods. To them, fire was not *a child of man's brain* but a gift from Prometheus.

idioms

Idioms are groups of words that have a special meaning apart from their literal meaning. Someone who "runs for office" in the United States, for example, need not be a track star. The same person would "stand for office" in England. In both nations, the individual is seeking public office; only the idioms of the two countries differ. This difference indicates why idioms give foreign writers and speakers trouble.

EXAMPLE   The judge *threw the book at* the convicted arsonist.

The foreigner must memorize such expressions; they cannot logically be understood. The native writer has little trouble understanding idioms and need not attempt to avoid them in writing, provided the reader is equally at home with them. Idioms are often helpful shortcuts, in fact, that can make writing more vigorous and natural.

If there is any chance that your writing might be translated into another language or read in other English-speaking countries, eliminate obvious idiomatic expressions that might puzzle readers.

Idioms are the reason certain prepositions follow certain verbs, nouns, and adjectives. Since there is no sure system to explain such usages, the best advice is to check a dictionary. The following are some common pairings that give writers trouble:

absolve from (responsibility)	adapt from (change)
absolve of (crimes)	agree on (terms)
accordance with	agree to (a plan)
according to	agree with (a person)
accountable for (actions)	angry with (a person)
accountable to (a person)	angry at, about (a thing)
accused by (a person)	apply for (a position)
accused of (a deed)	apply to (contact)
adapt for (a purpose)	argue for, against (a policy)
adapt to (a situation)	argue with (a person)

arrive in (a city, country)

arrive at (a specific location, conclusion)

blame for (an action)

blame on (a person)

compare to (things that are similar but not the same kind)

compare with (things of the same kind to determine similarities and differences)

concur in (consensus)

concur with (a person)

convenient for (a purpose)

convenient to (a place)

correspond to, with (a thing)

correspond with (a person)

differ about, over (an issue)

differ from (a thing)

differ with (a person)

differ on (amounts, terms)

disagree on (an issue, plan)

disagree with (a person)

divide between, among

divide into (parts)

expect from (things)

expect of (people)

impatient for (something)

impatient with (someone)

necessary for (an action)

necessary to (a state of being)

occupied by (things, people)

occupied with (actions)

opposite of (qualities)

opposite to (positions)

part from (a person)

part with (a thing)

proceed with (a project)

proceed to (begin)

profit by (things)

profit from (actions)

qualify as (a person)

qualify by (experience, actions)

qualify for (a position, award)

reward for (an action)

reward with (a gift)

surrounded by (people)

surrounded with (things)

talk to (a group)

talk with (a person)

wait at (a place)

wait for (a person, event)

intensifiers

Intensifiers are adverbs that emphasize degree, such as *very, quite, rather, such,* and *too.* Although they serve a legitimate and necessary function, they can also seduce the unwary writer who is not on guard against overusing them. Too many intensifiers weaken your writing. When revising your draft, either eliminate intensifiers that do not make a definite contribution, or replace them with specific details.

> CHANGE The team was *quite* happy to receive the *very* good news that it had been awarded a *rather* substantial monetary prize for its design.
>
> TO The team was happy to learn the good news that it had been awarded a $5,000 prize for its design.

The difference is not that the first example is wrong and the second one right, but that the intensifiers in the first example add nothing to the sentence and are therefore superfluous.

Some words (such as *unique, perfect, impossible, final, permanent, infinite,* and *complete*) do not logically permit intensification because they do not permit degrees of comparison. Although usage sometimes ignores this logical restriction, the writer should be aware that to ignore it is, strictly speaking, to defy the basic meanings of these words.

> CHANGE   It was *quite* impossible for the part to fit into its designated position.

> TO   It was impossible for the part to fit into its designated position.

jargon

Jargon is a highly specialized business slang that is unique to an occupational group. If all your readers are members of a particular occupational group, jargon may provide a time-saving and efficient means of communicating with them. For example, finding and correcting the errors in a computer program is referred to by programmers as "debugging." If you have any doubt that your entire reading audience is a part of this group, however, avoid using jargon.

long variants

Guard against inflating plain words beyond their normal value by adding extra prefixes or suffixes, a practice that creates long variants. The following is a list of some normal words followed by their inflated counterparts:

use	utilize
visit	visitation
priority	prioritization
orient	orientate
finish	finalize
connect	interconnect
analysis	analyzation
certified	certification
commercial	commercialistic

(See also the entry on **word choice** in this tabbed section.)

nominalizations

We have a natural tendency to want to make our on-the-job writing sound very formal—even "impressive." One practice that contributes to this tendency is the use of nominalizations, or a weak verb (*make, do, conduct, perform,* and so forth) combined with a noun, when the verb form of the noun would communicate the same idea more effectively in fewer words.

> CHANGE   The quality assurance team will *perform an evaluation* of the new software.

> TO   The quality assurance team will *evaluate* the new software.

You may occasionally find a legitimate use for a nominalization. You might, for example, use a nominalization to slow down the pace of your writing. But if you use nominalizations thoughtlessly or carelessly or just to make your writing sound more formal, the result will be affectation.

parallel structure

Parallel sentence structure requires that sentence elements that are alike in function be alike in construction as well, as in the following example (in which similar actions are stated in similar phrases):

> EXAMPLE   We need a supplementary work force to *handle* peak-hour activity, *free* full-time employees from routine duties, *relieve* operators during lunch breaks, and *replace* vacationing employees.

Parallel structure achieves an economy of words, clarifies meaning, pleases the reader aesthetically, and expresses the equality of its ideas. This technique assists readers because they are able to anticipate the meaning of a sentence element on the basis of its parallel construction. When they recognize the similarity of word order (or construction), readers know that the relationship between the new sentence element and the subject is the same as the relationship between the last sentence element and the subject. Because of this they can go from one idea to another more quickly and confidently.
   Parallel structure can be achieved with words, phrases, or clauses.

> EXAMPLES   The computer instruction contains *fetch, initiate,* and *execute* stages. (parallel words)
>
> The computer instruction contains *a fetch stage, an initiate stage,* and *an execute stage.* (parallel phrases)
>
> *The computer instruction contains a fetch stage, it contains an initiate stage,* and *it contains an execute stage.* (parallel clauses)

Parallelism is most frequently accomplished by the use of phrases.

> EXAMPLES   I was convinced of their competence *by their conduct, by their reputation,* and *by their survival* in a competitive business. (prepositional phrases)
>
> *Filling the gas tank, testing the windshield wipers,* and *checking tire pressure* are essential to preparing for a long trip. (gerund phrases)

From childhood the artist had made it a habit *to observe people, to store up the impressions they made upon him,* and *to draw conclusions about human beings from them.* (infinitive phrases)

Correlative conjunctions *(either . . . or, neither . . . nor, not only . . . but also)* should always be followed by parallel structure. Both members of these pairs should be followed immediately by the same grammatical form: two words, two similar phrases, or two similar clauses.

EXAMPLES   Viruses carry either *DNA* or *RNA,* never both. (words)

Clearly, neither *serologic tests* nor *virus isolation studies* alone would have been adequate. (phrases)

Either *we must increase our operational efficiency* or *we must decrease our production goals.* (clauses)

To make a parallel construction clear and effective, it is often best to repeat a preposition, an article, a pronoun, a subordinating conjunction, a helping verb, or the mark of an infinitive.

EXAMPLES   The Babylonians had *a* rudimentary geometry and *a* rudimentary astronomy. (article)

My father and *my* teacher agreed that I was not really trying. (pronoun)

To run and be elected is better than *to* run and be defeated. (mark of the infinitive)

The driver *must* be careful to check the gauge and *must* move quickly when the light comes on. (helping verb)

New teams were being established *in* New York and *in* Hawaii. (preposition)

The history of factories shows both *the* benefits and *the* limits of standardization. (article)

Parallel structure is especially important in creating your outline, your table of contents, and your heads because it enables your reader to know the relative value of each item in your table of contents and each head in the body of your document.

positive writing

Presenting positive information as though it were negative is a trap that business writers fall into quite easily because of the complexity of the information they must write about. It is a practice that confuses the reader, however, and one that should be avoided.

CHANGE   If the error does *not* involve data transmission, the special function will *not* be used.

TO   The special function is used only if the error involves data transmission.

In the first sentence, the reader must reverse two negatives to understand the exception that is being stated; the second sentence presents the exception to a rule in a straightforward manner.

On the other hand, negative facts or conclusions should be stated negatively; stating a negative fact or conclusion positively can mislead the reader.

> CHANGE   For the first quarter of this year, employee exposure to airborne lead has been maintained to within 10 percent of acceptable state health standards.

> TO   For the first quarter of this year, employee exposure to airborne lead continues to be 10 percent above acceptable state health standards.

Even if what you are saying is negative, do not use any more negative words than are necessary.

> CHANGE   We are withholding your shipment until we receive your payment.

> TO   We will forward your shipment as soon as we receive your payment.

repetition

The deliberate use of repetition to build a sustained effort or emphasize a feeling or idea can be quite powerful.

> EXAMPLE   Similarly, atoms *come and go* in a molecule, but the molecule *remains;* molecules *come and go* in a cell, but the cell *remains;* cells *come and go* in a body, but the body *remains;* persons *come and go* in an organization, but the organization *remains.*

> —Kenneth Boulding, *Beyond Economics* (Ann Arbor: U of Michigan P, 1968) 131.

Repeating key words from a previous sentence or paragraph can also be used effectively to achieve transition.

> EXAMPLE   For many years, *oil* has been a major industrial energy source. However, *oil* supplies are limited, and other sources of energy must be developed.

Be consistent in the word or phrase you use to refer to something. In business writing, it is generally better to repeat a word (so there will be no question in the reader's mind that you mean the same thing) than to use a synonym in order to avoid repeating it. Your primary goal in business writing is effective and precise communication rather than elegance.

> CHANGE   Several recent *analyses* support our conclusion. These *studies* cast doubts on the feasibility of long-range forecasting. The *reports*, however, are strictly theoretical.

> TO   Several recent theoretical *studies* support our conclusion. These *studies* cast doubts on the feasibility of long-range forecasting. They are, however, strictly theoretical.

Purposeless repetition, however, makes a sentence awkward and hides its key ideas.

> CHANGE He *said that* the customer *said that* the order was canceled.
>
> TO He *said that* the customer canceled the order.

The harm caused to your writing by careless repetition is not limited to words and phrases; the needless repetition of ideas can be equally damaging.

> CHANGE In this modern world of ours today, the well-informed, knowledgeable executive will be well ahead of the competition.
>
> TO To succeed, the contemporary executive must be well informed.

sentence variety

Sentences may be long or short; loose or periodic; simple, compound, complex, or compound-complex; declarative, interrogative, exclamatory, or imperative—even elliptical. There is never a legitimate excuse for letting your sentences become tiresomely alike. However, sentence variety is best achieved during revision; do not let it concern you when you are writing the draft.

SENTENCE LENGTH

Varying sentence length makes writing more interesting to the reader because a long series of sentences of the same length is monotonous. For example, avoid stringing together a number of short independent clauses. Either connect them with subordinating connectives, thereby making some dependent clauses, or make some clauses into separate sentences.

> CHANGE The river is 60 miles long, *and* it averages 50 yards in width, *and* its depth averages 8 feet.
>
> TO This river, *which* is 60 miles long and averages 50 yards in width, has an average depth of 8 feet.
>
> OR This river is 60 miles long. It averages 50 yards in width and 8 feet in depth.

Short sentences can often be effectively combined by converting verbs into adjectives.

> CHANGE The steeplejack *fainted.* He collapsed on the scaffolding.
>
> TO The *fainting* steeplejack collapsed on the scaffolding.

Although too many short sentences make your writing sound choppy and immature, a short sentence can be effective at the end of a passage of long ones.

EXAMPLE   During the past two decades, many changes have occurred in American life, the extent, durability, and significance of which no one has yet measured. *No one can.*

In general terms, short sentences are good for emphatic, memorable statements. Long sentences are good for detailed explanations and support. There is nothing inherently wrong with a long sentence, or even with a complicated one, as long as its meaning is clear and direct. Sentence length becomes an element of style when varied for emphasis or contrast; a conspicuously short or long sentence can be used to good effect.

WORD ORDER

When a series of sentences all begin in exactly the same way (usually with an article and a noun) the result is likely to be monotonous. You can make your sentences more interesting by occasionally starting with a modifying word, phrase, or clause. But overdoing this technique can be monotonous, so use it in moderation.

EXAMPLES   *Exhausted,* the project director slumped into a chair. (single modifier)

To reach the top job, she presented constructive alternatives when current policies failed to produce results. (phrase)

Because we now know the result of the survey, we may proceed with certainty. (clause)

Inverted sentence order can be an effective way to achieve variety, but be careful not to overdo it.

EXAMPLE   Then occurred the event that gained us the contract.

LOOSE/PERIODIC/INSERTION SENTENCES

A loose sentence makes its major point at the beginning and then adds subordinate phrases and clauses that develop or modify the point. A periodic sentence delays its main idea until the end by presenting modifiers or subordinate ideas first, thus holding the reader's interest until the end.

EXAMPLES   The attitude of the American citizen toward automation has undergone a profound change during the last decade or so. (loose)

During the last decade or so, the attitude of the American citizen toward automation has undergone a profound change. (periodic)

Experiment in your own writing, especially during revision, with shifts from loose sentences to periodic sentences. Avoid the sing-song monotony of a long series of loose sentences, particularly a series containing coordinate clauses joined by conjunctions. Subordinating some thoughts to others makes your sentences more interesting.

CHANGE   The auditorium was filled to capacity, *and* the chairman of the board came onto the stage. The meeting started at eight o'clock, *and* the president made his report of the company's operations during the past year. The audience of stockholders was obviously unhappy, *but* the members of the board of directors all were reelected.

TO   By eight o'clock, *when* the chairman of the board came onto the stage and the meeting began, the auditorium was filled to capacity. *Although* the audience of stockholders was obviously unhappy with the president's report of the company's operations during the past year, the members of the board of directors all were reelected.

For variety, you may also alter the normal sentence order with an inserted phrase or clause.

EXAMPLE   Titanium fills the gap, *both in weight and strength,* between aluminum and steel.

The technique of inserting such a phrase or clause is good for emphasis, for providing detail, for breaking monotony, and for regulating pace.

stacked modifiers

Some writing is unclear or difficult to read because it contains stacked modifiers, or strings of modifiers preceding nouns.

CHANGE   Your *staffing level authorization reassessment* plan should result in a major improvement.

In this sentence the noun *plan* is preceded by four modifiers; this string of modifiers slows the reader and makes the sentence awkward and clumsy. Stacked modifiers often result from an overuse of jargon or vogue words. Occasionally, they occur when writers mistakenly attempt to be concise by eliminating short prepositions or connectives—exactly the words that help to make sentences clear and readable. See how breaking up the jammed modifiers makes the previous example easier to read.

TO   Your plan for the reassessment of staffing-level authorizations should result in a major improvement.

telegraphic style

Telegraphic style condenses writing by omitting *articles, pronouns, conjunctions,* and *transitional expressions.* Although conciseness is important in writing, writers sometimes make their sentences too brief by omitting these words. Telegraphic style forces the reader to mentally supply the missing words. Compare the following two passages, and notice how much easier the revised version reads (the added words are italicized).

CHANGE Take following action when treating serious burn. Remove loose clothing on or near burn. Cover injury with clean dressing and wash area around burn. Secure dressing with tape. Separate fingers/toes with gauze/cloth to prevent sticking. Do not apply medication unless doctor prescribes.

TO Take *the* following action when treating a serious burn. Remove *any* loose clothing on or near *the* burn. Cover *the* injury with *a* clean dressing, *and* wash *the* area around *the* burn. Then secure *the* dressing with tape. Separate fingers *or* toes with gauze *or* cloth to prevent *them from* sticking *together.* Do not apply medication unless *a* doctor prescribes *it.*

Telegraphic style can also produce ambiguity, as the following example demonstrates.

CHANGE Grasp knob and adjust lever before raising boom.

Does this sentence mean that the reader should *adjust the lever* or *grasp an adjust lever?*

TO Grasp the knob and the adjust lever before raising the boom.

OR Grasp the knob and adjust the lever before raising the boom.

As a writer, remember that although you may save yourself work by writing telegraphically, your readers will have to work that much harder to read—or decipher—your writing.

vague words

A vague word is one that is imprecise in the context in which it is used. Some words encompass such a broad range of meanings that there is no focus for their definition. Words such as *real, nice, important, good, bad, contact, thing,* and *fine* are often called "omnibus words" because they can mean everything to everybody. In speech we sometimes use words that are less than precise, but our vocal inflections and the context of our conversation make their meanings clear. Since writing cannot rely on vocal inflections, avoid using vague words. Be concrete and specific.

CHANGE It was a *meaningful* meeting, and we got a *lot* done.

TO The meeting resolved three questions: pay scales, fringe benefits, and work loads.

word choice

As Mark Twain once said, "The difference between the right word and almost the right word is the difference between 'lightning' and 'lightning bug.'" The most important goal in choosing the right word in business writing is the preciseness implied by Twain's comment. Vague words and abstract words defeat preciseness because they do not convey the writer's meaning directly and clearly.

> CHANGE It was a *meaningful* meeting.

>> TO The meeting helped both sides understand each other's position.

In the first sentence, *meaningful* ironically conveys no meaning at all. See how the revised sentence says specifically what made the meeting meaningful. Although abstract words may at times be appropriate to your topic, their unnecessary use creates dry and lifeless writing.

> ABSTRACT work, fast, food

> CONCRETE sawing, 110 m.p.h., steak

Being aware of the connotation and denotation of words will help you anticipate the reader's reaction to the words you choose. *Connotation* is the suggested or implied meaning of a word beyond its dictionary definition. *Denotation* is the literal, or primary, dictionary meaning of a word.

Understanding antonyms and synonyms will increase your ability to choose the proper word. *Antonyms* are words with nearly the opposite meaning (fresh/stale), and *synonyms* are words with nearly the same meaning (notorious/infamous).

Trite language consists of stale and worn phrases and clichés.

> CHANGE We will finish the project *quick as a flash.*

>> TO We will finish the project *quickly.*

Avoid using jargon unless you are certain that all of your readers understand the terms. Avoid choosing words with the objective of impressing your reader; also avoid using long variants, which are elongated forms of words used only to impress *(utilize* for *use).* Using a euphemism (an inoffensive substitute for a word that is distasteful or offensive) may help you avoid embarrassment, but the overuse of euphemisms becomes affectation. Using more words than necessary *(in the neighborhood of* for *about, for the reason that* for *because, in the event that* for *if)* is certain to interfere with clarity.

OVERVIEW

Grammar is the systematic description of the way words work together to form a coherent language; in this sense, it is an explanation of the structure of a language. However, grammar is popularly taken to mean the set of "rules" that governs how a language ought to be spoken and written; in this sense, it refers to the usage conventions of a language.

These two meanings of grammar—how the language functions and how it ought to function—are easily confused. To clarify the distinction, consider the expression *ain't*. Unless used purposely for its colloquial flavor, *ain't* is unacceptable to careful speakers and writers because a convention of usage prohibits its use. Yet taken strictly as a part of speech, the term functions perfectly well as a verb; whether it appears in a declarative sentence ("I *ain't* going.") or an interrogative sentence ("*Ain't* I going?"), it conforms to the normal pattern for all verbs in the English language. Although we may not approve of its use in a sentence, we cannot argue that it is ungrammatical.

Parts of speech is a term used to describe the class of words to which a particular word belongs, according to its function in a sentence; that is, each function in a sentence (naming, asserting, describing, joining, acting, modifying, exclaiming) is performed by a word belonging to a certain part of speech. If a word's function is to name something, for example, it is a noun or pronoun. If a word's function is to make an assertion about something, it is a verb. If its function is to describe or modify something, the word is an adjective or an adverb. If its function is to join or link one element of the sentence to another, it is a conjunction or a preposition.

To achieve clarity, writers need to know both grammar (as a description of the way words work together) and the conventions of usage. Knowing the conventions of usage helps writers select the appropriate over the inappropriate word or expression. A knowledge of grammar helps them diagnose and correct problems arising from how words and phrases function in relation to one another.

In addition to the entries in this tabbed section, you may wish to see the USAGE and STYLE AND CLARITY tabs for entries related to this important subject.

adjectives

An adjective makes the meaning of a noun or pronoun more specific by pointing out one of its qualities (descriptive adjective) or by imposing boundaries on it (limiting adjective).

> **EXAMPLES** a *hot* iron (descriptive)
>
> *ten* automobiles (limiting)
>
> *his* desk (limiting)

Limiting adjectives include articles *(a, an, the)*, demonstrative adjectives *(this, that, these, those)*, possessive adjectives *(my, his, her, your, our, their)*, interrogative and relative adjectives *(whose, which, what)*, numeral adjectives *(two, first)*, and indefinite adjectives *(all, none, some, any)*.

COMPARISON OF ADJECTIVES

Most one-syllable adjectives add the suffix *-er* to show comparison with one other item and the suffix *-est* to show comparison with two or more other items.

> **EXAMPLES** The first ingot is *bright.* (positive form)
>
> The second ingot is *brighter.* (comparative form)
>
> The third ingot is *brightest.* (superlative form)

Many two-syllable adjectives and most three-syllable adjectives are preceded by *more* or *most* to form the comparative or the superlative.

> **EXAMPLES** The new facility is *more impressive* than the old one.
>
> The new facility is the *most impressive* in the city.

A few adjectives have irregular forms of comparison *(much, more, most; little, less, least; some, more, most; many, more, most; bad, worse, worst; good, better, best)*.

Absolute words *(round, unique)* are not logically subject to comparison.

PLACEMENT OF ADJECTIVES

Within a sentence, adjectives may appear before the nouns they modify (the attributive position) or after the nouns they modify (the predicative position).

> **EXAMPLES** The *small* jobs are given priority. (attributive position)
>
> Tests are taken even when exposure is *brief.* (predicative position)

When an adjective follows a linking verb, it is called a predicate adjective.

> **EXAMPLES** The warehouse is *full.*
>
> The lens is *convex.*
>
> His department is *efficient.*

adverbs

An adverb modifies the action or condition expressed by a verb.

> **EXAMPLE** The recording head hit the surface of the disc *hard*. (The adverb tells *how* the recording head hit the disc.)

An adverb may also modify an adjective, another adverb, or a clause.

> **EXAMPLES** The graphics department used *extremely* bright colors. (modifying an adjective)
>
> The redesigned brake pad lasted *much* longer. (modifying another adverb)
>
> *Surprisingly,* the machine failed. (modifying a clause)

An adverb answers one of the following questions:

Where? (adverb of place)

> **EXAMPLE** Move the throttle *forward* slightly.

When? (adverb of time)

> **EXAMPLE** Replace the thermostat *immediately*.

How? (adverb of manner)

> **EXAMPLE** Add the chemical *cautiously*.

How much? (adverb of degree)

> **EXAMPLE** The *nearly* completed report was lost in the move.

COMPARISON OF ADVERBS

One-syllable adverbs use the comparative ending *-er* and the superlative ending *-est*.

> **EXAMPLES** This copier is *faster* than the old one.
>
> This copier is the *fastest* of the three tested.

Most adverbs with two or more syllables end in *-ly*, and most adverbs ending in *-ly* are compared by inserting the comparative *more* or *less* or the superlative *most* or *least* in front of them.

> **EXAMPLES** He moved *more quickly* than the other company's salesman.
>
> *Most surprisingly,* the engine failed during the test phase.

There are a few irregular adverbs that require a change in form to indicate comparison (*well, better, best; badly, worse, worst; far, farther, farthest*).

> **EXAMPLES** The training program functions *well*.
>
> Our training program functions *better* than most others in the industry.
>
> Many consider our training program the *best* in the industry.

PLACEMENT OF ADVERBS

The adverb should usually be placed in front of the verb it modifies.

> EXAMPLE The pilot *meticulously* performed the preflight check.

An adverb may, however, follow the verb (or the verb and its object) that it modifies.

> EXAMPLES The gauge dipped *suddenly*.
>
> They repaired the computer *quickly*.

An adverb may be placed between a helping verb and a main verb.

> EXAMPLE In this temperature range, the pressure will *quickly* drop.

Such adverbs as *nearly, only, almost, just,* and *hardly* should be placed immediately before the words they limit.

> CHANGE The punch press with the auxiliary equipment *only* costs $47,000.
>
> TO The punch press with the auxiliary equipment costs *only* $47,000.

The first sentence is ambiguous because it might be understood to mean that only the punch press *with auxiliary equipment* costs $47,000.

agreement

Agreement, grammatically, means the correspondence in form between different elements of a sentence to indicate *person, number, gender,* and *case.* A pronoun must agree with its antecedent, and a verb must agree with its subject.

A subject and its verb must agree in number and in person.

> EXAMPLES The *design is* an acceptable one. (The first-person singular subject, *design,* requires the first-person singular verb, *is.*)
>
> The new *products are* going into production soon. (The third-person plural subject, *products,* requires the third-person plural form of the verb *are.*)

A pronoun and its antecedent must agree in person, number, and gender.

> EXAMPLES The *employees* report that *they* become less efficient as the humidity rises. (The third-person plural subject, *employees,* requires the third-person plural pronoun, *they.*)
>
> *Mr. Joiner* said that *he* would serve as a negotiator. (The third-person singular, masculine subject, *Mr. Joiner,* requires the third-person singular, masculine form of the pronoun, *he.*)

articles

As a part of speech, articles are considered to be adjectives because they modify the items they designate by either limiting them or making them more precise. There are two kinds of articles, indefinite and definite.

The indefinite articles *a* and *an* denote an unspecified item.

> EXAMPLE *A* program was run on our new computer. (Not a specific program, but an unspecified program.)

The definite article *the* denotes a particular item.

> EXAMPLE *The* program was run on the computer. (Not just any program, but *the* specific program.)

The choice between *a* and *an* depends on the sound rather than the letter following the article. Use *a* before words beginning with a consonant sound (*a* person, *a* happy person, *a* historical event). Use *an* before words beginning with a vowel sound (*an* uncle, *an* hour). With abbreviations, use *a* before initial letters having a consonant sound (*a* TWA flight). Use *an* before initial letters having a vowel sound (*an* SLN report).

> EXAMPLES The year's activities are summarized in *a* one-page report. (The *o* in *one* is a consonant sound, so the article *a* precedes the word.)
>
> He wrote *a* manual on that subject.
>
> It was *a* historic event for the laboratory. (The *h* in *historic* is a consonant sound.)
>
> The project manager felt that it was *a* unique situation. (The *u* in *unique* is the consonant sound of *y*, as in *you*.)

Do not capitalize articles when they appear in titles except as the first word of the title.

> EXAMPLE *Time* magazine reviewed *The Old World's New Order.*

clauses

A clause is a syntactical construction, or group of words, that contains a subject and a predicate and functions as part of a sentence. Every subject-predicate word group in a sentence is a clause, and every sentence must contain at least one independent clause.

A clause that could stand alone as a simple sentence is an *independent clause.*

> EXAMPLE *The scaffolding fell* when the rope broke.

A clause that could not stand alone if the rest of the sentence were deleted is a *dependent clause.*

> **EXAMPLE** I was at the St. Louis branch *when the decision was made.*

A clause may be connected with the rest of its sentence by a coordinating conjunction, a subordinating conjunction, a relative pronoun, or a conjunctive adverb.

> **EXAMPLES** It was 500 miles to the facility, *so* we made arrangements to fly. (coordinating conjunction)
>
> Mission control will have to be alert *because* at launch the space laboratory will contain a highly flammable fuel. (subordinating conjunction)
>
> It was Robert M. Fano *who* designed and developed the earliest "Multiple Access Computer" system at M.I.T. (relative pronoun)
>
> It was dark when we arrived; *nevertheless,* we began the tour of the factory. (conjunctive adverb)

collective nouns

Although collective nouns are grammatically singular in form, they name a group or collection of persons, places, or things.

> **EXAMPLES** army, committee, crowd, team, public, class, jury, humanity, herd, flock

When a collective noun refers to a group as a whole, it is treated as singular for purposes of grammatical agreement.

> **EXAMPLE** The jury *was* deadlocked; *it* had to be disbanded.

When a collective noun refers to individuals within a group, it is treated as plural.

> **EXAMPLE** The jury *were* allowed to go to *their* homes for the night.

complements

A complement is a word, phrase, or clause used in the predicate of a sentence to complete the meaning of the sentence.

> **EXAMPLES** Pilots fly *airplanes.* (word)
>
> To live is *to risk death.* (phrase)
>
> John knew *that he would be late.* (clause)

Four kinds of complements are generally recognized: *direct object, indirect object, objective complement,* and *subjective complement.*

A *direct object* is a noun or noun equivalent that receives the action of a transitive verb; it answers the question *what* or *whom* after the verb.

EXAMPLES John built *an antenna.* (noun)

I like *to work.* (verbal)

I like *it.* (pronoun)

I like *what I saw.* (noun clause)

An *indirect object* is a noun or noun equivalent that occurs with a direct object after certain kinds of transitive verbs such as *give, wish, cause,* and *tell.* It answers the question *to whom* or *for whom* (or *to what* or *for what*).

EXAMPLES We should buy *the Milwaukee office* a color copier. (*color copier* is the direct object)

An *objective complement* completes the meaning of a sentence by revealing something about the object of its transitive verb. An objective complement may be either a noun or an adjective.

EXAMPLES They call him *a genius.* (noun)

We painted the building *white.* (adjective)

A *subjective complement,* which follows a linking verb rather than a transitive verb, describes the subject. A subjective complement may be either a noun or an adjective.

EXAMPLES His sister is *an engineer.* (noun)

His brother is *ill.* (adjective)

conjunctions

A conjunction connects words, phrases, or clauses and can also indicate the relationship between the two elements it connects.

A *coordinating conjunction* joins two sentence elements that have identical functions. The coordinating conjunctions are *and, but, or, for, nor, yet,* and *so.*

EXAMPLES Nature *and* technology are only two conditions that affect petroleum operations around the world. (joining two nouns)

To hear *and* to obey are two different things. (joining two phrases)

He would like to include the test results, *but* that would make the report too long. (joining two clauses)

Correlative conjunctions are used in pairs. The correlative conjunctions are *either . . . or, neither . . . nor, not only . . . but also, both . . . and,* and *whether . . . or.*

EXAMPLE The inspector will arrive *either* on Wednesday *or* on Thursday.

A *subordinating conjunction* connects sentence elements of different weights, normally independent and dependent clauses. The most frequently used are *so, although, after, because, if, where, than, since, as, unless, before, that, though, when,* and *whereas.*

> **EXAMPLE** I left the office *after* I had finished writing the report.

A *conjunctive adverb* is an adverb that has the force of a conjunction because it is used to join two independent clauses. The most common conjunctive adverbs are *however, moreover, therefore, further, then, consequently, besides, accordingly, also,* and *thus.*

> **EXAMPLE** The engine performed well in the laboratory; *however,* it failed under road conditions.

Conjunctions in the titles of books, articles, plays, and movies should not be capitalized unless they are the first or last word in the title.

> **EXAMPLE** The book *Amateur and Professional Writing* was edited by Herman Waldren.

Occasionally, a conjunction may begin a sentence and even a paragraph, as in the following example.

> **EXAMPLE** The executive is impressed by the marvels of computer technology before him; he has difficulty in understanding the programming endeavor that makes the computer run. He walks away feeling that the annual report will look better because of these machines.
>
> *But* the balloon bursts the first time the system requires a modification, and the lead programmer is no longer with the company or cannot recall the details of the program due to the passage of time. . . .
>
> —William L. Harper, *Data Processing Documentation* (Englewood Cliffs, NJ: Prentice, 1980) 145.

dangling modifiers

Phrases that do not clearly and logically refer to the proper noun or pronoun are called *dangling modifiers.* Dangling modifiers usually appear at the beginning of a sentence as an introductory phrase.

> **CHANGE** *While eating lunch in the cafeteria,* the computer malfunctioned. (The problem, of course, is that the sentence neglects to mention *who* was eating lunch in the cafeteria.)
>
> **TO** While *the operator* was eating lunch in the cafeteria, the computer malfunctioned.

They can, however, appear at the end of the sentence as well.

CHANGE The program gains in efficiency *by eliminating the superfluous instructions.* (An action is stated, but no one is identified who could perform the stated action.)

TO The program gains in efficiency *when you* eliminate the superfluous instructions.

To test whether a phrase is a dangling modifier, turn it into a clause with a subject and a verb. If the expanded phrase and the independent clause do not have the same subject, the phrase is dangling.

CHANGE After finishing the research, the paper was easy to write. (The implied subject of the phrase is intended to be *I*, and the subject of the independent clause is *paper;* therefore, the sentence contains a dangling modifier.)

TO After finishing the research, *I found that* the paper was easy to write. (Changing the subject of the independent clause to agree with the implied subject of the introductory phrase eliminates the dangling modifier.)

OR After I finished the research, the paper was easy to write. (This version changes the phrase to a dependent clause with an explicit subject.)

demonstrative adjectives

The demonstrative adjectives *this, these, that,* and *those* "point to" the thing they modify, specifying its position in space or time.

EXAMPLES *This* proposal is the one we accepted.

That proposal would have been impracticable.

These problems remain to be solved.

Those problems are not insurmountable.

Demonstrative adjectives often cause problems when they modify the nouns *kind, type,* and *sort.* The demonstrative adjectives used with these nouns should agree with them in number.

EXAMPLES this kind/these kinds

that type/those types

this sort/these sorts

Confusion often develops when the preposition *of* is added ("this kind *of*," "these kinds *of*") and the object of the preposition is not made to conform in number to the demonstrative adjective and its noun.

CHANGE *This kind of* hydraulic *cranes* is best.

TO *This kind of* hydraulic *crane* is best.

CHANGE *These kinds of* hydraulic *crane* are best.

TO *These kinds of* hydraulic *cranes* are best.

English as a second language (ESL)

Learning to write well in a second language takes a great deal of effort and practice. The most effective way to improve your written command of English is to read widely beyond the reports and professional articles required by your job. Read magazine and newspaper articles, novels, biographies, short stories, or any other writing that interests you.

Persistent problem areas for nonnative speakers include the following:

- count and noncount nouns
- articles
- gerunds and infinitives
- adjective clauses
- present perfect verb tense

COUNT AND NONCOUNT NOUNS

Count nouns refer to things that can be counted: *tables, pencils, projects, specialists.* Noncount nouns identify things that cannot be counted: *electricity, water, oil, air, wood, love, loyalty, pride, harmony.*

The distinction between whether something can or cannot be counted determines the form of the noun to use (singular or plural), the kind of article that precedes it (*a, an, the,* or no article), and the kind of limiting adjective it requires (*fewer* or *less, much* or *many,* and so on). This distinction can be confusing with such words as *electricity* or *oil.* Although we can count watt hours of electricity or barrels of oil, counting becomes inappropriate when we use the words *electricity* and *oil* in a general sense, as in "Oil is a limited resource."

ARTICLES

This discussion of articles applies only to common nouns (not to proper nouns, such as the names of people) because count and noncount nouns are always common nouns.

The general rule is that every count noun must be preceded by an article (*a, an,* or *the*), a demonstrative adjective (*this, that, these*), a possessive adjective (*my, her, their,* and so on), or some expression of quantity (such as *one, two, several, many, a few, a lot of, some,* and *no*). The article, adjective, or expression of quantity appears either directly in front of the noun or in front of the whole noun phrase.

EXAMPLES Mary read *a* book last week. (The article *a* appears directly in front of the noun *book.*)

Those books Mary read were long and boring. (The demonstrative adjective *those* appears directly in front of the noun *books*.)

Their book was long and boring. (The possessive adjective *their* appears directly in front of the noun *book*.)

Some books Mary read were long and boring. (The indefinite adjective *some* appears directly in front of the noun *books*.)

The articles *a* and *an* are used with nouns that refer to any one thing out of the whole class of those items.

EXAMPLE Bill has *a* pen. (Bill could have *any* pen.)

The article *the* is used with nouns that refer to a specific item that both the reader and writer can identify.

EXAMPLE Bill has *the* pen. (Bill has a *specific* pen and both the reader and the writer know which specific one it is.)

The only exception to this rule occurs when the writer is making a generalization. When making generalizations with count nouns, writers can either use *a* or *an* with a singular count noun, or they can use no article with a plural count noun. Consider the following generalization using an article.

EXAMPLE An egg is a good source of protein. *(any egg, all eggs, eggs in general)*

However, the following generalization uses a plural noun with no article.

EXAMPLE Eggs are good sources of protein. *(any egg, all eggs, eggs in general)*

When making generalizations with noncount nouns, do not use an article in front of the noncount noun.

EXAMPLE Sugar is bad for your teeth.

See also the entry on **articles** in this tabbed section.

GERUNDS AND INFINITIVES

Nonnative writers are often puzzled by which form of a verbal (a verb used as another part of speech) to use when it functions as the direct object of a verb. No consistent rule exists for distinguishing between the use of an infinitive or a gerund after a verb when it is used as an object. Sometimes a verb takes an infinitive as its object, sometimes it takes a gerund, and sometimes it takes either an infinitive or a gerund. At times, even the base form of the verb is used.

GERUND AS A COMPLEMENT

EXAMPLE He enjoys *working*.

INFINITIVE AS A COMPLEMENT

EXAMPLE He promised *to fulfill* his part of the contract.

GERUND OR AN INFINITIVE AS A COMPLEMENT

EXAMPLES It began *raining* soon after we arrived. (gerund)

It began *to rain* soon after we arrived. (infinitive)

BASIC VERB FORM AS A COMPLEMENT

EXAMPLE The president had the technician *reassigned* to another project.

To make these distinctions accurately, you must rely on what you hear native speakers use or what you read.

ADJECTIVE CLAUSES

Because of the variety of ways adjective clauses are constructed in different languages, they can be particularly troublesome for nonnative speakers. You need to remember a few guidelines when using adjective clauses in order to form them correctly.

Place an adjective clause directly after the noun it modifies.

> **CHANGE** The tall man is a vice-president of the company *who is standing across the room.*
>
> **TO** The tall man *who is standing across the room* is a vice-president of the company.

The adjective clause *who is standing across the room* modifies *man,* not *company,* and thus comes directly after *man.*

Avoid using a relative pronoun with another pronoun in an adjective clause.

> **CHANGE** The man *who he* sits at that desk is my boss.
>
> **TO** The man *who* sits at that desk is my boss.
>
> **CHANGE** The man *whom* we met *him* at the meeting is on the board of directors.
>
> **TO** The man *whom* we met at the meeting is on the board of directors.

PRESENT PERFECT VERB TENSE

As a general rule, use the present perfect tense when referring to events completed in the past, but at nonspecified times. When a specific time is mentioned, use the simple past. Notice the difference in the two sentences following.

> **EXAMPLES** I *wrote* the letter yesterday. (simple past tense—the time when the action took place is specified.)
>
> I *have written* the letter. (present perfect tense—no specific time is mentioned.)

Use the present perfect tense to describe actions that were repeated several or many times in the unspecified past.

> **EXAMPLES** She *has written* that report three times.
>
> The president and his chief advisor *have met* many times over the past few months.

Use the present perfect with a *since* or *for* phrase when describing actions that began in the past and continue up to the present.

> **EXAMPLES** This company *has been* in business *for* ten years.
>
> This company *has been* in business *since* 1983.

gerunds

A gerund is a verbal ending in -*ing* that is used as a noun. A gerund may be used as a *subject*, a *direct object*, an *object of a preposition*, a *subjective complement*, or an *appositive*.

> **EXAMPLES** *Estimating* is an important managerial skill. (subject)
>
> I find *estimating* difficult. (direct object)
>
> We were unprepared for their *coming*. (object of a preposition)
>
> Seeing is *believing*. (subjective complement)
>
> My primary departmental function, *programming*, occupies about two-thirds of my time on the job. (appositive)

Only the possessive form of a noun or pronoun should precede a gerund.

> **EXAMPLES** *John's* working has not affected his grades.
>
> *His* working has not affected his grades.

indefinite pronouns

Indefinite pronouns do not specify a particular person or thing; they specify any one of a class or group of persons or things. *Any, another, anyone, anything, both, each, either, everybody, few, many, most, much, neither, none, several, some* and *such* are indefinite pronouns. Most require singular verbs.

> **EXAMPLES** If *either* of the vice-presidents *is* late, we will delay the meeting.
>
> *Neither* of them *was* available for comment.
>
> *Each* of the writers *has* a unique style.
>
> *Everyone* in our department *has* completed the form.

But some indefinite pronouns require plural verbs.

> **EXAMPLES** *Many are* called, but *few are* chosen.
>
> *Several* of them *are* aware of the problem.

And a few indefinite pronouns may take either plural or singular verbs, depending on whether the nouns they stand for are plural or singular.

> **EXAMPLES** *Most* of the employees *are* pleased, but *some are* not.
>
> *Most* of the oil *is* imported, but *some is* domestic.

infinitives

An infinitive is the root form of a verb *(go, run, fall, talk, dress, shout)* without the restrictions imposed by person and number. Along with the gerund and participle, it is one of the verbals, or nonfinite verb forms. The infinitive is generally preceded by the word *to,* which, although not an inherent part of the infinitive, is considered to be the sign (or mark) of an infinitive.

> **EXAMPLE** We met in the conference room *to talk* about the new project.

An infinitive may function as a *noun,* an *adjective,* or an *adverb.*

> **EXAMPLES** *To expand* is not the only objective. (noun)
>
> These are the instructions *to follow.* (adjective)
>
> The company struggled *to survive.* (adverb)

The most common mistake made with infinitives is to use the present perfect tense when the simple present tense is sufficient.

> **CHANGE** I should not have tried *to have gone* so early.
>
> **TO** I should not have tried *to go* so early.

SPLITTING INFINITIVES

A split infinitive is one in which an adverb is placed between the mark of the infinitive, *to,* and the infinitive itself. Because they make up a grammatical unit, the infinitive and its sign are better left intact than separated by an intervening adverb.

> **CHANGE** *To* initially *build* the table in the file, you must input transaction records containing the data necessary to construct the record and table.
>
> **TO** *To build* the table in the file initially, you must input transaction records containing the data necessary to construct the record and table.

However, it is better to split an infinitive occasionally than to allow a sentence to become awkward or ambiguous.

misplaced modifiers

A modifier is misplaced when it modifies the wrong word or phrase. Place modifiers as close as possible to the words they are intended to modify. A misplaced modifier can be a word, a phrase, or a clause.

Adverbs are especially likely to be misplaced because they can appear in several positions within a sentence.

EXAMPLES   We *almost* lost all of the parts.

We lost *almost* all of the parts.

The first sentence means that all of the parts were *almost* lost (but they were not), and the second sentence means that a majority of the parts *(almost all)* were in fact lost. To avoid confusion, place words, phrases, and clauses as close as possible to the words they modify. Note the two meanings possible when the phrase is shifted in the following sentences:

EXAMPLES   The equipment *without the accessories* sold the best. (Different types of equipment were available, some with and some without accessories.)

The equipment sold the best *without the accessories.* (One *type* of equipment was available, and the accessories were optional.)

mixed constructions

A mixed construction occurs when a sentence contains grammatical forms that are inconsistent with one another. The most common types of mixed constructions result from the following causes.

TENSE

CHANGE   The pilot *lowered* the landing gear and *is approaching* the runway. (shift from past to present tense)

TO   The pilot *lowered* the landing gear and *approached* the runway.

OR   The pilot *has lowered* the landing gear and *is approaching* the runway.

PERSON

CHANGE   The *technician* should take care in choosing *your* equipment. (shift from third to second person)

TO   The *technician* should take care in choosing *his or her* equipment.

OR   *You* should take care in choosing *your* equipment.

NUMBER

CHANGE   My *car,* though not as fast as the others, *operate* on regular gasoline. (singular subject with plural verb form)

TO   My *car,* though not as fast as the others, *operates* on regular gasoline.

VOICE

CHANGE   *I will check* your report, and then *it will be returned* to you. (shift from active to passive voice)

TO   *I will check* your report and then *return* it to you.

modifiers

Modifiers are words, phrases, or clauses that expand, limit, or make more precise the meaning of other elements in a sentence. Although we can create sentences without modifiers, we often need the detail and clarification they provide.

> EXAMPLES Production decreased. (without modifiers)
>
> *Automobile* production decreased *rapidly.* (with modifiers).

Most modifiers function as *adjectives* or *adverbs.*

An adjective makes the meaning of a noun or pronoun more precise by pointing out one of its qualities or by imposing boundaries on it.

> EXAMPLES *ten* automobiles   *this* crane
>
> an *educated* person   *loud* machinery

An adverb modifies an adjective, another adverb, a verb, or an entire clause.

> EXAMPLES Under test conditions, the brake pad showed *much* less wear than it did under actual conditions. (modifying the adjective *less*)
>
> The wear was *very* much less than under actual conditions. (modifying another adverb, *much*)
>
> The recording head hit the surface of the disc *hard.* (modifying the verb *hit*)
>
> *Surprisingly,* the machine failed even after all the tests that it had passed. (modifying a clause)

mood

The grammatical term *mood* refers to the verb functions that indicate whether the verb is intended to (1) make a statement or ask a question *(indicative mood)*, (2) give a command *(imperative mood)*, or (3) express a hypothetical possibility *(subjunctive mood).*

The *indicative mood* refers to an action or a state that is conceived as fact.

> EXAMPLE The setting *is* correct.

The *imperative mood* expresses a command, suggestion, request, or entreaty. In the imperative mood, the implied subject "you" is not expressed.

> EXAMPLE *Install* the wiring today.

The *subjunctive mood* expresses something that is contrary to fact, conditional, hypothetical, or purely imaginative; it can also express a wish, a doubt, or a possibility. The subjunctive mood may change the form of the verb *be.*

EXAMPLES The senior partner insisted that he (I, you, we, they) *be* in charge of the project.

If we *were* to close the sale today, we would meet our monthly quota.

The most common use of the subjunctive mood is to express clearly whether or not we consider a condition contrary to fact. If so, we use the subjunctive; if not, we use the indicative.

EXAMPLES If I *were* president of the firm, I would change several personnel policies. (subjunctive)

Although I *am* president of the firm, I don't feel that I control every aspect of its policies. (indicative)

nouns

A noun names a person, place, thing, concept, action, or quality. The two basic types of nouns are *proper nouns* and *common nouns.*

Proper nouns, which should be capitalized, name specific persons, places, and things.

EXAMPLES Abraham Lincoln, New York, U.S. Army, Nobel Prize

Common nouns, which should not be capitalized unless they begin sentences, name general classes or categories of persons, places, and things. Common nouns include all types of nouns except proper nouns.

EXAMPLES human, college, knife, bolt, string, faith, copper

Collective nouns are common nouns that indicate a group or collection of persons, places, things, concepts, actions, or qualities. They are plural in meaning but singular in form.

EXAMPLES audience, jury, brigade, staff, committee

Abstract nouns are common nouns that refer to something intangible that cannot be discerned by the five senses.

EXAMPLES love, loyalty, pride, valor, peace, devotion, harmony

Concrete nouns are common nouns used to identify those things that can be discerned by the five senses.

EXAMPLES house, carrot, ice, tar, straw, grease

A *count noun* is a type of concrete noun that identifies things that can be separated into countable units.

EXAMPLES desks, chisels, envelopes, engines, pencils

There were four *calculators* in the office.

A *mass noun* is a type of concrete noun that identifies things that comprise a mass, rather than individual units, and cannot be separated into countable units.

EXAMPLES   electricity, water, sand, wood, air, uranium, gold, oil, wheat, cement

Nouns may function as subjects of verbs, as objects of verbs and prepositions, as complements, or as appositives.

EXAMPLES   The *metal* bent as *pressure* was applied to it. (subjects)

The bricklayer cemented the *blocks* efficiently. (direct object)

The company awarded our *department* a plaque for safety. (indirect object)

The event occurred within the *year.* (object of a preposition)

An equestrian is a *horseman.* (subjective complement)

We elected the sales manager *chairman.* (objective complement)

George Thomas, the *treasurer,* gave his report last. (appositive)

Words normally used as nouns may also be used as adjectives and adverbs.

EXAMPLES   It is *company* policy. (adjective)

He went *home.* (adverb)

See the **possessive case** entry in this tabbed section for a discussion of how nouns form the possessive case.

Most nouns *form the plural* by adding *s.*

EXAMPLE   *Dolphins* are capable of communicating with people.

Those ending in *s, z, x, ch,* and *sh* form the plural by adding *es.*

EXAMPLES   How many size *sixes* did we produce last month?

The letter was sent to all the *churches.*

Technology should not inhibit our individuality; it should fulfill our *wishes.*

Those ending in a consonant plus *y* form the *plural* by changing *y* to *ies.*

EXAMPLE   The store advertises prompt delivery but places a limit on the number of *deliveries* in one day.

Some nouns ending in *o* add *es* to form the plural, but others add only *s.*

EXAMPLES   One tomato plant produced twelve *tomatoes.*

We installed two *dynamos* in the plant.

Some nouns ending in *f* or *fe* add *s* to form the plural; others change the *f* or *fe* to *ves.*

EXAMPLES   cliff/cliffs, fife/fifes, knife/knives

Some nouns require an internal change to form the plural.

> **EXAMPLES** woman/women, man/men, mouse/mice, goose/geese

Some nouns do not change in the plural form.

> **EXAMPLE** *Fish* swam lazily in the clear brook while a few wild *deer* mingled with the *sheep* in a nearby meadow.

Compound nouns form the plural in the main word.

> **EXAMPLES** sons-in-law, high schools

Compound nouns written as one word add *s* to the end.

> **EXAMPLE** Use seven *tablespoonfuls* of freshly ground coffee to make seven cups of coffee.

objects

There are three kinds of objects: *direct object, indirect object,* and *object of a preposition.* All objects are nouns or noun equivalents (pronoun, gerund, infinitive, noun phrase, noun clause).

The *direct object* answers the question "what?" or "whom?" about a verb and its subject.

> **EXAMPLE** John built a *business.*

An *indirect object* is a noun or noun equivalent that occurs with a direct object after certain kinds of transitive verbs, such as *give, wish, cause, tell.* The indirect object answers the question "to whom or what?" or "for whom or what?" The indirect object always precedes the direct object.

> **EXAMPLE** Their attorney wrote *our firm* a follow-up letter.

As the *object of a preposition,* a noun or pronoun combines with a preposition to form a prepositional phrase.

> **EXAMPLE** *After the meeting,* the district managers adjourned *to the executive dining room.*

See also the **complements** entry in this tabbed section.

person

Person refers to the form of a personal pronoun that indicates whether the pronoun represents the speaker, the person spoken to, or the person or thing spoken about. A pronoun representing the speaker is in the *first* person.

> **EXAMPLE** *I* could not find the answer in the manual.

A pronoun representing the person or persons spoken to is in the *second* person.

> **EXAMPLE** *You* are going to be a good supervisor.

A pronoun representing the person or persons spoken about is in the *third* person.

> **EXAMPLE** *They* received the news quietly.

The following table shows first, second, and third person pronouns.

Person	Singular	Plural
First	I, me, my	we, ours, us
Second	you, your	you, your
Third	he, him, his she, her, hers its, its	they, them, their

phrases

Below the level of the sentence, there are two ways to combine words into groups: by forming clauses, which combine subjects and verbs, and by forming phrases, which are based on nouns, nonfinite verb forms, or verb combinations without subjects.

> **EXAMPLE** He encouraged his staff (clause) *by his calm confidence.* (phrase)

A phrase may function as an *adjective,* an *adverb,* a *noun,* or a *verb.*

> **EXAMPLES** The subjects *on the agenda* were all discussed. (adjective)
>
> We discussed the project *with great enthusiasm.* (adverb)
>
> *Working hard* is her way of life. (noun)
>
> The chief engineer *should have been notified.* (verb)

Even though phrases function as adjectives, adverbs, nouns, or verbs, they are normally named for the kind of word around which they are constructed—preposition, participle, infinitive, gerund, verb, or noun. A phrase that begins with a preposition is a *prepositional phrase;* a phrase that begins with a participial is a *participial phrase,* and so on.

possessive case

A noun or pronoun is in the possessive case when it represents a person or thing owning or possessing something.

> **EXAMPLE** A recent scientific analysis of *New York City's* atmosphere concluded that New Yorkers on the street took into their lungs the equivalent in toxic materials of 38 cigarettes per person daily.

Singular nouns show the possessive by adding an apostrophe and *s*.

   EXAMPLE company/company's

Nouns that form their plurals by adding an *s* show the possessive by placing an apostrophe after the *s* that forms the plural.

   EXAMPLE a managers' meeting

The following list shows the relationships among singular, plural, and possessive nouns that form their plurals by adding *s* or changing *y* to *ies*.

singular	company	employee
singular possessive	company's	employee's
plural	companies	employees
plural possessive	companies'	employees'

Nouns that do not add *s* to form their plurals add an apostrophe and an *s* to show possession in both the plural and the singular forms.

singular	child	man
singular possessive	child's	man's
plural	children	men
plural possessive	children's	men's

Singular nouns that end in *s* form the possessive either by adding only an apostrophe or by adding both an apostrophe and an *s*.

   EXAMPLES a *waitress'* uniform/an *actress'* career

   a *waitress's* uniform/an *actress's* career

Singular nouns of one syllable always form the possessive by adding both an apostrophe and an *s*.

   EXAMPLE The *boss's* desk was cluttered.

When several words make up a single term, add *'s* to the last word only.

   EXAMPLE The *chairman of the board's* statement was brief.

With coordinate nouns, the last noun takes the possessive form to show joint possession.

   EXAMPLE *Michelson and Morely's* famous experiment on the velocity of light was made in 1887.

To show individual possession with coordinate nouns, each noun should take the possessive form.

   EXAMPLE The difference between *Thomasson's* and *Silson's* test results were statistically insignificant.

To form the possessive of a compound word, add *'s*.

> EXAMPLE the *vice-president's* car, the *pipeline's* diameter, the *antibody's* reaction.

When a noun ends in multiple consecutive *s* sounds, form the possessive by adding only an apostrophe.

> EXAMPLES Jesus' disciples, Moses' journey

Do not use an apostrophe with possessive pronouns.

> EXAMPLES *yours, its, his, ours, whose, theirs*

Several indefinite pronouns (*all, any, each, few, most, none,* and *some*) require *of* phrases to form the possessive case.

> EXAMPLE Both dies were stored in the warehouse, but rust had ruined the surface *of each*.

Others, however, use an apostrophe.

> EXAMPLE *Everyone's* contribution is welcome.

Only the possessive form of a pronoun should be used with a gerund.

> EXAMPLES The safety officer insisted in *my* wearing a respirator.
>
> *Our* monitoring was not affected by changing weather conditions.

predicates

The predicate is that part of a sentence that contains the main verb and any other words used to complete the thought of the sentence (the verb's modifiers and complements). The principal part of the predicate is the verb, just as a noun (or noun substitute) is the principal part of the subject.

> EXAMPLE Bill *piloted the airplane.*

The *simple predicate* is the verb (or verb phrase) alone; the complete predicate is the verb and its modifiers and complements. A compound predicate consists of two or more verbs with the same subject. It is an important device for economical writing.

> EXAMPLE The company *tried* but *did not succeed* in that field.

A *predicate nominative* is a noun construction that follows a linking verb and renames the subject.

> EXAMPLES She is my *lawyer.* (noun)
>
> His excuse was *that he had been sick.* (noun clause)

prepositions

A preposition is a word that links a noun or pronoun (its object) to another sentence element, by expressing such relationships as direction *(to, into, across, toward)*, location *(at, in, on, under, over, beside, among, by, between, through)*, time *(before, after, during, until, since)*, or figurative location *(for, against, with)*. Together, the preposition, its object, and the object's modifiers form a prepositional phrase that acts as a modifier.

The object of a preposition (the word or phrase following it) is always in the objective case. This situation gives rise to a problem in such constructions as "between you and *me*," a phrase that is frequently and incorrectly written as "between you and *I*." *Me* is the objective form of the pronoun, and *I* is the subjective form.

Many words that function as prepositions also function as adverbs. If the word takes an object and functions as a connective, it is a preposition; if it has no object and functions as a modifier, it is an adverb.

> **EXAMPLES** The manager sat *behind* the desk *in* his office. (prepositions)
>
> The customer lagged *behind;* then she came *in* and sat down. (adverbs)

Do not use redundant prepositions, such as "off *of*," "in back *of*," "inside *of*," and "at *about*."

> **CHANGE** The client arrived *at about* four o'clock.
>
> **TO** The client arrived *at* four o'clock. (to be exact)
>
> **OR** The client arrived *about* four o'clock. (to be approximate)

Do not omit necessary prepositions.

> **CHANGE** He was oblivious and not distracted by the view from his office window.
>
> **TO** He was oblivious *to* and not distracted *by* the view from his office window.

If a preposition falls naturally at the end of a sentence, leave it there.

> **EXAMPLE** I don't remember which file I put it *in.*

However, a preposition at the end of a sentence can be an indication that the sentence is awkwardly constructed.

> **CHANGE** The branch office is where he was *at.*
>
> **TO** He was at the branch office.

When a preposition appears in a title, it is capitalized only if it is the first word in the title or if it has four letters or more.

> **EXAMPLE** *Composition for the Business World* was reviewed recently by the *Journal of Business Communication.*

pronoun reference

Avoid vague and uncertain references between a pronoun and its antecedents.

> CHANGE   We made the sale and delivered the product. *It* was a big one.
>
> TO   We made the sale, which was a big one, and delivered the product.

For the sake of coherence, pronouns should be placed as close as possible to their antecedents because the danger of creating an ambiguous reference increases with distance.

> CHANGE   The house in the meadow at the base of the mountain range was resplendent in *its* coat of new paint.
>
> TO   The house, resplendent in *its* coat of new paint, was nestled in a meadow at the base of the mountain range.

Do not repeat an antecedent in parentheses following the pronoun. If you feel that you must identify the pronoun's antecedent in this way, you need to rewrite the sentence.

> CHANGE   The senior partner first met Bob Evans when he (Evans) was a trainee.
>
> TO   Bob Evans was a trainee when the senior partner first met him.

The use of the masculine personal pronoun to refer to both sexes implies sexual bias to many people. Avoid the problem by substituting an article or changing the statement from singular to plural.

> CHANGE   Each employee is to have *his* annual X-ray taken by Friday.
>
> TO   Each employee is to have *the* annual X-ray taken by Friday.
>
> OR   All employees are to have *their* annual X-rays taken by Friday.

pronouns

A pronoun is a word that is used as a substitute for a noun (the noun for which a pronoun substitutes is called its *antecedent*). Using pronouns in place of nouns relieves the monotony of repeating the same noun over and over.

Personal pronouns refer to the person or persons speaking (*I, me, my, mine; we, us, our, ours*), the person or persons spoken to (*you, your, yours*), or the person or thing spoken of (*he, him, his; she, her, hers; it, its; they, them, their, theirs*).

> EXAMPLES   *I* wish *you* had told *me* that *she* was coming with *us*.
>
> If *their* figures are correct, *ours* must be in error.

Demonstrative pronouns (*this, these, that, those*) indicate or point out the thing being referred to.

EXAMPLES   *This* is my desk.

These are my coworkers.

That will be a difficult job.

Those are incorrect figures.

Relative pronouns (who, whom, which, and *that)* perform a dual function: (1) they take the place of nouns, and (2) they connect and establish the relationship between a dependent clause and its main clause.

EXAMPLE   The personnel manager decided *who* would be hired.

Interrogative pronouns (who or *whom, what,* and *which)* are used only to ask questions.

EXAMPLE   *What* is the trouble?

Indefinite pronouns specify a class or group of persons or things rather than a particular person or thing. *All, any, another, anyone, anything, both, each, either, everybody, few, many, most, much, neither, nobody, none, several, some,* and *such* are indefinite pronouns.

EXAMPLE   Not *everyone* liked the new procedures; *some* even refused to follow them.

A *reflexive pronoun,* which always ends with the suffix *-self* or *-selves,* indicates that the subject of the sentence acts upon itself.

EXAMPLE   The electrician accidentally shocked *herself.*

The reflexive pronouns are *myself, yourself, himself, herself, itself, oneself, ourselves, yourselves,* and *themselves.*
   Myself is not a substitute for *I* or *me* as a personal pronoun.

CHANGE   John and *myself* completed the report on time.

TO   John and *I* completed the report on time.

CHANGE   The assignment was given to Wally and *myself.*

TO   The assignment was given to Wally and *me.*

Intensive pronouns are identical in form with the reflexive pronouns, but they perform a different function: to give emphasis to their antecedents.

EXAMPLE   I *myself* asked the same question.

Reciprocal pronouns (one another and *each other)* indicate the relationship of one item to another. *Each other* is commonly used when referring to two persons or things and *one another* when referring to more than two.

EXAMPLES   They work well with *each other.*

The crew members work well with *one another.*

CASE

Pronouns have forms to show the *subjective, objective,* or *possessive case,* as the following chart shows.

	Subjective	Objective	Possessive
1st person singular	I	me	my, mine
2nd person singular	you	you	your, yours
3rd person singular	he, she, it	him, her, it	his, her, hers, its
1st person plural	we	us	our, ours
2nd person plural	you	you	your, yours
3rd person plural	they	them	their, theirs

A pronoun that is used as the subject of a clause or sentence is in the *subjective case (I, we, he, she, it, you, they, who).* The subjective case is also used when the pronoun follows a linking verb.

> **EXAMPLES** *She* is my boss.
>
> My boss is *she.*

A pronoun that is used as the object of a verb or preposition is in the *objective case (me, us, him, her, it, you, them, whom).*

> **EXAMPLES** Mr. Davis hired Tom and *me.* (object of verb)
>
> Between you and *me,* he's wrong. (object of preposition)

A pronoun that is used to express ownership is in the *possessive case (my, mine, our, ours, his, hers, its, your, yours, their, theirs, whose).*

> **EXAMPLES** He took *his* notes with him on the business trip.
>
> We took *our* notes with us on the business trip.

A pronoun appositive takes the case of its antecedents.

> **EXAMPLES** Two systems analysts, Joe and *I,* were selected to represent the company. (*Joe and I* is in apposition to the subject, *systems analysts,* and must therefore be in the subjective case.)
>
> The systems analysts selected two members—Joe and *me.* (*Joe and me* is in apposition to *two members,* which is the object of the verb *selected,* and therefore must be in the objective case.)

If compound pronouns cause problems in determining case, try using them singly.

> **EXAMPLES** In his letter, John mentioned *you* and *me.*
>
> In his letter, John mentioned *you.*
>
> In his letter, John mentioned *me.*

They and *we* must discuss the terms of the merger.

They must discuss the terms of the merger.

We must discuss the terms of the merger.

When a pronoun modifies a noun, try it without the noun to determine its case.

EXAMPLES *(We/Us)* pilots fly our own planes.

We fly our own planes. (You would not write "*Us* fly our own planes.")

He addressed his remarks directly to *(we/us)* technicians.

He addressed his remarks directly to *us*. (You would not write "He addressed his remarks directly to *we.*")

GENDER

A pronoun must agree in gender with its antecedent. A problem sometimes occurs because the masculine pronoun has traditionally been used to refer to both sexes. To avoid the sexual bias implied in such usage, use *he or she* or the plural form of the pronoun, *they.*

CHANGE *Each* may stay or go as *he* chooses.

TO *Each* may stay or go as *he or she* chooses.

OR *All* may stay or go as *they* choose.

If you use the plural form of the pronoun, be sure to change the indefinite pronoun *each* to its plural form, *all.*

NUMBER

Number is a frequent problem with only a few indefinite pronouns *(each, either, neither;* and those ending with *-body,* or *-one,* such as *anybody, anyone, everybody, everyone, nobody, no one, somebody, someone),* which are normally singular and so require singular verbs and are referred to by singular pronouns.

EXAMPLE As *each arrives* for the meeting and is seated, please hand *him or her* a copy of the confidential report. *Everyone* is to return the copy before *he or she* leaves. *No one* should be offended by these precautions when the importance of secrecy has been explained to *him or her.* I think *everybody* on the committee *understands* that *neither* of our major competitors *is* aware of the new process that we have developed.

PERSON

Third-person personal pronouns usually have antecedents.

EXAMPLE John presented the report to the members of the board of directors. *He* [John] first read *it* [the report] to *them* [the directors] and then asked for questions.

First- and second-person personal pronouns do not normally require antecedents.

> EXAMPLES   *I* like my job.
>
> *You* were there at the time.
>
> *We* all worked hard on the project.

restrictive and nonrestrictive elements

Modifying phrases and clauses may be either restrictive or nonrestrictive.

A *nonrestrictive phrase* or *clause* provides additional information about what it modifies, but it does not restrict the meaning of what it modifies. Therefore, the nonrestrictive phrase or clause can be removed without changing the essential meaning of the sentence. It is, in effect, a parenthetical element, and it is set off by commas to show its loose relationship with the rest of the sentence.

> EXAMPLES   This instrument, *called a backscatter gauge,* fires beta particles at an object and counts the particles that bounce back. (nonrestrictive phrase)
>
> The annual report, *which was distributed yesterday,* shows that sales increased 20 percent last year. (nonrestrictive clause)

A *restrictive phrase or clause* limits, or restricts, the meaning of what it modifies. If it were removed, the essential meaning of the sentence would be changed. Because a restrictive phrase or clause is essential to the meaning of the sentence, it is never set off by commas.

> EXAMPLES   All employees *wishing to donate blood* may take Thursday afternoon off. (restrictive phrase)
>
> Companies *that adopt the plan* nearly always show profit increases. (restrictive clause)

It is important for writers to distinguish between nonrestrictive and restrictive elements. The same sentence can take on two entirely different meanings depending on whether a modifying element is set off by commas (because nonrestrictive) or not set off (because restrictive). The results of a slip by the writer can be not only misleading but also downright embarrassing.

> CHANGE   I think you will be impressed by our systems engineers who are thoroughly experienced in projects like yours.
>
> TO   I think you will be impressed by our systems engineers, who are thoroughly experienced in projects like yours.

The problem with the first sentence is that it suggests that "you may not be so impressed by our other, less experienced, systems engineers."

Which should be used to introduce nonrestrictive clauses.

EXAMPLE   After John left the restaurant, *which* is one of the finest in New York, he came directly to my office.

That should be used to introduce restrictive clauses.

EXAMPLE   Companies *that* diversify usually succeed.

sentence faults

A number of problems can create sentence faults, including faulty subordination, clauses with no subjects, rambling sentences, and omitting verbs.

Faulty subordination occurs when (1) a grammatically subordinate element, such as a dependent clause, actually contains the main idea of the sentence or (2) a subordinate element is so long or detailed that it dominates or obscures the main idea. Avoiding the main idea being expressed in a subordinate element depends on the writer's knowing which idea is the main one. Note that both of the following sentences appear logical; which one really is logical depends on which of two ideas should be emphasized.

EXAMPLES   Although the new filing system saves money, many of the staff are unhappy with it.

The new filing system saves money, although many of the staff are unhappy with it.

In this example, if the writer's main point is that *the new filing system saves money,* the second sentence is correct. If the main point is that *many of the staff are unhappy,* then the first sentence is correct.

The other major problem with subordination is loading so much detail into a subordinate element that it "crushes" the main point by its sheer size and weight.

CHANGE   Because the noise level on a typical street in New York City on a weekday is as loud as an alarm clock ringing three feet away, New Yorkers often have hearing problems.

TO   Because the noise level in New York City is so high, New Yorkers often have hearing problems.

Writers sometimes inappropriately assume a subject that is not stated in a clause.

CHANGE   Your application program can request to end the session after the next command. (Request *who* or *what* to end the session?)

TO   Your application program can request *the host program* to end the session after the next command.

Sentences that contain more information than the reader can comfortably absorb in one reading are known as *rambling sentences.* The obvious remedy for a rambling sentence is to divide it into two or more sentences. In doing so, however, put the main message of the rambling sentence into the first of the revised sentences.

> CHANGE The payment to which a subcontractor is entitled should be made promptly in order that in the event of a subsequent contractual dispute we, as general contractors, may not be held in default of our contract by virtue of nonpayment.

> TO Pay subcontractors promptly. Then if a contractual dispute should occur, we cannot be held in default of our contract because of nonpayment.

The assertion made by a sentence's predicate about its subject must be logical. "Mr. Wilson's *job* is a salesman" is not logical, but "*Mr. Wilson* is a salesman" is. "Jim's *height* is six feet tall" is not logical, but "*Jim* is six feet tall" is.

Do not omit a required verb.

> CHANGE I never have and probably never will write the annual report.

> TO I never have *written* and probably never will *write* the annual report.

sentence fragments

A sentence fragment is an incomplete grammatical unit that is punctuated as a sentence.

> EXAMPLES He quit his job. (sentence)
>
> And quit his job. (fragment)

Sentence fragments are often introduced by relative pronouns (*who, which, that*) or subordinating conjunctions (such as *although, because, if, when,* and *while*).

> CHANGE The new manager instituted several new procedures. *Many of which are impractical.*

> TO The new manager instituted several new procedures, many of which are impractical.

A sentence must contain a finite verb; verbals do not function as verbs. The following examples are sentence fragments because their verbals (*providing, to work, waiting*) cannot perform the function of a finite verb.

> EXAMPLES *Providing* all employees with hospitalization insurance.
>
> *To work* a forty-hour week.
>
> The customer *waiting* to see you.

sentence types

Sentences may be classified according to *structure* (simple, compound, complex, compound-complex); *intention* (declarative, interrogative, imperative, exclamatory); and *stylistic use* (loose, periodic, minor).

BY STRUCTURE

A *simple sentence* consists of one independent clause. At its most basic, the simple sentence contains only a subject and a predicate.

> **EXAMPLES** Profits (subject) rose (predicate).
>
> The strike (subject) finally ended (predicate).

A *compound sentence* consists of two or more independent clauses connected by a comma and a coordinating conjunction, by a semicolon, or by a semicolon and a conjunctive adverb.

> **EXAMPLES** Drilling is the only way to collect samples of the layers of sediment below the ocean floor, *but* it is by no means the only way to gather information about these strata. (comma and coordinating conjunction)
>
> There is little similarity between the chemical composition of sea water and that of river water; the various elements are present in entirely different proportions. (semicolon)
>
> It was 500 miles to the site; *therefore,* we made arrangements to fly. (semicolon and conjunctive adverb)

The *complex sentence* contains one independent clause and at least one dependent clause that expresses a subordinate idea.

> **EXAMPLE** The generator will shut off automatically (independent clause) if the temperature rises above a specified point (dependent clause).

A *compound-complex* sentence consists of two or more independent clauses plus at least one dependent clause.

> **EXAMPLE** Productivity is central to controlling inflation (independent clause), for when productivity rises (dependent clause), employers can raise wages without raising prices (independent clause).

BY INTENTION

By intention, a sentence may be *declarative, interrogative, imperative,* or *exclamatory.*

A *declarative sentence* conveys information or makes a factual statement.

> **EXAMPLE** This motor powers the conveyor belt.

An *interrogative sentence* asks a direct question.

> **EXAMPLE** Does the conveyor belt run constantly?

An *imperative sentence* issues a command.

> **EXAMPLE** Start the generator.

An *exclamatory sentence* is an emphatic expression of feeling, fact, or opinion. It is a declarative sentence that is stated with great feeling.

> **EXAMPLE** The heater exploded!

BY STYLISTIC USE

A *loose sentence* makes its major point at the beginning and then adds subordinate phrases and clauses that develop the major point. A loose sentence could be ended at one or more points before it actually does.

> **EXAMPLE** It went up (.), a great ball of fire about a mile in diameter (.), changing colors as it kept shooting upward (.), an elemental force freed from its bonds (.) after being chained for billions of years.

A *periodic sentence* delays its main idea until the end by presenting subordinate ideas or modifiers first.

> **EXAMPLE** During the last decade or so, the attitude of the American citizen toward automation has undergone a profound change.

A *minor sentence* is an incomplete sentence. It makes sense in its context because the missing element is clearly implied by the preceding sentence.

> **EXAMPLE** In view of these facts, is automation really useful? *Or economical?*

spelling

The use of a computer spelling checker helps enormously with spelling problems; however, it does not solve all spelling problems. It cannot detect a spelling error if the error spells a valid word; for example, if you mean *to* but inadvertently write *too*, the spelling checker cannot detect the error. You still must carefully proofread your document.

Whether or not you have access to a personal computer, the following system will help you learn to spell correctly.

1. Keep your dictionary handy, and use it regularly. If you are unsure about the spelling of a word, don't rely on memory or guesswork—consult the dictionary. When you look up a word, focus on both its spelling and its meaning.
2. After you have looked in the dictionary for the spelling of the word, write the word from memory several times. Then check the accuracy of your spelling. If you have misspelled the word, repeat this step. If

you do not follow through by writing the word from memory, you lose the chance of retaining it for future use. Practice is essential.
3. Keep a list of the words you commonly misspell, and work regularly at whittling it down. Do not load the list with exotic words; many of us would stumble over *asphyxiation* or *pterodactyl.* Concentrate instead on words like *calendar, maintenance,* and *unnecessary.* These and other frequently used words should remain on your list until you have learned to spell them.
4. Check all your writing for misspellings by proofreading.

subjects of sentences

The subject of a sentence is a noun or pronoun (and possibly its modifiers) about which the predicate of the sentence makes a statement. Although a subject may appear anywhere in a sentence, it most often appears at the beginning.

EXAMPLES   *To increase sales* is our goal.

The wiring is defective.

Grammatically, a subject must agree with its verb in number.

EXAMPLES   The *departments have* much in common.

The *department has* several advantages.

The subject is the actor in active-voice sentences.

EXAMPLE   The *aerosol bomb* propels the liquid as a mist.

A compound subject has two or more substantives as the subject of one verb.

EXAMPLE   *The president* and *the treasurer* agreed to withhold the information.

tense

Tense is the grammatical term for verb forms that indicate time distinctions. There are six tenses in English: past, past perfect, present, present perfect, future, and future perfect, and each has a corresponding progressive form.

Tense	Basic	Progressive
Past	I began	I was beginning
Past Perfect	I had begun	I had been beginning
Present	I begin	I am beginning
Present Perfect	I have begun	I have been beginning
Future	I will begin	I will be beginning
Future Perfect	I will have begun	I will have been beginning

Perfect tenses allow you to express a prior action or condition that continues in a present, past, or future time.

EXAMPLES *I have begun* to write the annual report, and I will work on it for the rest of the month. (present perfect)

I had begun to read the manual when the lights went out. (past perfect)

I will have begun this project by the time funds are allocated. (future perfect)

Past Tense

The simple past tense indicates that an action took place in its entirety in the past. The past tense is usually formed by adding *-d* or *-ed* to the root form of the verb.

EXAMPLE We *closed* the office early yesterday.

Past Perfect Tense

The past perfect tense indicates that one past event preceded another. It is formed by combining the helping verb *had* with the past participle form of the main verb.

EXAMPLE He *had finished* by the time I arrived.

Present Tense

The simple present tense represents action occurring in the present, without any indication of time duration.

EXAMPLE I *use* the beaker.

A general truth is always expressed in the present tense.

EXAMPLE He learned that the saying "time *heals* all wounds" is true.

The present tense can be used to present actions or conditions that have no time restrictions.

EXAMPLE Water *boils* at 212 degrees Fahrenheit.

The present tense can be used to indicate habitual action.

EXAMPLE I *pass* the paint shop on the way to my department every day.

The present tense can be used as the "historical present" to make things that occurred in the past more vivid.

EXAMPLE He *asks* for more information on production statistics and *receives* a detailed report on every product manufactured by the company.

Then he *asks,* "Is each department manned at full strength?" In his office, surrounded by his staff, he *goes* over the figures and *plans* for the coming year.

Present Perfect Tense

The present perfect tense describes something from the recent past that has a bearing on the present—a period of time before the present but after the simple past. The present perfect tense is formed by combining a form of the helping verb *have* with the past principle form of the main verb.

> **examples**   He *has retired,* but he visits the office frequently.
>
> We *have finished* the draft and are ready to begin revising it.

Future Tense

The simple future tense indicates a time that will occur after the present. It uses the helping verb *will* (or *shall*) plus the main verb.

> **example**   I *will finish* the job tomorrow.

Do not use the future tense needlessly.

> **change**   This system *will be* explained on page 3.
>
> **to**   This system *is* explained on page 3.
>
> **change**   When you press this button, the card *will be* moved under the read station.
>
> **to**   When you press this button, the card *is* moved under the read station.

Future Perfect Tense

The future perfect tense indicates action that will have been completed at a future time. It is formed by linking the helping verbs *will have* to the past participle form of the main verb.

> **example**   He *will have driven* the test car 40 miles by the time he returns.

Be consistent in your use of tense. The only legitimate shift in tense records a real change in time. When you choose a tense stay with that tense. Illogical shifts in tense will only confuse your reader.

> **change**   Before he *installed* the printed circuit, the technician *cleans* the contacts.
>
> **to**   Before he *installed* the printed circuit, the technician *cleaned* the contacts.

verbs

A verb is a word that describes an action (The antelope *bolted* at the sight of the hunters), states the way in which something or someone is affected by an action (He *was saddened* by the death of his friend), or affirms a state of existence (He *is* a wealthy man now).

TYPES OF VERBS

Verbs may be described as being either transitive verbs or intransitive.

A *transitive verb* is a verb that requires a direct object to complete its meaning.

> EXAMPLES They *laid* the foundation on October 24. (*foundation* is the direct object of the transitive verb *laid*)
>
> George Anderson *wrote* the treasurer a letter. (*letter* is the direct object of the transitive verb *wrote*)

An *intransitive verb* is a verb that does not require an object to complete its meaning. It is able to make a full assertion about the subject without assistance (although it may have modifiers).

> EXAMPLE The engine *ran*.
>
> The engine *ran* smoothly and quietly.

Linking verbs are intransitive verbs that link a complement to the subject. When the complement is a noun or pronoun, it refers to the same person or thing as the noun or pronoun that is the subject.

> EXAMPLES The winch *is* rusted. (*Rusted* is an adjective modifying *winch*.)
>
> A calculator *remains* a useful tool. (*A useful tool* is a subjective complement renaming *calculator*.)

Such intransitive verbs as *be, become, seem,* and *appear* are almost always linking verbs. A number of others, such as *look, sound, taste, smell,* and *feel,* may function as either linking verbs or simple intransitive verbs. If you are unsure about whether one of them is a linking verb, try substituting *seem;* if the sentence still makes sense, the verb is probably a linking verb.

> EXAMPLES Their antennae *feel* delicately for their prey. (simple intransitive verb)
>
> Their antennae *feel* delicate. (linking verb; you could substitute *seem*)

FORMS OF VERBS

By form, verbs may be described as being either *finite* or *nonfinite.*

A *finite verb* is the main verb of a clause or sentence and it makes an assertion about its subject. *Nonfinite verbs* are verbals, which, although they are derived from verbs, actually function as nouns, adjectives, or adverbs.

When the *-ing* form of a verb is used as a noun, it is called a *gerund.*

EXAMPLE *Seeing* is *believing.*

An infinitive, which is the root form of a verb (usually preceded by *to*), can be used as a noun, an adverb, or an adjective.

EXAMPLES He hates *to complain.* (noun, direct object of *hates*)

The valve closes *to stop* the flow. (adverb, modifies *closes*)

This is the proposal *to select.* (adjective, modifies *proposal*)

A participle is a verb form used as an adjective.

EXAMPLES His *closing* statement was very *convincing.*

The *rejected* proposal was ours.

PROPERTIES OF VERBS

Person is the grammatical term for the form of a personal pronoun that indicates whether the pronoun refers to the speaker, the person spoken to, or the person (or thing) spoken about. Verbs change their forms to agree in person with their subjects.

EXAMPLES I *see* (first person) a yellow tint, but he *sees* (third person) a yellow-green hue.

I *am* (first person) convinced, and you *are* (second person) not convinced.

Voice refers to the two forms of a verb that indicate whether the subject of the verb acts or receives the action. If the subject of the verb acts, the verb is in the *active voice;* if it receives the action, the verb is in the *passive voice.*

EXAMPLES The aerosol bomb *propels* the liquid as a mist. (active)

The liquid *is propelled* as a mist by the aerosol bomb. (passive)

Number refers to the two forms of a verb that indicate whether the subject of a verb is singular or plural.

EXAMPLES The machine *was* in good operating condition. (singular)

The machines *were* in good operating condition. (plural)

Tense refers to verb forms that indicate time distinctions. There are six tenses: present, past, future, present perfect, past perfect, and future perfect. See the **tense** entry in this tabbed section for a detailed discussion of tense.

voice

In grammar, voice indicates the relation of the subject to the action of the verb. When the verb is in the *active voice,* the subject acts; when it is in the *passive voice,* the subject is acted upon.

EXAMPLES David Cohen *wrote* the advertising copy. (active)

The advertising copy *was written* by David Cohen. (passive)

The sentences say the same thing, but each has a different emphasis: In the first sentence emphasis is on the subject, *David Cohen*, whereas in the second sentence the focus is on the object, *the advertising copy*.

Always use the active voice unless you have a good reason to use the passive. Because they are wordy and indirect, passive-voice sentences are more difficult for the reader to understand.

CHANGE Things *are seen* by the normal human eye in three dimensions: length, width, and depth.

TO The human eye *sees* things in three dimensions: length, width, and depth.

Passive-voice sentences are wordy because they always use a helping verb in addition to the main verb, as well as an extra preposition if they identify the doer of the action specified by the main verb. The passive-voice version is also indirect because it puts the doer of the action behind the verb instead of in front of it.

ACTIVE Employees *resent* changes in policy.

PASSIVE Changes in policy *are resented by* employees.

There are, however, certain instances when the passive voice is effective or even necessary. Indeed, for reasons of tact and diplomacy, you might need to use the passive voice to *avoid* identifying the doer of the action.

CHANGE Your sales force didn't meet the quota last month. (active)

TO The quota wasn't met last month. (passive)

When the performer of the action is either unknown or unimportant, use the passive voice.

EXAMPLES The copper mine *was discovered* in 1929.

Fifty-six barrels *were processed* in two hours.

When the performer of the action is less important than the receiver of that action, the passive voice is sometimes more appropriate.

EXAMPLE Ann Bryant *was presented* with an award by the president.

Whether you use the passive or the active voice, however, be careful not to *shift* voices in a sentence.

CHANGE Ms. McDonald *corrected* the malfunction as soon as it *was identified* by the technician.

TO Ms. McDonald *corrected* the malfunction as soon as the technician *identified* it.

who/whom

Who and *whom* cause much trouble in determining case. *Who* is the sub-jective case form, whereas *whom* is the objective case form. When in doubt about which form to use, try substituting a personal pronoun to see which one fits. If *he* or *they* fits, use *who*.

EXAMPLES *Who* is the congressman for the 45th district?

He is the congressman for the 45th district.

If *him* or *them* fits, use *whom*

EXAMPLES It depends on *whom?*

It depends on *them.*

Understanding punctuation and mechanics is essential for writers because it enables them to communicate clearly and precisely.

Punctuation is a system of symbols that helps the reader understand the structural relationship within (and the intention of) a sentence. Marks of punctuation may link, separate, enclose, indicate omissions, terminate, and classify sentences. (See the GRAMMAR tab for more on sentence structure.)

The use of punctuation is determined by grammatical conventions and the writer's intention—in fact, punctuation often substitutes for the writer's facial expressions.

Detailed information on each mark of punctuation is given in its own entry. The following are the thirteen marks of punctuation:

This tabbed section also contains entries on **abbreviations and acronyms, capital letters, contractions, dates, ellipses, italics,** and **numbers.**

abbreviations and acronyms

Abbreviations may be shortened versions of words, or they may be formed by the first letters of words.

EXAMPLES   company/co.

         boulevard/blvd.

         electromotive force/emf

         horsepower/hp

> National Institute of Standards and Technology/NIST
> cash on delivery/c.o.d.

Although abbreviations and acronyms can be important space savers, use them only if you are certain that your reader will understand them as readily as he or she would the terms they represent. In general, use abbreviations only in charts, tables, graphs, footnotes, bibliographies, and other places where space is at a premium. Spell in full the term represented by an acronym the first time you use it, with the acronym enclosed in parentheses following it; thereafter, use the acronym alone.

> EXAMPLE The National Aeronautics and Space Administration (NASA) has accomplished much in its short history. NASA will now develop a permanent orbiting space laboratory.

Do not add an additional period at the end of a sentence that ends with an abbreviation.

> EXAMPLE The official name of the company is Data Base, Inc.

FORMING ABBREVIATIONS

Measurements. The following list contains some common abbreviations used with units of measurement. Notice that except for *in.* (inch), *tan.* (tangent), and others that form words, abbreviations of measurements do not require periods.

amp, ampere	Hz, hertz
bbl, barrel	in., inch
Btu, British thermal unit	kg, kilogram
bu, bushel	km, kilometer
cm, centimeter	lb, pound
cos, cosine	min, minute
doz or dz, dozen	oz, ounce
F, Fahrenheit	pt, pint
fig., figure (illustration)	qt, quart
ft, foot (or feet)	sec, second or secant
gal., gallon	tan., tangent
hp, horsepower	yd, yard
hr, hour	yr, year

Abbreviations of units of measure are identical in the singular and plural: one *cm* and three *cm* (not three *cms*).

Personal Names and Titles. Personal names should generally not be abbreviated.

> CHANGE Chas., Thos., Wm., Geo.
>   TO Charles, Thomas, William, George

An academic, civil, religious, or military title should be spelled out when it does not precede a name.

EXAMPLE The doctor asked for the patient's chart.

When they precede names, some titles are customarily abbreviated.

EXAMPLES Dr. Smith, Mr. Mills, Mrs. Katz

An abbreviation of a title may follow the name; however, be certain that it does not duplicate a title before the name.

CHANGE Dr. William Smith, Ph.D.

TO Dr. William Smith

OR William Smith, Ph.D.

Names of Organizations. Many companies include in their names such terms as *Brothers, Incorporated, Corporation,* and *Company.* If these terms appear as abbreviations in the official company names, use them in their abbreviated forms: *Bros., Inc., Corp.,* and *Co.* If not abbreviated in the official names, such terms should be spelled out in most writing other than addresses, footnotes, bibliographies, and lists, where abbreviations may be used. A similar guideline applies for use of an ampersand (&); this symbol should be used only if it appears in an official company name. Titles of divisions within organizations, such as Department (Dept.) and Division (Div.) should be abbreviated only when space is limited.

Dates and Time. The following are common abbreviations.

A.D.	*anno Domini* (beginning of calendar time—A.D. 1790)	Jan.	January
B.C.	before Christ (before the beginning of calendar time—647 B.C.)	Feb.	February
		Mar.	March
		Apr.	April
a.m.	*ante meridiem,* "before noon"	Aug.	August
p.m.	*post meridiem,* "after noon"	Sept.	September
		Dec.	December

Months should always be spelled out when only the month and year are given. The standard and alternative forms of abbreviations appear in current dictionaries, either in regular alphabetical order (by the letters of the abbreviation) or in a separate index.

apostrophes

The apostrophe (') is used to show possession, to mark the omission of letters, and sometimes to indicate the plural of Arabic numbers, letters, and acronyms. Do not confuse the apostrophe used to show the plural with the apostrophe used to show possession.

EXAMPLES The entry required five 7's in the appropriate columns. (The apostrophe here is used to indicate the *plural,* not possession.)

The *letter's* purpose was clearly evident in its opening paragraph. (The apostrophe here is used to show *possession,* not the plural.)

TO SHOW POSSESSION

An apostrophe is used with an *s* to form the possessive case of some nouns.

EXAMPLE A recent scientific analysis of *New York City's* atmosphere concluded that a New Yorker on the street took into his or her lungs the equivalent in toxic materials of 38 cigarettes a day.

With coordinate nouns, the last noun takes the possessive form to show joint possession.

EXAMPLE *Michelson and Morley's* famous experiment on the velocity of light was made in 1887.

To show individual possession with coordinate nouns, each noun should take the possessive form.

EXAMPLE The difference between *Tom's* and *Mary's* test results is statistically insignificant.

Singular nouns ending in *s* may form the possessive either by an apostrophe alone or by *'s.* Whichever way you do it, however, be consistent.

EXAMPLES an actress' career

an actress's career

Singular nouns of one syllable form the possessive by adding *'s.*

EXAMPLE The *boss's* desk was cluttered.

Use only an apostrophe with plural nouns ending in *s.*

EXAMPLE a managers' meeting

When adding *'s* would result in a noun ending in multiple consecutive *s* sounds, add only an apostrophe.

EXAMPLES The Joneses' test result

Do not use the apostrophe with possessive pronouns.

EXAMPLES yours, its, his, ours, whose, theirs

It's is a contraction of *it is; its* is the possessive form of the pronoun. Be careful not to confuse the two words.

EXAMPLE *It's* important that the sales force meet *its* quota.

In names of places and institutions, the apostrophe is usually omitted.

EXAMPLES Harpers Ferry, Writers Book Club

To Show Omission

An apostrophe is used to mark the omission of letters in a word or date.

EXAMPLES can't, I'm, I'll

the class of '61

To Form Plurals

An apostrophe and an *s* may be added to show the plural of a word as a word.

EXAMPLE There were five *and's* in his first sentence.

If the term is in all capital letters or ends with a capital letter, however, the apostrophe is not required to form the plural.

EXAMPLE The university awarded seven *Ph.D.s* in engineering last year.

Do not use an apostrophe to indicate the plural of numbers and letters unless confusion would result without one.

EXAMPLES 5s, 30s, two 100s, seven i's

brackets

The primary use of brackets is to enclose a word or words inserted by an editor or writer into a quotation from another source.

EXAMPLE The text stated, "Fissile and fertile nuclei spontaneously emit characteristic nuclear radiations [such as neutrons and gamma rays] that are sufficiently energetic to penetrate the container or cladding."

Brackets are also used to set off a parenthetical item within parentheses.

EXAMPLE We should be sure to give Emanuel Foose (and his brother Emilio [1812–1882] as well) credit for his role in founding the institute.

Brackets are also used in academic writing to insert the Latin word *sic,* which indicates that the writer has quoted material exactly as it appears in the original, even though it contains an obvious error.

EXAMPLE Dr. Smith pointed out that "The earth does not revolve around the son *[sic]* at a constant rate."

capital letters

The use of capital letters (or uppercase letters) is determined by custom and tradition. Capital letters are used to call attention to certain words, such as proper nouns and the first word of a sentence. Care must be exercised in using capital letters because they can affect the meaning of words (march/ March, china/China, turkey/Turkey). Thus, capital letters can help eliminate ambiguity.

Proper Nouns

Proper nouns name a specific person, place, thing, concept, or quality and therefore are capitalized.

> **EXAMPLES** Physics 101, General Electric, John Doe

Common Nouns

Common nouns name a general class or category of persons, places, things, concepts, or qualities rather than specific ones and therefore are not capitalized.

> **EXAMPLES** a physics class, a company, a person

First Words

The first letter of the first word in a sentence is always capitalized.

> **EXAMPLE** Of all the plans you mentioned, the first one seems the best.

The first word after a colon may be capitalized if the statement following is a complete sentence or if it introduces a formal resolution or question.

> **EXAMPLE** Today's meeting will deal with only one issue: What is the firm's role in environmental protection?

If a subordinate element follows the colon, however, or if the thought is closely related, use a lowercase letter following the colon.

> **EXAMPLE** We had to keep working for one reason: our deadline was upon us.

The first word of a complete sentence in quotation marks is capitalized.

> **EXAMPLE** Dr. Vesely stated, "It is possible to postulate an imaginary world in which no decisions are made until all the relevant information is assembled."

Complete sentences contained as numbered items within a sentence may also be capitalized.

> **EXAMPLE** To make correct decisions, you must do three things: (1) Identify the information that would be pertinent to the decision anticipated, (2) Establish a systematic program for acquiring this pertinent information, and (3) Rationally assess the information so acquired.

The first word in the salutation and complimentary close of a letter is capitalized.

EXAMPLES   Dear Mr. Smith:

Sincerely yours,

Best regards,

SPECIFIC GROUPS

Capitalize names of ethnic groups and nationalities.

EXAMPLES   American Indian, Italian, Jew, Chicano

Thus Italian immigrants contributed much to the industrialization of the United States.

Do not capitalize names of social and economic groups.

EXAMPLES   middle class, working class, ghetto dwellers

SPECIFIC PLACES

Capitalize the names of all political divisions.

EXAMPLES   Chicago, Cook County, Illinois, Ontario, Iran, Ward Six

Capitalize the names of geographical divisions.

EXAMPLES   Europe, Asia, North America, the Middle East, the Orient

Do not capitalize geographic features unless they are part of a proper name.

EXAMPLE   The mountains in some areas, such as the Great Smoky Mountains, make television transmission difficult.

The words *north, south, east,* and *west* are capitalized when they refer to sections of the country. They are not capitalized when they refer to directions.

EXAMPLES   I may travel *south* when I relocate to Delaware.

We may build a new plant in the *South* next year.

Capitalize the names of stars, constellations, and planets.

EXAMPLES   Saturn, Andromeda, Jupiter, Milky Way

Do not capitalize *earth, sun,* and *moon,* however, except when they are used with the names of other planets.

EXAMPLES   Although the *sun* rises in the east and sets in the west, the *moon* may appear in any part of the evening sky when darkness settles over the *earth.*

Mars, Pluto, and *Earth* were discussed at the symposium.

SPECIFIC INSTITUTIONS, EVENTS, AND CONCEPTS

Capitalize the names of institutions, organizations, and associations.

> **EXAMPLE** The American Society of Mechanical Engineers and the Department of Housing and Urban Development are cooperating on the project.

An organization usually capitalizes the names of its internal divisions and departments.

> **EXAMPLES** Faculty, Board of Directors, Engineering Department

Types of organizations are not capitalized unless they are part of an official name.

> **EXAMPLE** Our group decided to form a writers' association; we called it the American Association of Writers.

Capitalize historical events.

> **EXAMPLE** Dr. Jellison discussed the Boston Tea Party at the last class.

Capitalize words that designate specific periods of time.

> **EXAMPLES** Labor Day, the Renaissance, the Enlightenment, January, Monday, the Great Depression, Lent

Do not, however, capitalize seasons of the year.

> **EXAMPLES** spring, autumn, winter, summer

Capitalize scientific names of classes, families, and orders, but do not capitalize species or English derivatives of scientific names.

> **EXAMPLES** Mammalia, Carnivora/mammal, carnivorous

TITLES OF BOOKS, ARTICLES, PLAYS, FILMS, REPORTS, AND SUBJECT LINES IN MEMOS

Capitalize the initial letters of the first and last words of a title of a book, article, play, or film, as well as all major words in the title. Do not capitalize articles *(a, an, the)*, conjunctions *(and, but, if)*, or short prepositions *(at, in, on, of)* unless they begin the title. Capitalize prepositions that contain more than four letters *(between, because, until, after)*.

> **EXAMPLE** The microbiologist greatly admired the book *The Lives of a Cell*.

PERSONAL, PROFESSIONAL, AND JOB TITLES

Titles preceding proper names are capitalized.

> **EXAMPLES** Miss March, Professor Galbraith

Appositives following proper names are not normally capitalized. (The word *President* is usually capitalized when it refers to the chief executive of a national government.)

> EXAMPLES Frank Jones, senator from New Mexico (but Senator Jones)
>
> The President called a news conference.

The only exception is an epithet, which actually renames the person.

> EXAMPLES Alexander the Great, Solomon the Wise

Job titles used with personal names are capitalized.

> EXAMPLE John Reems, Division Manager, will meet with us on Wednesday.

Job titles used without personal names are not capitalized.

> EXAMPLE The division manager will meet with us on Wednesday.

Use capital letters to designate family relationships only when they occur before a name or substitute for a name.

> EXAMPLES One of my favorite people is *Uncle Fred.*
>
> Jim and my *uncle* went along.

ABBREVIATIONS

Capitalize abbreviations if the words they stand for would be capitalized.

> EXAMPLES UCLA (University of California at Los Angeles)
>
> p. (page)

LETTERS

Capitalize letters that serve as names or indicate shapes.

> EXAMPLES X-ray, vitamin B, T-square, U-turn, I-beam

MISCELLANEOUS CAPITALIZATIONS

The word *Bible* is capitalized when it refers to the Jewish or Christian Scriptures; otherwise, it is not capitalized.

> EXAMPLE He quoted a verse from the *Bible,* then read from Blackstone, the lawyer's *bible.*

All references to deities (Allah, God, Jehovah, Yahweh) are capitalized.

> EXAMPLE *God* is the *One* who sustains us.

A complete sentence enclosed in dashes, brackets, or parentheses is not capitalized when it appears as part of another sentence.

EXAMPLES We must make an extra effort in safety this year *(accidents last year were up 10 percent).*

Extra effort in safety should be made this year. *(Accidents were up 10 percent.)*

Certain units, such as parts and chapters of books and rooms in buildings, when specifically identified by number, are normally capitalized.

EXAMPLES Chapter 5, Ch. 5; Room 72, Rm. 72

Minor divisions within such units are not capitalized unless they begin a sentence.

EXAMPLES page 11, verse 14, seat 12

colons

The colon is a mark of anticipation and introduction that alerts the reader to the close connection between the first statement and the one that follows it.

A colon may be used to connect a list or series to the clause, word, or phrase with which it is in apposition.

EXAMPLE Three decontamination methods are under consideration: a zeolite-resin system, an evaporation and resin system, and a filtration and storage system.

Do not, however, place a colon between a verb and its objects.

CHANGE The three fluids for cleaning pipettes are: water, alcohol, and acetone.

TO The three fluids for cleaning pipettes are water, alcohol, and acetone.

One common exception is made when a verb is followed by a stacked list.

EXAMPLE The corporations that manufacture computers include:

Apple	Compaq	DEC
IBM	Unisys	Gateway

Do not use a colon between a preposition and its object.

CHANGE I would like to be transferred to: Tucson, Boston, or Miami.

TO I would like to be transferred to Tucson, Boston, or Miami.

A colon may be used to link one statement to another that develops, explains, amplifies, or illustrates the first.

EXAMPLE Any large organization is confronted with two separate, though related, information problems: it must maintain an effective internal communication system, and it must see that an effective overall communication system is maintained.

A colon may be used to link an appositive phrase to its related statement if greater emphasis is needed.

> **EXAMPLE** There is only one thing that will satisfy Mr. Sturgess: our finished report.

Colons are used to link numbers signifying different identifying nouns.

> **EXAMPLES** Matthew 14:1 (chapter 14, verse 1)
>
> 9:30 a.m. (9 hours, 30 minutes)

In proportions, the colon indicates the ratio of one amount to another.

> **EXAMPLE** The cement is mixed with the water and sand at 7:5:14. (In this case, the colon replaces *to.*)

Colons are often used in mathematical ratios.

> **EXAMPLE** $7:3 = 14:x$

In bibliography, footnote, and reference citations, colons may link the place of publication with the publisher and perform other specialized functions.

> **EXAMPLE** Watson, R. L. *Statistics for Electrical Engineers.* Englewood, CA: EEE, 1992.

A colon follows the salutation in business letters, even when the salutation refers to a person by name.

> **EXAMPLES** Dear Ms. Jeffers:
>
> Dear Manager:
>
> Dear George:

The initial capital letter of a quotation is retained following a colon if the quoted material originally began with a capital letter.

> **EXAMPLE** The senator issued the following statement: "We are not concerned about the present. We are worried about the future."

A colon always goes outside quotation marks.

> **EXAMPLE** This was the real meaning of his "suggestion": the division must show a profit by the end of the year.

When quoting material that ends in a colon, drop the colon and replace it with ellipses.

> **CHANGE** "Any large corporation is confronted with two separate, though related, information problems:"
>
> **TO** "Any large corporation is confronted with two separate, though related, information problems . . ."

The first word after a colon may be capitalized if (1) the statement following is a complete sentence or (2) it introduces a formal resolution or question.

> EXAMPLE   The members attending this year's conference passed a single resolution: Voting will be open to associate members next year.

If a subordinate element follows the colon, however, use a lowercase letter following the colon.

> EXAMPLE   There is only one way to stay within our present budget: to reduce expenditures for research and development.

commas

DIRECTORY

Like all punctuation, the comma helps readers understand the writer's meaning and prevents ambiguity. Notice how the comma helps make the meaning clear in the following example:

> CHANGE   To be successful managers with MBAs must continue to learn. (At first glance, this sentence seems to be about "successful managers with MBAs.")
>
> TO   To be successful, managers with MBAs must continue to learn. (The comma makes clear where the main part of the sentence begins.)

As this example illustrates, effective use of the comma depends on your understanding of sentence construction.

LINKING INDEPENDENT CLAUSES

Use a comma before a coordinating conjunction *(and, but, or, nor,* and sometimes *so, yet,* and *for)* that links independent clauses.

> EXAMPLE   Human beings have always prided themselves on their unique capacity to create and manipulate symbols, *but* today computers are manipulating symbols.

Although many writers omit the comma when the clauses are short and closely related, the comma can never be wrong.

> EXAMPLES The cable snapped and the power failed.
>
> The cable snapped, and the power failed.

ENCLOSING ELEMENTS

Commas are used to enclose nonrestrictive clauses and parenthetical elements. (For other means of punctuating parenthetical elements, see the **dashes** and **parentheses** entries in this tabbed section.)

> EXAMPLES Our new Detroit factory, *which began operations last month,* should add 25 percent to total output. (nonrestrictive clause)
>
> The lathe operator, *working quickly and efficiently,* finished early. (nonrestrictive phrase)
>
> We can, *of course,* expect their lawyer to call us. (parenthetical element)

(See also the **restrictive and nonrestrictive elements** entry on the GRAMMAR tab.)

Yes and *no* are set off by commas in such uses as the following:

> EXAMPLES I agree with you, *yes.*
>
> *No,* I do not think we can finish as soon as we would like.

A direct address should be enclosed in commas.

> EXAMPLE You will note, *Mark,* that the surface of the brake shoe complies with the specifications.

Phrases in apposition (which help identify another expression) are enclosed in commas.

> EXAMPLE Our company, *The Blaylok Precision Company,* did well this year.

Interrupting transitional words or phrases are usually set off with commas.

> EXAMPLE We must wait for the written authorization to arrive, *however,* before we can begin work on the project.

Commas are omitted when the word or phrase does not interrupt the continuity of thought.

> EXAMPLE I *therefore* suggest that we begin construction.

INTRODUCING ELEMENTS

Clauses and Phrases. It is generally a good rule of thumb to put a comma after an introductory clause or phrase. Identifying where the introductory element ends helps indicate where the main part of the sentence begins.

Always place a comma after a long introductory clause.

> **EXAMPLE** *Since many rare fossils seem never to occur free from their matrix,* it is wise to scan every slab with a hand lens.

When long modifying phrases precede the main clause, they should always be followed by a comma.

> **EXAMPLE** *During the first series of field-performance tests last year at our Colorado proving ground,* the new motor failed to meet our expectations.

When an introductory phrase is short and closely related to the main clause, the comma may be omitted.

> **EXAMPLE** *In two seconds* a 20 degrees Fahrenheit temperature is created in the test tube.

A comma should always follow an introductory absolute phrase.

> **EXAMPLE** *The tests completed,* we organized the data for the final report.

Words and Quotations. Certain types of introductory words are followed by a comma. One such is a proper noun used in direct address.

> **EXAMPLE** *Bill,* enclosed is the article you asked me to review.

An introductory interjection (such as *oh, well, why, indeed, yes,* and *no*) is followed by a comma.

> **EXAMPLES** *Yes,* I will make sure your request is approved.
>
> *Indeed,* I will be glad to send you further information.

A transitional word or phrase like *moreover* or *furthermore* is usually followed by a comma to connect the following thought with the preceding clause or sentence.

> **EXAMPLES** *Moreover,* steel can withstand a humidity of 99 percent, provided that there is no chloride or sulphur dioxide in the atmosphere.
>
> *In addition,* we can expect a better world market as a result of this move.
>
> *However,* we should expect some shortages due to the overall economic climate.

When adverbs closely modify the verb or the entire sentence, however, they should not be followed by a comma.

> **EXAMPLES** *Perhaps* we can still solve the environmental problem. *Certainly* we should try.

Use a comma to separate a direct quotation from its introduction.

> **EXAMPLE** Morton and Lucia White said, "Men live in cities but dream of the countryside."

Do not use a comma, however, when giving an indirect quotation.

> **EXAMPLE** Morton and Lucia White said that men dream of the countryside, even though they live in cities.

SEPARATING ITEMS IN SERIES

Although the comma before the last word in a series is sometimes omitted, it is generally clearer to include it. The confusion that may result from omitting the comma is illustrated in the following sentence:

> **CHANGE** Random House, Irwin, Doubleday and Dell are publishing companies. (Is "Doubleday and Dell" one company or two?)
>
> **TO** Random House, Irwin, Doubleday, and Dell are publishing companies.

The presence of the comma removes the ambiguity.

Phrases and clauses in coordinate series, like words, are punctuated with commas.

> **EXAMPLE** It is well known that plants absorb noxious gases, act as receptors of dirt particles, and cleanse the air of other impurities.

When adjectives modifying the same noun can be reversed and make sense, or when they can be separated by *and* or *or,* they should be separated by commas.

> **EXAMPLE** The drawing was of a *modern, sleek, swept-wing* airplane.

When an adjective modifies a phrase, no comma is required.

> **EXAMPLE** He was investigating his *damaged radar beacon system. (damaged* modifies the phrase *radar beacon system)*

Never separate a final adjective from its noun.

> **CHANGE** He is a conscientious, honest, reliable, worker.
>
> **TO** He is a conscientious, honest, reliable worker.

CLARIFYING AND CONTRASTING

If you find you need a comma to separate the consecutive use of the same word to prevent misreading, rewrite the sentence.

> **CHANGE** The assets we had, had surprised us.
>
> **TO** We were surprised at the assets we had.

Use a comma to separate two contrasting thoughts or ideas.

> **EXAMPLE** The project was finished on time, but not within the budget.

Use a comma following an independent clause that is only loosely related to the dependent clause that follows it.

> **EXAMPLE** I should finish the plan by July, even though I lost time because of illness.

SHOWING OMISSIONS

A comma sometimes replaces a verb in certain elliptical constructions.

> **EXAMPLE** Some were punctual; *others, late.* (replaces *were*)

However, it is better to avoid such constructions in on-the-job writing.

USING WITH OTHER PUNCTUATION

Conjunctive adverbs (*however, nevertheless, consequently, for example, on the other hand*) joining independent clauses are preceded by a semicolon and followed by a comma. Such adverbs function as both modifiers and connectives.

> **EXAMPLE** Your idea is good; *however,* your format is poor.

Use a semicolon to separate phrases or clauses in a series when one or more of the phrases or clauses contains commas.

> **EXAMPLE** Among those present were John Howard, president of the Howard Paper Company; Thomas Martin, president of Copco Corporation; and Larry Stanley, president of Stanley Papers.

A comma always goes inside quotation marks.

> **EXAMPLE** The operator placed the discharge bypass switch at "normal," which triggered a second discharge.

When an introductory phrase or clause ends with a parenthesis, the comma separating the introductory phrase or clause from the rest of the sentence always appears outside the parenthesis.

> **EXAMPLE** Although we left late (at 7:30 p.m.), we arrived in time for the keynote address.

Except with abbreviations, a comma should not be used with a period, question mark, exclamation mark, or dash.

> **CHANGE** "Have you finished the project?," I asked.
>
> **TO** "Have you finished the project?" I asked. (omit the comma)

Using with Numbers and Names

Commas are conventionally used to separate distinct items. Use commas between the elements of an address written on the same line.

EXAMPLE Walter James, 4119 Mill Road, Dayton, Ohio 45401

A date can be written with or without a comma following the year if the date is in the month–day–year format.

EXAMPLES October 26, 19--, was the date the project began.

October 26, 19-- was the date the project began.

If the date is in the day–month–year format, do not set off the date with commas.

EXAMPLE The date was 26 October 19-- when the project began.

Use commas to separate the elements of Arabic numbers.

EXAMPLE 1,528,200

Use a space rather than a comma in metric values, because many countries use the comma as the decimal marker.

EXAMPLE 1 528 200

A comma may be substituted for the colon in a personal letter. Do not use a comma in a business letter, however, even if you use the person's first name.

EXAMPLES Dear John, (personal letter)

Dear John: (business letter)

Use commas to separate the elements of geographical names.

EXAMPLE Toronto, Ontario, Canada

Use a comma to separate names that are reversed or that are followed by an abbreviation.

EXAMPLE Smith, Alvin

Jane Rogers, Ph.D.

LMB, Inc.

Use commas to separate certain elements of footnote, reference, and bibliography entries.

EXAMPLES Bibliography—Barnett, Walter, ed. *Handbook of Correspondence.* Westport, CT: Greenwood, 1992.

Footnote—[1]Barnett, Walter, ed. *Handbook of Correspondence.* (Westport, CT: Greenwood, 1992) 30.

Reference—1. Barnett, Walter, ed. *Handbook of Correspondence.* Westport, CT: Greenwood Press, 1992.

AVOIDING UNNECESSARY COMMAS

A number of common writing errors involve placing commas where they do not belong. These errors often occur because writers assume that a pause in a sentence should be indicated by a comma. It is true that commas usually signal pauses, but it is not true that pauses necessarily call for commas.

Be careful not to place a comma between a subject and verb or between a verb and its object.

CHANGE   The cold conditions at the test site in the Arctic, made accurate readings difficult.

TO   The cold conditions at the test site in the Arctic made accurate readings difficult.

CHANGE   He has often said, that one company's failure is another's opportunity.

TO   He has often said that one company's failure is another's opportunity.

Do not use a comma between the elements of a compound subject or a compound predicate consisting of only two elements.

CHANGE   The director of the engineering department, and the supervisor of the quality-control section both were opposed to the new schedules.

TO   The director of the engineering department and the supervisor of the quality-control section both were opposed to the new schedules.

CHANGE   The director of the engineering department listed five major objections, and asked that the new schedule be reconsidered.

TO   The director of the engineering department listed five major objections and asked that the new schedule be reconsidered.

An especially common error is placing a comma after a coordinating conjunction such as *and* or *but*.

CHANGE   The chairman formally adjourned the meeting, but, the members of the committee continued to argue.

TO   The chairman formally adjourned the meeting, but the members of the committee continued to argue.

Do not place a comma before the first item or after the last item of a series.

CHANGE   We are considering a number of new products, such as, calculators, scanners, and cameras.

TO   We are considering a number of new products, such as calculators, scanners, and cameras.

CHANGE   It was a fast, simple, inexpensive, process.

TO   It was a fast, simple, inexpensive process.

Do not unnecessarily separate a prepositional phrase from the rest of the sentence with a comma.

> CHANGE We discussed the final report, on the new project.
>
> TO We discussed the final report on the new project.

contractions

A contraction is a shortened spelling of a word or phrase with an apostrophe substituting for the missing letters.

> EXAMPLES cannot/can't
>
> will not/won't
>
> have not/haven't
>
> it is/it's

Contractions are often used in speech but should be used discriminatingly in reports, formal letters, and most business writing.

dashes

The dash is a versatile, yet limited, mark of punctuation. It is versatile because it can perform all the duties of punctuation (to link, to separate, and to enclose). It is limited because it is an especially emphatic mark that is easily overused. Use the dash cautiously, therefore, to indicate more informality or emphasis (a dash gives an impression of abruptness) than would be achieved by the conventional punctuation marks. In some situations, a dash is needed; in others, a dash is a forceful substitute for other marks.

A dash can emphasize a sharp turn in thought.

> EXAMPLE The project will end January 15—unless the company provides additional funds.

A dash can indicate an emphatic pause.

> EXAMPLE The job will be done—after we are under contract.

Sometimes, to emphasize contrast, a dash is also used with *but*.

> EXAMPLE We may have produced work more quickly—but the result was not as good.

A dash can be used before a final summarizing statement or before repetition that has the effect of an afterthought.

> EXAMPLE It was hot near the ovens—steaming hot.

Such a thought may also complete the meaning.

> **EXAMPLE** We try to speak as we write—or so we believe.

A dash can be used to set off an explanatory or appositive series.

> **EXAMPLE** Three of the applicants—John Evans, Mary Fontana, and Thomas Lopez—seem well qualified for the job.

Dashes set off parenthetical elements more sharply and emphatically than commas. Unlike dashes, parentheses tend to reduce the importance of what they enclose. Compare the following sentences:

> **EXAMPLES** Only one person—the president—can authorize such activity.
>
> Only one person, the president, can authorize such activity.
>
> Only one person (the president) can authorize such activity.

The first word after a dash is never capitalized unless it is a proper noun.

dates

In business and industry, dates have traditionally been indicated by the month, day, and year, with a comma separating the figures.

> **EXAMPLE** October 26, 19--

The day–month–year system used by the military does not require commas.

> **EXAMPLE** 26 October 19--

A date can be written with or without a comma following the year if the date is in the month–day–year format.

> **EXAMPLES** October 26, 19--, was the date the project began.
>
> October 26, 19-- was the date the project began.

The strictly numerical form for dates (10/26/95) should be used sparingly, and never on business letters or formal documents, since it is less immediately clear. When this form is used, the order in American usage is always month/day/year. For example, 5/7/95 is May 7, 1995.

CENTURIES

Confusion often occurs because the spelled-out names of centuries do not correspond to the numbers of the years.

> **EXAMPLE** The twentieth century is the 1900s (1900–1999).

When the century is written as a noun, do not use a hyphen.

> **EXAMPLE** The sixteenth century produced great literature.

When the century is written as an adjective, however, use a hyphen.

EXAMPLE Twentieth-century technology must rely on clear communications.

ellipses

When you omit words in quoted material, use a series of three spaced periods—called *ellipsis dots*—to indicate the omission.

EXAMPLES Material distributed for promotional use is sometimes charged for, particularly in high-volume distribution to schools, although prices for these publications are not uniformly based on the cost of developing them. (without omission)

Material distributed for promotional use is sometimes charged for . . . although prices for these publications are not uniformly based on the cost of developing them. (with omission)

When the omitted portion comes at the beginning of the sentence, begin the quotation with a lowercase letter.

EXAMPLES "When the programmer has determined a system of runs, he must create a system flowchart to provide a picture of the data flow through the system." (without omission)

The letter states that the programmer " . . . must create a system flowchart to provide a picture of the data flow through the system." (with omission)

When the omission comes at the end of a sentence and you continue the quotation following the omission, use four periods to indicate both the final period to end the sentence and the omission.

EXAMPLES In all publications departments except ours, publications funds— once they are initially allocated by higher management—are controlled by publications personnel. Our company is the only one to have nonpublications people control funding within a budget period. In addition, all publications departments control printing funds as well. (without omission)

In all publications departments except ours, publications funds— once they are initially allocated by higher management—are controlled by publications personnel. . . . In addition, all publications departments control printing funds as well. (with omission)

Use a full line of periods across the page to indicate the omission of one or more paragraphs.

EXAMPLES A computer system operates with two types of programs: the software programs supplied by the manufacturer and the programs created by the user. The manufacturer's software consists of a number of programs that enable the system to perform complicated manipulations of data from the relatively simple instructions specified in the user's program.

Programmers must take a systematic approach to solving any data-processing problem. They must first clearly define the problem, and then they must define a system of runs that will solve the problem. For example, a given problem may require a validation and sort run to handle account numbers or employee numbers, a computation and update run to manipulate the data for the output reports, and a print run to produce the output reports.

When a system of runs has been determined, the programmer must create a system flowchart to provide a picture of the data flow through the system. (without omission)

A computer system operates with two types of programs: the software programs supplied by the manufacturer and the programs created by the user. The manufacturer's software consists of a number of programs that enable the system to perform complicated manipulations of data from the relatively simple instructions specified in the user's program.

....

When a system of runs has been determined, the programmer must create a system flowchart to provide a picture of the data flow through the system. (with omission)

Do not use ellipsis dots for any purpose other than to indicate omission.

exclamation marks

The purpose of the exclamation mark (!) is to indicate the expression of strong feeling. It can signal surprise, indignation, or excitement. It cannot make an argument more convincing, lend force to a weak statement, or call attention to an intended irony.

Uses

The most common use of an exclamation mark is after an interjection, phrase, clause, or sentence to indicate surprise. Interjections are words that express strong emotion.

EXAMPLES Oh! Stop! Hurry!

An exclamation mark can also be used after a whole sentence, or even an element of a sentence.

EXAMPLES The subject of this meeting—please note it well!—is our budget deficit.

How exciting is Stravinsky's *Rite of Spring!*

An exclamation mark is sometimes used after a title that is an exclamatory word, phrase or sentence.

> EXAMPLES "Our Marketing Strategy Must Change!" is an article by Richard Moody.
>
> *The Cancer with No Cure!* is a book by Wilbur Moody.

When used with quotation marks, the exclamation mark goes outside, unless what is quoted is an exclamation.

> EXAMPLE The boss yelled, "Get in here!" Then Ben, according to Ray, "jumped like a kangaroo"!

hyphens

Although the hyphen functions primarily as a spelling device, it also functions to link and to separate words; in addition, it occasionally replaces the preposition *to* (0–100 for 0 *to* 100). The most common use of the hyphen, however, is to join compound words.

> EXAMPLES able-bodied, self-contained, carry-all, brother-in-law

A hyphen is used to form compound numbers from twenty-one to ninety-nine and fractions when they are written out.

> EXAMPLES twenty-one, one forty-second

When in doubt about whether or where to hyphenate a word, check your dictionary.

HYPHENS USED WITH MODIFIERS

Two-word and three-word unit modifiers that express a single thought are hyphenated when they precede a noun (an *out-of-date* car, a *clear-cut* decision). If each of the words can modify the noun without the aid of the other modifying word or words, however, do not use a hyphen (a *new digital* computer—no hyphen). Also, if the first word is an adverb ending in *-ly*, do not use a hyphen (a *hardly* used computer, a *badly* needed micrometer).

The presence or absence of a hyphen can alter the meaning of a sentence.

> EXAMPLE We need a biological waste management system.
>
> COULD MEAN We need a biological-waste management system.
>
> OR We need a biological waste-management system.

A modifying phrase is not hyphenated when it follows the noun it modifies.

> EXAMPLE Our office equipment is *out of date.*

A hyphen is always used as part of a letter or number modifier.

> **EXAMPLES** 5-cent, 9-inch, A-frame, H-bomb

In a series of unit modifiers that all have the same term following the hyphen, the term following the hyphen need not be repeated throughout the series; for greater smoothness and brevity, use the term only at the end of the series.

> **CHANGE** The third-floor, fourth-floor, and fifth-floor rooms have recently been painted.
>
> **TO** The third-, fourth-, and fifth-floor rooms have recently been painted.

Hyphens Used with Prefixes and Suffixes

A hyphen is used with a prefix when the root word is a proper noun.

> **EXAMPLES** *pre*-Sputnik, *anti*-Stalinist, *post*-Newtonian

A hyphen may optionally be used when the prefix ends and the root word begins with the same vowel.

> **EXAMPLES** re-elect, re-enter, anti-inflationary

A hyphen is used when *ex-* means "former."

> **EXAMPLES** ex-partners, ex-wife

A hyphen may be used to emphasize a prefix.

> **EXAMPLE** He was *anti-everything.*

The suffix *-elect* is hyphenated.

> **EXAMPLES** president-elect, commissioner-elect

Other Uses of the Hyphen

To avoid confusion, some words and modifiers should always be hyphenated. *Re-cover* does not mean the same thing as *recover,* for example; the same is true of *re-sent* and *resent, re-form* and *reform, re-sign* and *resign.*
Hyphens should be used between letters showing how a word is spelled.

> **EXAMPLE** In his letter he misspelled *believed* b-e-l-e-i-v-e-d.

A hyphen can stand for *to* or *through* between letters and numbers.

> **EXAMPLES** pp. 44-46
>
> the Detroit-Toledo Expressway
>
> A-L and M-Z

Finally, hyphens are used to divide words at the end of a line. Avoid dividing words whenever possible, but, if you must, use the following guidelines for hyphenation:

Divide

- Between syllables (but leave at least three letters on each line)
  EXAMPLE let-ter
- Between the compounding parts of compound words
  EXAMPLE time-table
- After a single-letter syllable in the middle of the root word
  EXAMPLE sepa-rate
- After a prefix
  EXAMPLE pre-view
- Before a suffix
  EXAMPLE cap-tion
- Between two consecutive vowels with separate sounds
  EXAMPLE gladi-ator

Do Not Divide

- A word that is pronounced as one syllable
  EXAMPLE shipped
- A contraction
  EXAMPLE you're
- An abbreviation or acronym
  EXAMPLE AOPA
- A proper noun
  EXAMPLE Jim Wilson

italics

Italics (indicated on the typewriter by underlining) is a style of type used to denote emphasis and to distinguish foreign expressions, book titles, and certain other elements. *This sentence is printed in italics.* You may need to italicize words that require special emphasis in a sentence.

> EXAMPLE Contrary to projections, sales have *not* improved since we started the new procedure.

Do not overuse italics for emphasis, however.

> CHANGE This will hurt *you* more than *me*.
>
> TO This will hurt you more than me!

TITLES

Italicize the titles of books, periodicals, newspapers, movies, and paintings.

> EXAMPLE The *Cincinnati Enquirer* is one of our oldest newspapers.

Abbreviations of such titles are italicized if their spelled-out forms would be italicized.

> EXAMPLE The *Journal of QA Technology* is an informative publication.

Titles of chapters or articles within publications and titles of reports are placed in quotation marks, not italicized.

> EXAMPLE "Clarity, the Business Writer's Tightrope" was an article in the *Wall Street Journal.*

Titles of holy books and legislative documents are not italicized.

> EXAMPLE The Bible and the Magna Carta changed the history of Western civilization.

Titles of long poems and musical works are italicized, but titles of short poems and musical works and songs are enclosed in quotation marks.

> EXAMPLES Milton's *Paradise Lost* (long poem)
>
> T.S. Eliot's "The Love Song of J. Alfred Prufrock" (short poem)

PROPER NAMES

The names of ships, trains, and aircraft (but not the companies that own them) are italicized.

> EXAMPLE They sailed to Africa on the Onassis *Clipper* but flew back on the United *New Yorker.*

Craft that are known by model or serial designations are exceptions. These are not italicized.

> EXAMPLES DC-7, Boeing 747

WORDS, LETTERS, AND FIGURES

Words, letters, and figures discussed as such are italicized.

> EXAMPLES The word *inflammable* is often misinterpreted.
>
> I should replace the *s* and the *6* keys on my dad's old typewriter.

FOREIGN WORDS

Foreign words that have not been assimilated into the English language are italicized.

 EXAMPLES *sine qua non, coup de grâce, in res, in camera*

Foreign words that have been fully assimilated into the language, however, need not be italicized.

 EXAMPLES cliché, etiquette, vis-à-vis, de facto, siesta

SUBHEADS

Subheads in a report are sometimes italicized.

 EXAMPLE There was no publications department as such, and the writing groups were duplicated at each plant or location. Wellington, for example, had such a large number of publications groups that their publication efforts can only be described as disorganized. Their duplication of effort must have been enormous.

  Training Writers

  We are certainly leading the way in developing first-line managers (or writing supervisors) who are not only professionally competent but can also train the writers under their direction and be responsible for writing quality as well.

numbers

GENERAL GUIDELINES

1. Write numbers from zero to ten as words and numbers above ten as figures.
2. Spell out approximate numbers.
3. In most writing, do not spell out ordinal numbers, which express degree or sequence (42nd), unless they are single words (tenth, sixteenth).
4. When several numbers appear in the same sentence or paragraph, express them alike, regardless of other rules and guidelines.

 EXAMPLE The company owned 150 trucks, employed 271 people, and rented 7 warehouses.

5. Spell out numbers that begin a sentence, even if they would otherwise be written as figures.

 EXAMPLE One hundred and fifty people attended the meeting.

If spelling out such a number seems awkward, rewrite the sentence so that the number does not appear at the beginning.

EXAMPLE The meeting was attended by 150 people.

6. Do not follow a word representing a number with a figure in parentheses representing the same number. This is redundant.

CHANGE Send five (5) copies of the report.

TO Send five copies of the report.

PLURALS

The plural of a written number is formed by adding *s* or *es* or by dropping *y* and adding *ies,* depending on the last letter, just as the plural of any other noun is formed.

EXAMPLES sixes, elevens, twenties

The plural of a figure may be written with *s* alone or with *'s.*

EXAMPLES 5s, 12s or 5's, 12's

DOCUMENT PARTS

In typed manuscript, page numbers are written as figures, but chapter or volume numbers may appear as figures or words.

EXAMPLES Page 37

Chapter 2 or Chapter Two

Volume 1 or Volume One

Figure and table numbers are expressed as figures.

EXAMPLE Figure 4 and Table 3

MEASUREMENTS

Units of measurement are expressed in figures.

EXAMPLES 3 miles, 45 cubic feet, 9 meters, 27 cubic centimeters, 4 picas

When numbers appear run together in the same phrase, write one as a figure and the other as a word.

CHANGE The order was for 12 6-inch pipes.

TO The order was for twelve 6-inch pipes.

Percentages are normally given as figures, and the word *percent* is written out, except when the number is in a table.

EXAMPLE Approximately 85 *percent* of the area has been sold.

FRACTIONS

Fractions are expressed as figures when written with whole numbers.

EXAMPLES 27½ inches, 4¼ miles

Fractions are spelled out when they are expressed without a whole number.

EXAMPLES one-fourth, seven-eighths

Numbers with decimals are always written as figures.

EXAMPLE 5.21 meters

TIME

Hours and minutes are expressed as figures when a.m. and p.m. follow.

EXAMPLES 11:30 a.m., 7:30 p.m.

When not followed by a.m. or p.m., however, time should be spelled out.

EXAMPLES four o'clock, eleven o'clock

DATES

The year and day of the month should be written as figures. Dates are usually written in a month–day–year sequence, in which the year may or may not be followed by a comma.

EXAMPLE The August 26, 19-- issue of *Computer World* announced the new system.

In the day–month–year sequence, commas are not used.

EXAMPLE The 26 August 19-- issue of *Computer World* announced the new system.

The slash form of expressing dates (8/24/95) is used in informal writing only.

ADDRESSES

Numbered streets from one to ten should be spelled out except when space is at a premium.

EXAMPLE East Tenth Street

Building numbers are written as figures. The only exception is the building number *one*.

EXAMPLES 4862 East Monument Street

One East Tenth Street

Highways are written as figures.

EXAMPLES U.S. 70, Ohio 271, I-94

parentheses

Parentheses ( ) are used to enclose words, phrases, or sentences. The material within parentheses can add clarity to a statement without altering its meaning. Parentheses de-emphasize (or play down) an inserted element. Parenthetical information may not be essential to a sentence, but it may be interesting or helpful to some readers.

> **EXAMPLE** Aluminum is extracted from its ore (called bauxite) in three stages.

Parenthetical material applies to the word or phrase immediately preceding it.

> **EXAMPLE** The development of International Business Machines (IBM) is a uniquely American success story.

Parentheses may be used to enclose figures or letters that indicate sequence. Enclose the figure or letter with two parentheses rather than using only one parenthesis.

> **EXAMPLE** The following sections deal with (1) preparation, (2) research, (3) organization, (4) writing, and (5) revision.

Parenthetical material does not affect the punctuation of a sentence. If a parenthesis closes a sentence, the ending punctuation should appear after the parenthesis. Also, a comma following a parenthetical word, phrase, or clause appears outside the closing parenthesis.

> **EXAMPLE** These oxygen-rich chemicals, as for instance potassium permanganate ($KMnO_4$) and potassium chromate ($KCrO_4$), were oxidizing agents (they added oxygen to a substance).

However, when a complete sentence within parentheses stands independently, the ending punctuation goes inside the final parenthesis.

> **EXAMPLE** The new marketing approach appears to be a success; most of our regional managers report sales increases of 15 to 30 percent. (The only important exceptions are the Denver and Houston offices.) Therefore, we plan to continue . . .

In some footnote forms, parentheses enclose the publisher, place of publication, and date of publication.

> **EXAMPLE** [1]J. Demarco, *Nuclear Reactor Theory* (Reading, MA: Addison, 1991) 9.

Use brackets to set off a parenthetical item that is already within parentheses.

> **EXAMPLE** We should be sure to give Emanuel Foose (and his brother Emilio [1812–1882] as well) credit for his part in founding the institute.

periods

A period usually indicates the end of a declarative sentence. Periods also link (when used as leaders) and indicate omissions (when used as ellipses).

Although the primary function of periods is to end declarative sentences, periods also end imperative sentences that are not emphatic enough for an exclamation mark.

> EXAMPLE Send me any information you may have on the subject.

Periods may also end questions that are really polite requests and questions to which an affirmative response is assumed.

> EXAMPLE Will you please send me the specifications.

IN QUOTATIONS

Do not use a period after a declarative sentence that is quoted in the context of another sentence.

> CHANGE "There is every chance of success." she stated.
>
> TO "There is every chance of success," she stated.

A period is conventionally placed inside quotation marks.

> EXAMPLES He liked to think of himself as a "tycoon."
>
> He stated clearly, "My vote is yes."

WITH PARENTHESES

A sentence that ends in a parenthesis requires a period *after* the parenthesis.

> EXAMPLE The institute was founded by Harry Denman (1902–1972).

If a whole sentence (beginning with an initial capital letter) is in parentheses, the period (or any other end mark) should be placed inside the final parenthesis.

> EXAMPLE The project director listed the problems facing her staff. (This was the third time she had complained to the board.)

CONVENTIONAL USES OF PERIODS

Use periods after initials in names.

> EXAMPLES W. T. Grant, J. P. Morgan

Use periods as decimal points with numbers.

> EXAMPLES 109.2, $540.26, 6.9

Use periods to indicate abbreviations.

EXAMPLES Ms., Dr., Inc.

When a sentence ends with an abbreviation that ends with a period, do not add another period.

EXAMPLE Please meet me at 3:30 p.m.

Use periods following the numbers in numbered lists.

EXAMPLE 1.
2.
3.

PERIOD FAULTS

The incorrect use of a period is sometimes referred to as a *period fault*. When a period is inserted prematurely, the result is a sentence fragment.

CHANGE After a long day at the office in which we finished the report. We left hurriedly for home.

TO After a long day at the office in which we finished the report, we left hurriedly for home.

When a period is left out, the result is a "fused," or run-on, sentence. Be careful never to leave out necessary periods.

CHANGE Bill was late for ten days in a row Ms. Sturgess had to fire him.

TO Bill was late for ten days in a row. Ms. Sturgess had to fire him.

question marks

The question mark (?) has the following uses:
Use a question mark to end a sentence that is a direct question.

EXAMPLE Where did you put the specifications?

Use a question mark to end any statement with an interrogative meaning (a statement that is declarative in form but asks a question).

EXAMPLE The report is finished?

Use a question mark to end an interrogative clause within a declarative sentence.

EXAMPLE It was not until July (or was it August?) that we submitted the report.

Retain the question mark in a title that is being cited, even though the sentence in which it appears has not ended.

EXAMPLE *Should Engineers Be Writers?* is the title of her book.

When used with quotations, the question mark indicates whether the writer who is doing the quoting or the person being quoted is asking the question. When the writer doing the quoting asks the question, the question mark is outside the quotation marks.

> **EXAMPLE** Did she say, "I don't think the project should continue"?

If, on the other hand, the quotation itself is a question, the question mark goes inside the quotation marks.

> **EXAMPLE** She asked, "When will we go?"

If the writer doing the quoting and the person being quoted both ask questions, use a single question mark inside the quotation marks.

> **EXAMPLE** Did she ask, "Will you go in my place?"

Question marks may follow a series of separate items within an interrogative sentence.

> **EXAMPLE** Do you remember the date of the contract? its terms? whether you signed it?

A question mark should never be used at the end of an indirect question.

> **CHANGE** He asked me whether sales had increased this year?
>
> **TO** He asked me whether sales had increased this year.

When a directive or command is phrased as a question, a question mark is usually not used. However, a request (to a customer or a superior, for instance) almost always requires a question mark.

> **EXAMPLES** Will you make sure that the machinery is operational by August 15.
>
> Will you please telephone me collect if your entire shipment does not arrive by June 10?

quotation marks

Quotation marks (" ") are used to enclose direct repetition of spoken or written words. They should not be used to emphasize. There are a variety of guidelines for using quotation marks.

Enclose in quotation marks anything that is quoted word for word (direct quotation) from speech.

> **EXAMPLE** She said clearly, "I want the progress report by three o'clock."

Do not enclose indirect quotations—usually introduced by *that*—in quotation marks. Indirect quotations are paraphrases of a speaker's words or ideas.

> **EXAMPLE** She said that she wanted the progress report by three o'clock.

Handle quotations from written material the same way: place direct quotations, but not indirect quotations, within quotation marks.

> EXAMPLE   The report stated, "The potential in Florida for our franchise is as great as in California."
>
> The report indicated that the potential for our franchise is as great in Florida as in California.

If you use quotation marks to indicate that you are quoting, you may not make any changes in the quoted material unless you clearly indicate what you have done. (See the **brackets** entry in this tabbed section.)

Quotations longer than four typed lines (at least fifty characters per line) are normally indented (*all* the lines) five spaces from the left margin, single-spaced, and *not* enclosed in quotation marks.

Unless it is indented as just described, a quotation of more than one paragraph is given quotation marks at the beginning of each new paragraph, but at the end of only the last paragraph.

Use single quotation marks (on a typewriter use the apostrophe key) to enclose a quotation that appears within a quotation.

> EXAMPLE   John said, "Jane told me that she was going to 'hang tough' until the deadline is past."

Use quotation marks to set off special words or terms only to point out that the term is used in context for a unique or special purpose (used, that is, in the sense of the *so-called*).

> EXAMPLE   Typical of deductive analyses in real life are accident investigations: What chain of events caused the sinking of an "unsinkable" ship such as the *Titanic* on its maiden voyage?

However, slang, colloquial expressions, and attempts at humor, although infrequent in on-the-job writing, seldom rate being set off by quotation marks.

> CHANGE   Our first six months in the new office amounted to little more than a "shakedown cruise" for what lay ahead.
>
> TO   Our first six months in the new office amounted to little more than a shakedown cruise for what lay ahead.

Use quotation marks to enclose titles of reports, short stories, articles, essays, radio and television programs, short musical works, paintings, and other art works.

> EXAMPLE   Did you see the article, "No-Fault Insurance and Your Motorcycle" in last Sunday's *Journal*?

Titles of books and periodicals are underlined (to be typeset in italics).

EXAMPLE Articles in the *Business Education Forum* and *The Wall Street Journal* quoted the same passage.

Some titles, by convention, are neither set off by quotation marks nor underlined, although they are capitalized.

EXAMPLES Business Writing (college course title), the Bible, the Constitution, Lincoln's Gettysburg Address, the Montgomery Ward Catalog

Commas and periods always go inside closing quotation marks.

EXAMPLE "Reading *Space Technology* gives me the insider's view," he says, adding "it's like having all the top officials sitting in my office for a bull session."

Semicolons and colons always go outside the closing quotation marks.

EXAMPLE The following are her favorite "sports": eating and sleeping.

All other punctuation follows the logic of the context: If the punctuation is a part of the material quoted, it goes inside the quotation marks; if the punctuation is not part of the material quoted, it goes outside the quotation marks.

Quotation marks may be used as ditto marks, instead of repeating a line of words or numbers. When used this way, the ditto marks should be directly beneath the word or set of words that it represents. In formal writing, this use is confined to tables and lists.

EXAMPLE   A is at a point equally distant from L and M.
          B   ”   ”   ”   ”   ”   S and T.
          C   ”   ”   ”   ”   ”   R and Q.

semicolons

The semicolon links independent clauses or other sentence elements of equal weight and grammatical rank, especially phrases in a series that have commas within them. The semicolon indicates a greater pause between clauses than a comma, but not as great a pause as a period would.

When the independent clauses of a compound sentence are not joined by a comma and a conjunction, they are linked by a semicolon.

EXAMPLE No one applied for the position; the job was too difficult.

Make sure, however, that such clauses balance or contrast with each other. The relationship between the two statements should be so clear that further explanation is not necessary.

EXAMPLE It is a curious fact that there is little similarity between the chemical composition of river water and that of sea water; the various elements are present in entirely different proportions.

Do not use a semicolon between a dependent clause and its main clause. Remember that elements joined by semicolons must be of equal grammatical rank or weight.

> **CHANGE** No one applied for the position; even though it was heavily advertised.
>
> **TO** No one applied for the position, even though it was heavily advertised.

USING A SEMICOLON WITH STRONG CONNECTIVES

In complicated sentences, a semicolon may be used before transitional words or phrases *(that is, for example, namely)* that introduce examples or further explanation.

> **EXAMPLE** The study group was aware of his position on the issue; that is, federal funds should not be used for the housing project.

A semicolon should also be used before conjunctive adverbs (such as *therefore, moreover, consequently, furthermore, indeed, in fact, however*) that connect independent clauses.

> **EXAMPLE** I won't finish today; *moreover,* I doubt that I will finish this week.

The semicolon in this example shows that *moreover* belongs to the second clause.

USING A SEMICOLON FOR CLARITY IN LONG SENTENCES

Use a semicolon between two independent clauses connected by a coordinating conjunction *(and, but, for, or, nor, yet)* if the clauses are long and contain other punctuation.

> **EXAMPLE** In most cases these individuals are corporate executives, bankers, Wall Street lawyers; *but* they do not, as the economic determinists seem to believe, simply push the button of their economic power to affect fields remote from economics.

A semicolon may also be used if items in a series contain commas within them.

> **EXAMPLE** Among those present were John Howard, president of the Omega Paper Company; Carol Martin, president of Alpha Corporation; and Larry Stanley, president of Stanley Papers.

Do not, however, use semicolons to enclose a parenthetical element that contains commas. Use parentheses or dashes for this purpose.

> **CHANGE** All affected job classifications; typists, secretaries, clerk-stenographers, and word processors; will be upgraded this month.
>
> **TO** All affected job classifications (typists, secretaries, clerk-stenographers, and word processors) will be upgraded this month.

Do not use a semicolon as a mark of anticipation or enumeration. Use a colon for this purpose.

CHANGE   Three decontamination methods are under consideration; a zeolite-resin system, an evaporation and resin system, and a filtration and storage system.

TO   Three decontamination methods are under consideration: a zeolite-resin system, an evaporation and resin system, and a filtration and storage system.

The semicolon always appears outside closing quotation marks.

EXAMPLE   The attorney said, "You must be accurate"; the client said, "I will."

slashes

The slash performs punctuating duties by separating and showing omission. The slash is called a variety of names, including *slant line, virgule, bar, solidus, shilling sign.*

The slash is often used to separate parts of addresses in continuous writing.

EXAMPLE   The return address on the envelope was Ms. Rose Howard/62 W. Pacific Court/Dalton/Ontario/Canada.

The slash can indicate alternative items.

EXAMPLE   David's telephone number is 549-2278/2335.

The slash often indicates omitted words and letters.

EXAMPLE   miles/hour for "miles per hour"

In fractions the slash separates the numerator from the denominator.

EXAMPLES   2/3 (2 of 3 parts), 3/4 (3 of 4 parts), 27/32 (27 of 32 parts)

In informal writing, the slash is also used to separate day from month and month from year in dates.

EXAMPLE   12/29/95

Index terms followed by page numbers refer to the titles of handbook entries. Terms without page numbers refer either to synonyms for entries or to topics discussed within an entry.